MINI SPORT

MINI SPORT

Second Edition

MIKE SLEAP

Lecturer in Education
University of Hull
England

Heinemann Educational Publishers
Halley Court, Jordan Hill, Oxford OX2 8EJ
a division of Reed Educational & Professional Publishing Ltd.

MELBOURNE AUCKLAND
FLORENCE PRAGUE MADRID ATHENS
SINGAPORE TOKYO SAO PAULO
CHICAGO PORTSMOUTH (NH) MEXICO
IBADAN GABORONE JOHANNESBURG
KAMPALA NAIROBI

ISBN 0 435 86591 9

Printed in Great Britain by Athenæum Press Ltd,
Gateshead, Tyne & Wear.

CONTENTS

ACKNOWLEDGEMENTS

I am indebted to the following for their contributions:

Pam   *Artwork Roughs*

Bucken Ltd, Watford, Herts   *Finished Artwork*
David Hely-Hutchinson ⎫
George Spillane   ⎬ *Photography*

Leslie Morrow   ⎫
Nieve O'Connor   ⎪
Jonathan O'Neill   ⎪
Jason Robinson   ⎬ *Demonstrations*
Dawn Sleap   ⎪
Nicholas Sleap   ⎪
Tiffany Sleap   ⎭

Henry Ellis   ⎫
Peter Hoare   ⎪
Paul Robinson   ⎬ *Advice*
Gordon Underwood   ⎭

Ebhlin Ni Ealaithe ⎫
Carmel Hall   ⎬ *Typing*

The All England Netball Association ⎫
The English Basketball Association ⎪
The English Mini Basketball Association ⎪
The English Schools' Badminton Association ⎪
The English Schools' Football Association ⎪
The English Schools' Netball Association ⎪
The English Schools' Volleyball Association ⎪
The English Volleyball Association ⎪
The Football Association ⎬ *Information*
The Girls' Schools' Lawn Tennis Association ⎪
The Hockey Association ⎪
The Lawn Tennis Association ⎪
The National Association of Youth Clubs ⎪
The National Cricket Association ⎪
The National Rounders Association ⎪
Professional Tennis Coaches' Association ⎪
The Rugby Football Union ⎭

PREFACE TO THE SECOND EDITION

There have been many developments in mini sport over the past two years. This second edition updates the rules, award schemes and other information that has changed since the first edition.

INTRODUCTION

'I have sometimes asked why children are not given the same games of skill as men; tennis, mall, billiards, archery, football, and musical instruments. I was told that some of these are beyond their strength, that the child's senses are not sufficiently developed for others. These do not strike me as valid reasons; a child is not as tall as a man, but he wears the same sort of coat; I do not want him to play with our cues at a billiard-table three feet high; I do not want him knocked about by our games, nor carrying one of our racquets in his little hand; but let him play in a room whose windows have been protected; at first only let him use soft balls, let his first racquets be of wood, then of parchment, and lastly of gut, according to his progress'.

Jean Jacques Rousseau

What are Mini Sports?

Our various sports have evolved with rules specifying sizes of playing areas, types of equipment which can or cannot be used and regulations concerning methods of play. Invariably these rules apply to adults and are largely 'inappropriate' for young children.

In the 'mini' game playing areas and equipment are 'scaled down' to suit shorter legs and lesser strengths. In addition methods of play are simplified to enable children to grasp games quicker and play happily without worrying about intricate and complex rules.

Since mini sports are based upon adult games and emphasize all the basic skills and methods of play they are the most logical way of preparing young children for the senior versions.

Who can play Mini Sports?

Mini sports are played mainly by children from 7-13 years although the activities, practices and game variations described in this book can almost always be modified to suit sports enthusiasts of any age.

The formal rules for each game are stated but, if necessary, these can be easily adapted to suit your particular situation.

This book aims to:

1 act as a comprehensive reference source for the mini versions of the senior games.

2 stimulate greater interest and participation in mini games.

3 help the teacher, coach and parent introduce mini games to young children.

There are ten sports:

mini badminton	mini rounders
mini basketball	mini rugby
mini cricket	mini soccer
mini hockey	mini tennis
mini netball	mini volleyball

Each section contains information on:

1 Playing Area and Equipment

Dimensions for mini pitches and mini courts are given together with suggestions as to how other sports areas could be adapted to suit the sport concerned.

The equipment needed for the mini game is described along with do-it-yourself construction methods to cut down on costs.

2 Rules

The main rules of the mini game are detailed. Supplementary notes are also provided to enable the newcomer to appreciate the meaning of these rules.

Some hints on refereeing and umpiring are also included.

3 Practices

This section offers a logical and progressive scheme to introduce the mini game to groups of young children. It is presented in the form of a variety of challenging and purposeful activities. A summary of pertinent points have also been added to aid in the coaching of fundamental skills.

4 Proficiency Awards

In recent years various sports have initiated Award Schemes. These schemes aim to stimulate interest and improve playing standards through the objective testing of practical skills and theoretical knowledge.

Many Proficiency Award Schemes are described although it should be noted that new developments are occurring in some sports and the reader should contact the relevant Association for the latest information.

5 Teaching/Coaching Qualifications

The teaching and coaching advice in this book is necessarily limited. However, the governing bodies organise comprehensive coaching schemes for their respective sport. The basic teaching and coaching awards often concentrate upon small sided games or the mini game and details of these qualifications are thus included.

6 Reference Information

Inevitably this book can only cover a certain amount of material. If further information is needed it is hoped that this section will provide the means of finding it.

HOW TO USE THIS BOOK

This section aims to show how a mini game might be introduced to children using the material in this book.

1 Your first consideration will be to note whether there is a suitable playing area and adequate equipment for the particular game involved. Although each game usually has regulation areas and equipment it is quite feasible to start off with modified conditions as described in the text.

2 The next task is to read through the rules of the mini game so that a basic knowledge of the general principles can be gained.

3 In the first activity session it may be sufficient to familiarise the children with basic movements and actions involved in the game. Examples of such familiarisation activities are offered for each sport.

4 It may be best to delay playing the full mini game in early sessions as the children may not be ready for it, and their individual participation will be limited in such a large group situation. It may be far more effective to start with some fundamental techniques which can be practised in pairs or small groups. This approach provides a sound base of fundamental skills and gives maximum opportunity for activity on the part of all children. Guidelines regarding the correct techniques and appropriate practices are suggested throughout the book.

5 If the correct skills are to be firmly established these practice situations need to be continued for a substantial period of time. Thus a variety of activities or practices are provided which enable a single skill to be reinforced without losing the interest of the children. However, these competence activities should only be continued for as long as the children remain stimulated and challenged.

6 The introduction of a competitive element can add an extra stimulus to the practice situation. Competitive activities not only serve to enhance the learning of techniques but also provide the child with an awareness of fundamental methods of play and basic tactical considerations. For example, within the 2 v 2 situation positioning, passing, supporting and other aspects of team play can easily be emphasised and developed.

7 The full mini game itself will need to be introduced at some time. The optimum time for this would seem to be after a few fundamental techniques have been learnt and after the children have experienced some small game situations. However, there are no 'hard and fast' rules on this point and individual circumstances will differ. The following section provides more detailed advice for individual teaching sessions.

ORGANISATION OF A TEACHING SESSION

The following two plans offer a framework for a teaching session of approximately 40 minutes. Where sessions are shorter:

  i) time allowances can be reduced proportionately

or

  ii) warm ups can be included in skills section.

Introductory session

Aim: To provide an active, challenging and enjoyable introduction to a game.

TIME	TYPE OF ACTIVITY	ACTIVITY EXAMPLE	REASON FOR INCLUSION
Min. 4 mins	Warm up	Relays/tag games	Psychological Physiological preparation
Max. 8 mins		Keep ball off ground	Ball familiarisation
Min. 4 mins Max. 8 mins	Teaching of specific skills	Demonstration Shadowing	Learning of fundamental skills
Min. 14 mins Max. 18 mins	Skills practice	Stationary passing in small groups Stationary passing, increased distance Passing whilst moving	Reinforcement of basic skills
Min. 10 mins or Max. 14 mins	Conditioned game or minor game	2 v 2 Passing competition Change opponents	Challenge and enjoyment of competitive element in game situation

TYPICAL ACTIVITY SESSION

Aim: To revise and reinforce basic passing and to introduce the correct timing of a pass.

TIMING	TYPE OF ACTIVITY	ACTIVITY EXAMPLE	REASON FOR INCLUSION
Min. 3 mins Max. 5 mins	Warm up	Beat your own record	Psychological Physiological preparation
Min. 10 mins Max. 14 mins	Revision of skill	Pass and move to new position Pressure on one player to pass quickly	Reinforcement of skill
Min. 12 mins Max. 16 mins	Teaching of fundamental tactics	3 v 1 — How many passes made before an interception	Where and when to pass Moving into a space
Min. 8 mins Max. 12 mins	Conditioned or full game	Game conditioned to emphasise accurate timing of pass	Development of skills and basic tactics in game situation

MARKING OF PLAYING AREA

The effectiveness of activity sessions can be greatly enhanced if playing areas are marked out with grid squares as shown below. The grid provides:

a *Lines for assembling pupils*   e.g. When giving demonstrations.

b *Lines for practice situations*   e.g. Pairs 10m apart, passing.

c *Lines for race distances*   e.g. Dribble to first line and return.

d *Separate, limited practice areas*   e.g. 2 v 1 in one square.

e *Corridors for passing movements
   and tackling practices*   e.g. Funnel ball.

f *Playing areas for small game
   situations*   e.g. 2 v 2 in two squares

The layout and size of grid squares will depend upon individual circumstances.

SYMBOLS USED IN DIAGRAMS

✦	Players
○ ✧	Targets
✳	Pass, catch or hit made at this point
‑ ‑ ‑ ‑ ➤	Pathway of ball
⎯⎯⎯➤	Pathway of player without ball
∿∿∿➤	Pathway of player with ball

Note: Diagrams and teaching points refer to *right handed* and *right footed* players. Activities are arranged in twos and threes for maximum participation. Where equipment, space or numbers prevent this organisation activities can easily be adapted for larger numbers.

MINI BADMINTON

MINI BADMINTON CONTENTS

1. PLAYING AREA

1.1 THE COURT

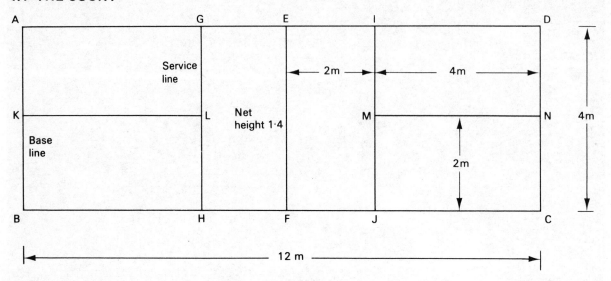

Marking Instructions

1 Use two lengths of string:
   (a) 12m long with a knot tied at 4m
   (b) 7.2m

2 Lay down the 12m string and mark line AD with mid-point E.

3 Fix one end of 12m string at A. Fix one end of 7.2m string at E. Hold 12m string at 4m knot and free end of 7.2m string. B is marked where both strings meet when taut.

4 Using D as the fixed point for the 12m string instead of A, mark C.

5 Mark lines AB, BC, CD, and mid-point F.

6 Mark G, H, I and J, each 4m from end-lines. Mark lines GH, EF and IJ.

7 Mark K, L, M and N, each 2m from side-lines. Mark lines KL and MN.

1.2 ADAPTATIONS OF OTHER PLAYING AREAS

————————————— original lines to be 'disregarded' in mini badminton

━━━━━━━━━━━━━ original lines to be 'utilised' in mini badminton

▬ ▬ ▬ ▬ ▬ ▬ additional temporary lines required

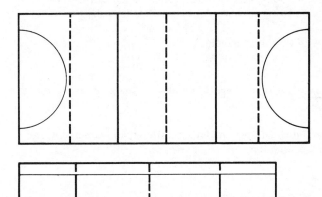

Junior Netball Court
6 Mini Badminton Courts
12m x 4.5m

Lawn Tennis Court
4 Mini Badminton Courts
11m x 6m

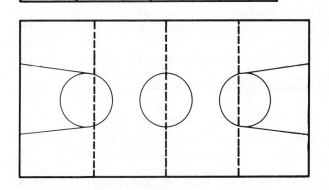

Basketball Court
4 Mini Badminton Courts
14m x 6.5m

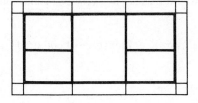

Badminton Court
1 Mini Badminton Court
12m x 5m

1.3 ANCILLARY EQUIPMENT

(a) Bat:

Either bat shapes or strung rackets can be used depending on circumstances. Bats can be easily made but make the game less like Senior Badminton. Badminton rackets are light enough for young children but more expensive.

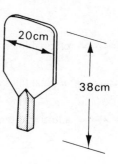

Bat shape cheaply constructed in woodwork department. Suitable materials:

1 Plastic frame with cork facing.
2 ½" marine plywood.

(b) Racket:

1 Approx. 66cm (26") long, weight 140gm (5oz), handle grip 9-10cm (3½") gut or nylon stringing, fibreglass or stainless steel shaft.

2 Strung racket with very short handle.

(c) Shuttle:

1 Feathered: Comes in varying weights and speeds. Cheapest satisfactory for mini badminton.

2 Plastic or nylon: Much cheaper and longer lasting than feathered. Quite suitable for mini badminton.

(d) Ball:

Airflow balls (as used for golf practice) make an adequate substitute if shuttles unavailable.

(e) Posts and Bases:

1 1.5m x 5cm diameter post of wood or metal. Attach sturdy hook to hold net. Encase in large paint tin filled with sand.

2 Longer posts 1.8m. Drill holes in playing area surface. Insert posts in socket during play. Cover holes with lids when not in use.

3 Utilise existing volleyball posts. Attach hooks at 1.5m.

4 Utilise existing badminton posts.

(f) Net:

1 Strong cord or tension wire enclosed in 5cm (2") webbing or tape, brightly coloured. Provides effective and cheap net height.

2 Tennis/badminton club throwouts. Handicraft department may be able to repair holes and cut to correct size. Even if nets are in a very bad condition the tape part may still be usable.

3 Tie a rope between posts and attach a fringe (i.e. thin strips of coloured material).

4 Utilise gymnastic beams at number 10, 1.5m.

2. RULES

The following rules are suggested for the game of mini badminton. The full rules of senior badminton can be found in *The Laws of Badminton* (see 6.2).

2.1 INTERPRETATION OF RULES

Rules	*Notes*

Object
(1) To play the shuttle into the opponents' area so that it is out of reach or such that it forces them to play the shuttle into the net or out of court.

(1) This principle needs little explanation and is usually grasped quickly.

The Teams
(2) Mini Badminton can either be played as *singles* *(1 v 1)* or *doubles (2 v 2)*.

(2) 2 v 2 probably most suitable in school situation.

Service
(3) The serve must be hit *underarm* with both feet touching the ground when service is made.

(3) Shuttle must be struck below waist level and the whole of the bat/racket head must be below the server's hand at impact.

(4) The first service in every game is taken from the *right* hand service court to the service court *diagonally opposite*.

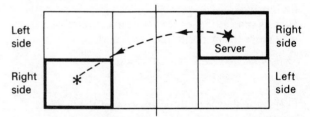

(5) Serves then taken from *alternate* sides every point.

(5) Emphasise this until rhythm of changing established.

(6) Each player serves consecutively *five* times before a change is made. The new server must serve on a *different diagonal* to the one last played.

(6) in *SINGLES*:
If A's fifth serve is from right to left B's first serve must be from left to right.

(7) Order of Service: *doubles*
(a) A starts right to left (A to X) serving 5 times from alternate sides. (Receivers do *not* change sides.)

(7)
(a)

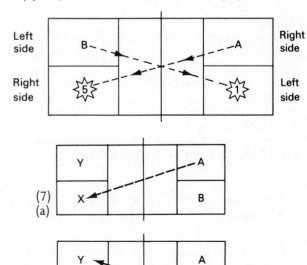

(b) B starts left to right (B to Y) serving 5 times from alternate sides.

(b)

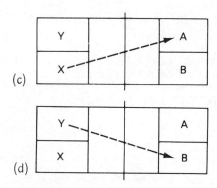

(c)

(d)

(c) X starts right to left (X to A) serving 5 times from alternate sides.

(d) Y starts left to right (Y to B) serving 5 times from alternate sides.

Continue repeating this sequence until game finishes.

Remember *both* members of the pair serve before the opposing pair begin serving.

(8) *ONE* serving attempt only allowed unless shuttle touches the net and lands in the correct service court.

(8) If the shuttle touches the net and lands in the service court a second service attempt (a let) is allowed.

(9) The receiver must stand in the service court diagonally opposite the server while awaiting service.

(9) The player needs to be positioned centrally in order that a long or short service can be dealt with effectively.

Shuttle in Play

(10) After the service the shuttle may be played in any manner (e.g. overarm, underarm) as long as a clean hit is made.

(10) Only one touch is allowed and the shuttle cannot be held or carried.

(11) As soon as the service has been delivered players may move to any position on the court.

(11) In doubles partners do *not* have to play the shuttle alternately.

(12)

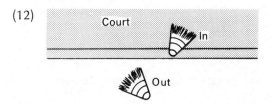

(12) If the shuttle lands on any part of the line it is counted as *IN*.

Scoring

(13) A player gains a point for every rally won whether serving or receiving. Play up to 15 points to win a set.

(13) If both sides have scored 14 points then play must continue with *alternate* serves until one side has a clear lead of 2 points (e.g. 19-17).

(14) It is suggested that matches are played over the best of three sets.
Note: Older children can be encouraged to change to the senior scoring system.

(14) Shorter sets (e.g. up to 11 points), may be more suitable in teaching sessions where a frequent change of opponent is desirable.

2.2 UMPIRING MINI BADMINTON

1 Get as much height as possible (e.g. stand on chair or bench).

2 Ensure that players serve from the correct side and that receivers are diagonally opposite.

3 Be alert for change of serve every 5 points, i.e. every

time the combined scores add up to a multiple of 5 (e.g. 7-3, 11-9).

4 State the score clearly after each rally.

5 Always give the server's score first.

6 Replay any doubtful points.

3. PRACTICES (ALL KEY POINTS REFER TO RIGHT HANDED PLAYERS)

3.1 SHUTTLE FAMILIARISATION

Activities

Key points

1 Continuous hitting of the shuttle approx. 1m into the air.

Shake hands with handle for grip, hold bat face flat (i.e. horizontal) when hitting.

2 Hit the shuttle very high into the air.

Whip-like action of the wrist, arm bends sharply at elbow, keep alert on the toes.

3 Play the shuttle very close to the bat.

Watch the flight of the shuttle closely, move the wrist up and down but keep the arm still.

4 Hit into the air with the back of the bat (i.e. palm facing ground).

Stand with the right foot slightly forward, flex the wrist.

5 Hit very high into the air with the back of the bat.

Start each stroke with the bat low to give adequate backswing.

6 Alternate bat face on every hit.

Turn wrist over quickly, gradually hit lower and lower.

7 Perform 1 to 6 whilst moving around. Start slowly and gradually increase speed.

Aim slightly ahead (i.e. angle the face of the bat away from body), watch out for others.

8 Keep shuttle in the air whilst moving backwards.

Look out for others out of corner of eye.

9 Keep shuttle in the air whilst moving in and out of other players.

Look for a clear pathway, gradually increase speed but keep shuttle under control.

10 On the spot, bend down and touch the floor between each hit.

Hit shuttle straight up in the air, watch it carefully, touch floor quickly.

11 Hit back and forth over object (e.g. partner's arm, net, beam).

Hit shuttle high rather than long. Alternate hitting with front and back of bat.

12 Continuous hitting of shuttle against a wall.

Stand close to wall, hit very high at first, be alert to rebound.

Examples of Competitive Challenges

(a)	Beat Your Own Record	How many consecutive hits can you make before shuttle falls to ground?
(b)	How Many Ways?	How many different ways can you hit the shuttle into the air?
(c)	Races	Keeping shuttle in the air, alternating bat face, walking over set distance.

3.2 BASIC HITTING WITH A PARTNER

Skill 1   Hitting with Hand Feed from Partner

Activities

1 3-4m apart, underarm throw to forehand side of partner. *Forehand* stroke played back for feeder to catch.

2 Feeder throws slightly further away making striker move and hit.

3 Feeder varies height of feed.

4 3-4m apart, underarm throw to backhand side of partner. *Backhand* stroke played for feeder to catch.

5 Same as 2 but now throwing further away on backhand side.

6 Same as 3 but now vary height on backhand.

7 Feeder mixes up throws to forehand and backhand.

Key points

Emphasise accurate feeding, preliminary throwing practice may be necessary. Striker stands sideways, left shoulder forward, hits with whip-like wrist action.

Move quickly to flight of shuttle, step on to left foot while drawing bat back in preparation for stroke. Bat aimed at shuttle with elbow bent. Keep the wrist loose.

Experiment by hitting
(a) shoulder height
(b) low with bat parallel to ground.
Always keep the head of the bat up.

Same principles as forehand except striker puts right shoulder forward, steps on to right foot and prepares earlier with slightly longer backswing.

Arm comes right across body, fling hand away as if sticky paper were stuck to it.

Right elbow points forward when preparing to hit, full and natural follow through.

Be ready to turn in either direction, always try to step on to correct leg.

Skill 2   Hitting in Pairs (without net)

1 4-5m apart, random hitting to each other, keep rally going.

Stress cooperation, hit carefully and accurately to each other.

2 Forehands only.

Hit across body aiming to forehand side of partner.

3 Backhands only.

Again hit across body, keep wrist loose, follow through further, aim for backhand side of partner.

4 Make partner move to hit shuttle. Hit slightly to one side.

Move feet quickly into position, try 'cocking' wrist back as far as possible and releasing forward just before impact.

Skill 3   Hitting in Pairs (playing over net)

Practices 1 to 4 of Skill 2

Ensure backhands are fully practised.

5 Hit shuttle very high over net.

Use a much stronger, snappy wrist and arm action, watch falling shuttle right on to the face of the bat.

6 Try to keep the shuttle low over net hitting with drive at shoulder height.

Quick reflex shots, again emphasise wrist action, try not to let shuttle drop below shoulder level.

7 Now vary the height of all shots.

Mix it up for partner, hitting very high and then very low.

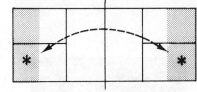

8 Play a rally of 'good length' shots.

Drive the shuttle so that it would land deep in the court (shaded area) if partner did not hit it.

9 Same as 8 using
   (a) Underarm stroke to hit shuttle high.
   (b) Shoulder height drive keeping shuttle low.

(a) Still use wristy action, hit over imaginary opponent at net.
(b) Drive shuttle firmly along flat path.

10 Alternate long and short shots.

Be alert, on your toes, use a 'fencer's lunge' when moving forwards quickly.

11 Take up any position but play the shuttle back and forth as quickly as possible.

Be alert at all times with the bat up ready, concentrate on making the wrist work rather than the arm.

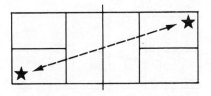

12 Play the shuttle cross court rather than straight.

Hit across body, always come back to central position on court.

13 Vary the strokes, e.g. long, short, cross-court, high, fast.

Try to move partner about the court, return to central position after every stroke.

Examples of Competitive Challenges

(a) Beat Your Own Record	Count number of consecutive strokes before rally breaks down.
(b) Time Challenges	Which pair can play most strokes in 30 secs.?
(c) Circle Shuttle	Small group in circle try to keep shuttle off the ground.
(d) Passing While Moving	Which pair can keep rally going whilst walking/jogging up and down playing area?
(e) Simple Conditioned Games	(1) Playing only in front section of court. Any player puts shuttle in play. Point scored for every rally won. Play to 11 and change opponents. (2) Same as (1) but use full court.
(f) Keep the Kettle Boiling	(1) Small team at both ends of court, first player plays and moves to back of team, next player steps forward and does the same, keep going until rally breaks down. (2) After hitting shuttle player moves to back of team at 'other' end of court. (3) Either of above but player loses 'life' when causing breakdown of rally.

3.3 SERVICE

Skill 1   Low Service

Activities

1 Take up stance ready to serve, standing within service court.

2 Practise serving short into court diagonally opposite.

3 Practise serving to land shuttle on target (e.g. box, shoe, stone).

4 Practise low service with opponent receiving.

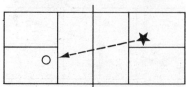

Key points

Left foot forward, holding shuttle by tips of the feathers slightly ahead of body, right hand holds bat down just behind right hip.

As shuttle drops, swing bat forward smoothly, arm slightly brushing side of body.

Make sure stance is relaxed, guide shuttle so that it just clears net.

Try to make it difficult for opponent to play attacking stroke (i.e. serve low over net).

Skill 2   High Service

1 Practise serving high and deep
  into service court diagonally
  opposite.

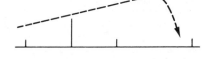

Action similar to that for low service
except for stronger and faster
movement of bat.

2 Practise serving to land shuttle on
  target at back of court.

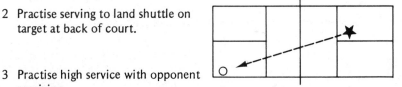

Take firmer stance, longer backswing, bring bat through faster
with whip-like action, full follow-
through.

3 Practise high service with opponent
  receiving.

Keep head down and eyes on
shuttle, avoid snatching and jerking.

Examples of Competitive Challenges

(a) Beat Your Own Record	Count number of consecutive services which land on the target.
(b) Server v Receiver	Competition to find which player can make most service winners. 10 serves each, any type of serve, receiver must return serve to specified area (e.g. left service court).
(c) Conditioned Game	Introduce serving rules (e.g. serves taken from alternate sides), 2 points for service winner, 1 point for every rally won. Play to 11 and change opponents.

3.4 OVERHEAD STROKES

Skill 1   Forehand Smash

Activities

1 Partner feeds high for player to
  smash downwards.

2 Same as 1 but smash played cross
  court on the diagonal.

3 Try to keep rally going by alternating smash and defensive
  underarm stroke.

Key points

Turn body sideways, left foot forward, bat taken behind back, throw
bat at shuttle to smash.

Sight the shuttle by pointing left
hand at it, bat in back-scratching
position, weight shifts forward to
left foot on impact.

Hit steeply downwards by getting
on top of shuttle, hit towards
partner in this instance.

Skill 2   Forehand Clear (High, deep overhead defensive stroke)

1 Players keep a rally of 'clears' going. Shuttle to be played deep to back of court.

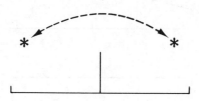

Same action as for smash except shuttle struck further back over right shoulder.

2 Same as 1 but clears must be played over high object (e.g. beam, rope, roof girder).

Important to hit shuttle on high upward pathway. Arm almost straight on impact.

3 Same as 1 but players must touch service line with bat between strokes.

'Fencer's lunge' forward, trot back on toes once service line has been touched.

Skill 3   Backhand Clear (More advanced)

1 Partner plays shuttle deep on backhand for player to attempt clear.

Right shoulder points towards net, drop bat over left shoulder, elbow pointing up towards shuttle, whip bat up to meet shuttle.

2 Players keep rally of backhand 'clears' going.

Take bat back very early to make sure full backswing is used.

Skill 4   Overhead Drop Shot

1 Partner feeds shuttle high for player to hit overhead drop shot.

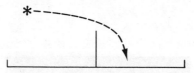

Same action as forehand smash except speed of arm checked just before impact.

2 Partner feeds shuttle high for player to hit overhead drop shot on to target.

Bat held firmly, follow through shortened. Avoid letting shuttle drop to head height.

Examples of Competitive Challenges

(a) Marathon	Who can keep rally of clears going the longest?
(b) Beat Your Own Record	Count number of consecutive backhand clears before rally breaks down.
(c) Smash v Defensive Stroke	Who can win rally?
(d) Clear v Clear	Who can win rally? Clears only to be played.
(e) Keep the Kettle Boiling	Forehand and backhand clears.

(f) Champion Rally

Same set up as keep the kettle boiling but first two players continue rally until winner is found. Loser moves to back of team, winner stays and rallies with new opponent. Teams can either score points or lose lives.

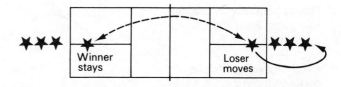

(g) Conditioned Games

For many excellent conditioned games see *Teaching Badminton* and *Teach your Child Badminton* (6.2).

(h) Mini Badminton

Full singles and doubles game can now be introduced if not done earlier.

3.5 NET SHOTS AND THE LOB

Skill 1   Net Shots

Activities

1 Partner feeds shuttle low over net for player to 'dab' downwards.

2 Same as 1 but feed played wide so that player must move to hit shuttle.

3 Net shots hit upward. Players keep rally going whilst playing close to net, shuttle hit from below height of net.

4 As 3 but play cross court shots also to make partner move along net.

Key points

Keep alert on the toes, knees slightly bent, bat held up firmly at tape height, hit downwards.

No backswing, bat pushed short distance forward, angle bat head sharply down, no follow through.

Bat angled upwards by cocking wrist back, hit lightly using very short backswing and little if any follow through.

Be ready to spring in either direction, drop bat underneath shuttle, gentle forward and upward push.

Skill 2   Underarm Lob

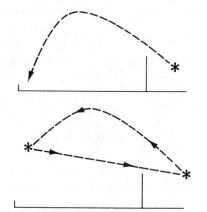

1 Underarm stroke played when shuttle dropped from hand. Partner catches and repeats.

Bat swung back behind body, left foot steps forward, bat sweeps forward and up, wrist held back.

2 Players keep rally of underarm lobs going. Forehand and backhand.

Fast wrist action needed, strong follow through vital.

3 Keep rally going, one player performs underarm lob while partner returns with overhead drop shot.

Aim to land shuttle just inside baseline (if partner did not hit it), try to use more wrist and less arm movement.

Examples of Competitive Challenges

(a)	Marathon	Who can keep rally of net shots going the longest?
(b)	Keep the Kettle Boiling	Net shots.
(c)	Conditioned Games	Use only the front section of court to encourage net shots. Point scored for every rally won. Play to 11 and change opponents. Otherwise normal rules.
(d)	Underarm Lob v Overhead Drop Shot	Who can win rally?
(e)	Lob v Smash Game	'A' plays net shot to 'B' who attempts a lob. 'A' smashes if possible. Point scored if either lob or smash is successful.

3.6 TACTICAL PLAY

General Points

1 Always try to keep the shuttle in play: consistency is more effective than erratic play.

2 Play the 'safe' shot rather than the 'big winner'. Statistical research shows that more points are won from opponents' errors than from winning strokes. Accurate placement of the shuttle is often more successful than sheer speed.

3 Manoeuvre your opponents by playing the shuttle away from them.

4 Play to the weakness of your opponents (e.g. net shots) and try to make them play to your strength.

5 Use a variety of strokes (e.g. short, long, straight, angled) to stretch your opponents and force an error.

6 Play the shuttle as soon as possible to achieve a downward angle: try not to let it drop below net level.

7 Never stand admiring your stroke, always be moving and preparing for the next one.

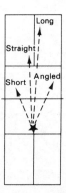

Singles

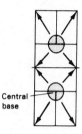

1 In general try to serve and receive at the positions shown.

2 Serve either low and short or right to the back of the court: avoid half-court serves which your opponent may easily smash.

3 Footwork is all important in singles: try to adopt a fast bouncing shuffle finishing with a large stride to achieve maximum reach.

4 Always return to the central base after playing a stroke. This position allows the player to cover all parts of the court.

5 A defensive clear should be played as high and deep as possible to allow sufficient recovery time. Remember also a poor clear makes an easy smash.

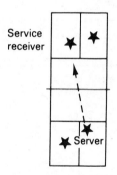

6 If you play the shuttle short move slightly closer to the net: your opponent is ideally placed to play a very short drop shot.

7 If you play a strong, deep stroke move up to the net and kill (smash) any weak return from your opponent.

Doubles

1 In the initial stages players should cover their respective sides of the court. Later they can attempt the more effective method of one up and one back in attack and a side-by-side formation in defensive play.

2 In general try to serve and receive service at the positions shown.

3 An attack down the middle of the opponents' court is often a successful strategy as it may lead to confusion on their part.

4 When receiving service try to attack immediately by attempting to play the shuttle downwards on the return.

5 Keep on your toes when your partner is playing a stroke.

6 Be prepared to cover for your partner sometimes but avoid 'poaching' shots which are not really yours.

7 Give a clear, early call if there is a doubt about who is to play a shot.

4.1 PROFICIENCY AWARDS

1 Award Scheme Title   Carlton Awards

2 Organising Body   English Schools' Badminton Association.

3 Aim

To encourage children at all levels to improve their own standard and give each child tangible recognition of his or her success.

4 Award Details

Note: For these awards the laws and scoring procedures relate to senior badminton

Primary Award

Requirements
1 Children must be 8 years old *before* start of current season (1st September).
2 Demonstrate: (a) Low Service   (d) Smash
                  (b) High Service   (e) Drop Shot
                  (c) Clear
3 Score a game of singles.

Assessment

By any teacher, or those qualified to assess Bronze Award.

Note: No specific standard available — all awards must be EARNED but Primary should be within reach of EVERY CHILD PLAYING IN SCHOOLS.

Bronze Award

Requirements

1 Children must be 10 years old *before* start of current season (1st September).
2 Hold Primary Award for at least six months. If already 11 years old before start of season, Primary Award need *not* be held.
3 Demonstrate: (a) Serves (excluding flick and drive)
                   (b) Returns of service
                   (c) Sequence of overhead shots
                   (d) Sequence of under-arm shots
4 Play a game of singles to show basic tactics.
5 Score a game.
6 Show an understanding of the laws of badminton.

Assessment
By any teacher who holds the E.S.B.A. Teachers' Badminton Award (see 5.1), or by any B.A. of E. coach.

Silver Award

Requirements

1 Children must be 11 years old *before* start of current season (1st September).
2 Hold Bronze Award for at least six months.
3 Demonstrate: Same shots as Bronze Award showing a much greater degree of competence plus
                   (a) Forehand and backhand drives
                   (b) Simple net shots
                   (c) Serves (including flick and drive)
4 Play a game of doubles to show basic tactics (attack and defence).
5 Score a game of doubles.
6 Show an understanding of the laws of badminton.
7 Know the E.S.B.A. Competitors' Code of Conduct.

Assessment

By any teacher who holds the E.S.B.A. Teachers' Badminton Award, or by any B.A. of E. coach.

Gold Award

Requirements

1 Children must be 12 years old *before* start of current season (1st September).
2 Hold Silver Award for at least six months.
3 Demonstrate: (a) Serves (including flicks and drives) and returns of these serves
                (b) Various backhand shots
                (c) Straight and cross court net shots
                (d) 'Tumble' net shots
4 Play a game to show the tactical use of these shots.
5 Demonstrate: A sequence of overhead and under-arm shots selected by the Assessor.
6 Answer a test (written or oral) on the laws of badminton and the E.S.B.A. Competitors' Code of Conduct.

Assessment

By a Badminton Association of England advanced coach (or above).

Supreme Award

Requirements

1 Children must be 14 years old *before* start of current season (1st September).
2 Hold Gold Award for at least twelve months.
3 Perform and maintain any *three* sequences of shots selected by the Assessor.
4 Play games of singles and level doubles. Candidates at this level will be expected to show a much higher standard than at Gold Award.
5 Show tactical appreciation, by analysis, of own and opponent's game.
6 Must show, by text and example, a comprehensive understanding of the E.S.B.A. Competitors' Code of Conduct.
7 Must be competing in age-group tournaments outside own county.

Assessment

By officials appointed by the County Schools' B.A. and registered with the E.S.B.A. Award Secretary; by Badminton Association of England Assessor Coaches; by other Examiners approved by E.S.B.A.

5 Award Secretary

All matters relating to the Award Scheme are dealt with by the E.S.B.A. Award Secretary, Mrs. A.C. Capon, 27 Malcolm Road, Shirley, Solihull, West Midlands, B90 2AH.

6 General Details

1 Children must be under 18 years on 1st September of the current season and still receiving full-time education.
2 Candidates must hold the previous Award for at least six months before attempting Silver or Gold.
3 Successful candidates receive badges and certificates.
4 A small fee is charged to cover costs.
5 All testing must be organised within the County in which the candidate's school is situated unless special permission is granted by E.S.B.A.

5. TEACHING/COACHING QUALIFICATIONS

5.1 CARLTON TEACHERS' BADMINTON AWARD

1 Organising Body English Schools' Badminton Association.

2 Aims To help teachers, students and sports instructors:

1 Introduce the game to any age group.
2 Coach elementary stroke techniques and basic tactics in singles and doubles. Correct basic faults.
3 Set up group practices, organise simple tournaments and help maintain interest in the sport.

3 Course Content

1 Introduction to the game and its laws.
2 Basic stroke production.
3 Basic tactics for singles and doubles games.
4 Group/class coaching — competitive practices.
5 Types of suggested coaching lessons.
6 Fitness training related to badminton.
7 How to help the better player.
8 The E.S.B.A. — its Award Scheme, organisation, opportunities.
9 Suggestions for running school clubs.
10 Literature, visual aids, etc.

4 Duration of Course 20 hours

5 Assessment Practical assessment of group handling and simple tests on the Laws of Badminton, tactics and points concerning coaching. Candidates are not assessed on their playing ability.

6 Applications L.E.A.s, Colleges of Education, Schools' County Badminton Associations and County Badminton Associations organise Teachers' Award Courses. Information regarding local courses can be obtained from the E.S.B.A. Hon. Secretary (see 6.1).

6. REFERENCE INFORMATION

6.1 USEFUL ADDRESSES

Badminton Association of England
Secretary: National Badminton Centre
Bradwell Road
Milton Keynes
Bucks MK8 9LA

International Badminton Federation
Secretary: Mrs V.S. Rowan
24 Winchcombe House
Winchcombe Street
Cheltenham
Gloucestershire GL52 2NA

English Schools' Badminton Association
The Secretary, E.S.B.A.
National Badminton Centre
Bradwell Road
Milton Keynes
Bucks MK8 9LA

6.2 BADMINTON REFERENCES

Publication					Description of Mini Game	Skill Descriptions	Teaching Practices	Tactics	Senior Rules
B.A.E.	1977	Laws of Badminton	B.A.E.	Booklet					*
B.A.E.	1976	Notes for Badminton Coaches	B.A.E.	Booklet		*		*	
Brown E.	1971	Badminton	Faber & Faber	Book		*		*	*
Crossley K.	1979	Progressive Badminton	Bell	Book		*		*	*
Davidson K. Smith L.C.	1971	Badminton	Bailey & Swinfen	Book		*			*
Davis P.	1979	Badminton Complete	Kaye & Ward	Book		*		*	
Davis P.	1980	The Badminton Coach	Kaye & Ward	Book		*	*	*	
Downey J.C.	1975	Better Badminton For All	Pelham	Book		*	*	*	*
Downey J.C.	1976	Teach Your Child Badminton	Lepus	Book		*	*	*	*
Downey J.	1978	Badminton for Schools	Pelham	Book		*	*	*	*
Gregory D. Webb G.	1974	Teaching Badminton	Surrey County School of Badminton	Book		*	*	*	
Internat. Badminton Federation	1974	Statute Book	Internat. Badminton Federation	Booklet					*
Johnson M.	1974	Badminton	Saunders	Book		*		*	*
Know the Game		Badminton	E.P. Pub. Co.	Booklet					*
Mills R.	1975	Badminton	E.P. Pub. Co.	Book		*		*	*
Mills R. Butler E.	1974	Tackle Badminton	Stanley Paul	Book		*		*	
Whetnall P. & S.	1975	Badminton	Pelham	Book		*	*	*	*

MINI BASKETBALL

CONTENTS

1. PLAYING AREA

1.1 THE COURT

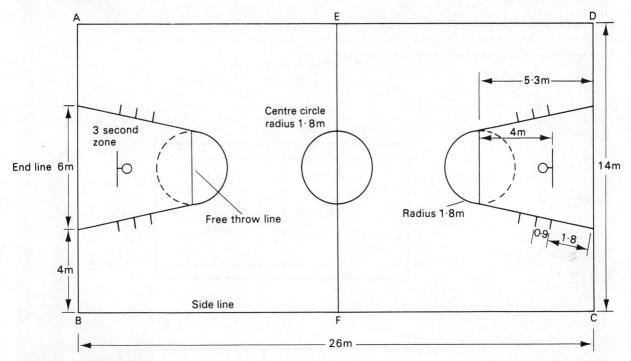

Since this is a regulation size court smaller dimensions may be found more suitable. However, the measurements must be in the same proportion to one another and the *free-throw* lines must always be drawn exactly 4m from the backboards.

Marking Instructions

1 Use two lengths of string:

   (a) 26m with a knot tied at 14m.
   (b) 19m with a knot tied at 1.8m.

2 Lay down the 26m string and mark line AD with mid-point E.

3 Fix one end of 26m string at A. Fix one end of 19m string at E. Hold 26m string at 14m knot and free end of 19m string. B is marked where both strings meet when taut.

4 Using D as the fixed point for the 26m string instead of A, mark C.

5 Mark lines AB, BC, CD and EF.

6 Fix the 26m string to the mid-points of endlines AB and CD. Mark the centres of each of the three circles (i.e. 5.3m from each end and the mid-point of EF).

7 Mark each circle by fixing one end of 19m string at the centre and walking round holding knot at 1.8m.

8 Mark the remainder of the zone lines using the measurements shown.

1.2 ADAPTATIONS OF OTHER PLAYING AREAS

———————————— original lines to be 'disregarded' in mini basketball

———————————— original lines to be 'utilised' in mini basketball

— — — — — — additional temporary lines required

Lawn Tennis Court
1 Mini basketball court
24m x 11 m

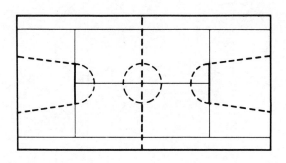

Junior Netball Court
1 Mini basketball court
26m x 14m

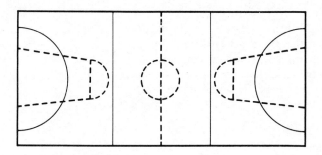

Volleyball Court
1 Mini basketball court
18m x 9m

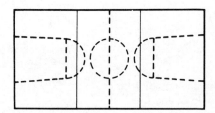

1.3 ANCILLARY EQUIPMENT

(a) Goal Posts:

1 Portable stands complicated and difficult to construct but a challenging project for woodwork/metalwork department.

2 Single or double pole stands can only be used if suitable deep sockets can be constructed.

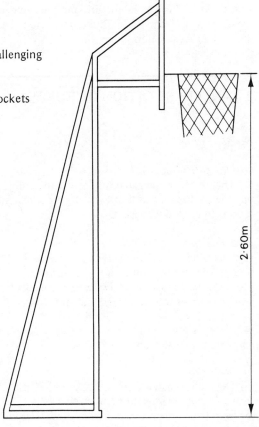

3 Wall fixings can be used and are probably easiest to construct.

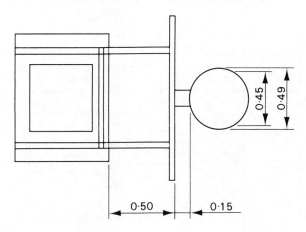

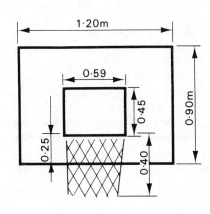

(b) Ball:

May be covered with leather, synthetic material or rubber.

Circumference: 0.68-0.73m (27-29")
Weight: 450-500gm (16-18 oz)

2. RULES

Mini Basketball is a game for girls and boys under 13 years of age. The following rules outline the game showing the differences from Senior Basketball. The full set of rules can be found in the Rule Book of the English Mini Basket Ball Association (see 6.2).

2.1 INTERPRETATION OF RULES

Rules

Notes

Object (and Scoring)
(1) The object of the game is to throw the ball into the opponents' basket and to prevent the opponents from scoring in one's own basket.

(1) Basket made . . . . 2 points
Free throw made . . . . 1 point

The Teams
(2) Each side has *5 players*. (For matches a team consists of 10 players: 5 on court, 5 substitutes)
(3) Each team should have a *referee* and a *coach* to give advice and arrange players' substitutions.

(4) Players should wear shirts of the same colour with *numbers* back and front.

(2) Each member of the team must play at least one ten minute period (see 'time in play').
(3) In order to help teachers, older pupils (e.g. secondary school team members) should be encouraged to act as referees and coaches.
(4) Players' numbers are important to identify scorers and to observe the number of fouls committed.

Time in Play
(5) The match is divided into *2 halves of 20 minutes*, with a *10 minute interval* between them.
(6) Each half is divided into *2 periods of 10 minutes*, with a compulsory interval of *2 minutes* between them.
(7) Each member of the team must play at least *one 10 minute period*.
(8) During the first 3 periods, substitutions can only take place *during an interval*. During these first 3 periods each of the ten players of a team must have played in the match for at least one period but not more than two. During the 4th period, one *time out* of one minute may be granted to each of the teams, upon a request by the coach. During these time outs both coaches may substitute players.

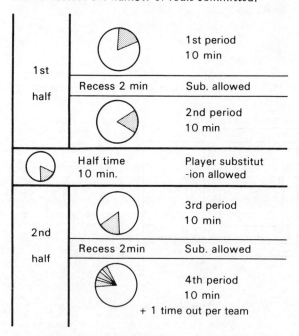

1st half	1st period 10 min	
	Recess 2 min	Sub. allowed
	2nd period 10 min	
	Half time 10 min.	Player substitut -ion allowed
2nd half	3rd period 10 min	
	Recess 2min	Sub. allowed
	4th period 10 min + 1 time out per team	

Ball in Play
(9) To start play in every period a jump ball is taken between 2 opponents in the centre circle.

(10) A player who holds the ball can only take *2 steps* and must shoot or pass before executing a third step.

(9) The referee tosses the ball vertically between the two players concerned. They can tap the ball after it has reached the peak of its flight.
(10) This rule is sometimes difficult for young players but must be adhered to fairly rigidly to be fair to all.

(11) A player who receives the ball when standing still, or stops correctly after catching it, is allowed to *pivot*.

(12) When a player wants to advance with the ball he may *dribble*. But he may not:

    (a) dribble with 2 hands at same time;

    (b) allow the ball to rest in one hand while dribbling;

    (c) dribble again after the ball comes to rest in his hands.

(13) To strike the ball with *fist* or *foot* is a violation (unless it occurs accidentally).

(14) A player may not remain longer than *3 seconds* in the opponents' 'restricted area' when his team has possession of the ball.

(11) Pivoting means moving one foot in any direction whilst the other remains in contact with the ground.

(12) Dribbling means bouncing the ball to the ground with one hand.

    (b) refers to the common fault of carrying the ball as opposed to merely exerting downward pressure with the hand;

    (c) commonly called a double dribble i.e. dribble, stop and hold the ball and dribble again.

(13) The ball is held and played only with the hands.

(14)

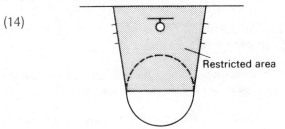

Restricted area

(15) In the following situations the player has *5 seconds* to play the ball:

    (a) passing the ball into play from the sideline or backline;

    (b) when closely guarded;

    (c) taking a free throw.

(16) When a team has possession it must take a shot at the basket *within 30 seconds*.

(17) When the ball is put into play from the sideline at a spot between midcourt and the opponents' end-line, the *referee* should hand the ball to the player who is to put it into play.

Fouls

(18) Mini Basketball is a *no-contact* game. The player who is to blame for any contacts commits a *personal foul*.

(19) A player who commits *5 personal fouls* is automatically expelled from the game.

(20)   Accidental contact (Normal foul).

Deliberate contact (Intentional foul).

Blatent, unsportsmanlike foul (Disqualifying foul).

(15) The time is counted from the moment the ball has been given to the player. If violated the referee should call a jump ball. If a ball is put out of bounds by two opponents, or if the referee is in doubt as to who put the ball out of bounds, the referee will declare a jump-ball.

(16) If the ball goes out-of-bounds during the 30 seconds and the same team keeps possession, a new 30 second period begins.

(17) If this does not occur the referee can either order the pass to be retaken or have an opposing player make the pass.

(18) The main contact fouls are obstruction, holding, pushing, hacking and charging. Opposing team given possession unless foul committed during the act of shooting. Two free throws awarded if shot was unsuccessful.

(19) A substitute may take his place.

(20) Opposing team puts ball into play from *sideline* unless foul committed during the act of shooting. In this case two free throws to fouled player unless a score was made.

Two free throws unless a score was made at the time the foul was committed. Immediate *expulsion* from the game. A substitute may take his place.

Immediate *expulsion* from the game. A substitute may take his place

Free Throw

(21) Shooter receives ball from the referee. The other players may stand as shown. No player can enter the restricted area before the ball has touched the rim or backboard.

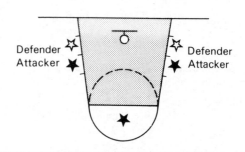

2.2 MINI BASKETBALL OFFICIATING

1 In Mini Basketball the referee should be a 'friend' and should not be too severe.

2 In addition to learning the rules and hand signals study the publication *Referees' Manual* (see 6.2).

3 Be positive and co-operative, helping the players observe the rules rather than seeming to treat them as criminals.

4 Ensure that the players are clear as to why the whistle has gone.

5 Vary your positioning to gain a clear view of play.

6 Check that the timekeeper and scorer understand their respective duties.

7 Take special note of the rules concerning jump balls, free throws and fouls. Remember, the substitution rules for Mini Basketball are different from Senior Basketball.

8 Make an effort to learn the respective duties of the leading and trailing officials. (Either referee may be the leading or trailing official depending upon the position of play at any given time.)

Brief Summary of Duties

Leading Official

(a) Always ahead of play by moving to the right.

While play is developing

(b) Watches movements of players away from the ball.

When ball is in restricted area

(c) Watches below shoulder height.

Trailing Official

(a) Always behind the play by moving to the left.

(b) Watches ball and players around it.

(c) Watches above shoulder height, i.e. backboard, basket, ball and 3 sec rule.

(d) Before each jump ball or free throw the officials change sides of the court.

3. TEACHING POINTS AND PRACTICES

3.1 BALL FAMILIARISATION

Activities	*Key points*
1 Pairs ● 2-3m apart, pass ball in as many ways as possible; e.g. one handed, two handed, underarm.	Watch ball carefully, keep hands and wrists relaxed, bring ball close to body quickly when catching.
2 Pairs ● As above but ball must bounce before reaching partner.	Take weight on to left foot whilst making pass. Bounce low, bounce high.
3 Pairs ● Players aim for part of body nominated by teacher; e.g. chest, knee, elbow. Partner attempts catch.	Use different types of throw, try to find the most effective. Catchers must be alert for difficult catches.
4 Pairs ● Any of 1 to 3 but ball is thrown slightly wide of partner.	Stretch with one hand to start catching action while other hand is placed quickly on ball to control it.
5 Pairs ● 2-3m apart, passing back and forth whilst moving down playing area.	Pass slightly ahead of partner, try not to take too many steps with the ball.
6 Pairs ● All pairs intermingle in playing area. Make a pass when clear.	Keep moving in and out of others, only pass when certain of reaching partner.
7 Fours ● In grid square, mix up passes; e.g. high, low, bounce, fast.	Be alert for pass at any time, use all types of throw explored earlier.
8 Fours ● As 7 but group now moves around grid square.	Move into a space, call for a pass, catch ball, look for player who is clear.

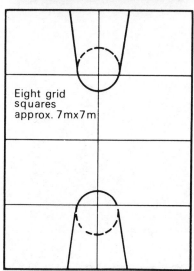

Eight grid squares approx. 7m x 7m

Examples of Competitive Challenges

(a) Beat Your Own Record	How many consecutive passes before ball falls to ground?
(b) Time Challenges	How many one-handed passes in 30 secs?
(c) How Many Ways?	How many ways can you bounce pass to partner?

3.2 PASSING

Skill 1 Two Handed Pass

Activities

1 Class • Shadow/copy two handed chest pass as demonstrated by teacher.

2 Pairs • 2-3m apart, two handed chest pass to each other.

3 Pairs • Gradually increase distance to 5m, chest pass to each other.

4 Pairs • As 1 to 3 but make ball bounce before reaching partner.

5 Pairs • As 1 to 3 but use two handed overhead pass.

6 Threes • Two handed passing whilst crossing playing area. Try to avoid moving in a straight line.

7 Threes • Players as in diagram, random passing around triangle, then put pressure on one player.

8 Threes • In grid square, two players try to keep possession, third player attempts to intercept. (Use 3 v 1 if skill level is low).

Key points

Hold ball in front of chest, fingers spread pointing upwards, thumbs point at each other, elbows away from body.

Thrust hands away from body whilst stepping forward.

Thrust away faster when passing over greater distance, pass straight and low aiming for partner's chest.

Angle thrust downwards, aim to bounce ball 1-2m in front of partner.

Lift ball above head with arms straight, hands behind ball with fingers spread, strong thrust with fingers and wrists.

Explain route and boundaries carefully, two handed passing only. Restrict steps when holding ball.

Turn to face direction of pass, use chest, bounce and overhead passes, gradually increase speed.

'Pig in the middle' idea, pass and *move to space*, pass only if partner is free, defender tries to mark receiver.

Skill 2 One Handed Pass

1 Class • Shadow/copy one handed pass as demonstrated by teacher.

2 Pairs • 3m apart, practise one handed passing to each other.

Stand sideways, feet slightly apart, ball in two hands, turn shoulders taking weight on right foot.

Take ball back with both hands, release left hand, push right arm through turning right shoulder forward.

3 Pairs • 3m apart, catcher stands with one arm outstretched at any level, thrower aims at catcher's hand.

Throw ball along flat pathway avoiding a slow, lobbed pass. Make adjustments if throw is inaccurate.

4 Pairs • Catcher calls 'right, left, high, low'. Thrower aims for correct area.

Take aim quickly, try to increase speed from time call is made.

5 Pairs • 3m apart, moving along playing area. Receiver signals where and when ball is wanted.

Keep to prescribed route avoiding other pairs, indicate with hand when you are free and want pass.

6 Pairs • As 1 to 5 but now concentrate on one handed bounce pass.

Take arms back high, change throwing angle to thrust downwards strongly.

7 Threes • In grid square two players try to keep possession using one handed pass only. (Use 3 v 1 if skill level is low.)

Emphasis upon running into space to receive pass and confuse opponent.

8 Fours • One handed accurate pass to moving player. Thrower stands in middle whilst others move round circle.

Continuous passing to players running around circle, thrower aims just in front of running player. Change often.

Examples of Competitive Challenges

(a)	Time Challenges	Which pair can make most one handed passes in 30 sec?
(b)	Passing Races	Which group can finish first passing round circle three times?
(c)	Dodge Ball	Threes in grid square, middle player dodging to avoid being hit below knee by ball

(d) Circle Pass Out

Players pair off and form circle with one partner standing in front of other. Player in middle with ball tries to pass to a player on outer ring. Inner ring defenders try to intercept. Each team has 3-5 min.

(e) 2 v 2 Basketball

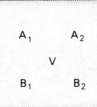

- 1 Use 7m x 7m grid square.
  2 Score by catching ball while standing on opponents' end line.
  3 Either team starts with possession, but when score has been made the team which did *not* score takes possession.
  4 No dribbling allowed.
  5 Play for 5 min. and change opponents.
  6 Otherwise normal basketball rules (e.g. no deliberate steps with ball).

3.3 FOOTWORK

Skill 1   Achieving Balance when Stopping

Activities

Key points

1 Class • Sprint, stop on whistle.

Thrust leading foot towards ground to act as brake.

2 Class • Sprint, jump and stop on whistle.

Emphasise bending of knee on landing.

3 Class • Sprint, jump and stop on whistle, move off in new direction.

Take smaller steps to slow down, thrust off from bent landing leg.

4 Pairs • 15m apart, jog towards partner who throws ball, stop as soon as catch is made.

Try to catch in mid-air and take only two steps before stopping. Count one, two as you step. Return ball and repeat.

5 Pairs • Player A on straight line, B 5m away. B throws to side of A who sprints, jumps to catch and stops.

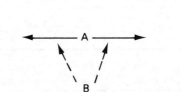

Catch in mid-air, land on one foot and place other wide to stop and maintain balance. Pivot on landing foot using other to step in direction of return throw. Accelerate quickly to lose imaginery opponent.

Skill 2   Dodging and Marking

Encourage quick, sharp dodging movements, flexing hard at knees and ankles.

1 Class • Basic tag with one or more chasers.

2 Pairs • Shadowing, dodge away from partner in restricted area.

Partner tries to stay within 2m, emphasise quick changes of direction, watch out for others.

3 Pairs • Tail tag, braid tucked in
   waistband at back. Try to get
   partner's tail without losing own.

4 Class • Hospital tag, chaser holds
   back of neck with left hand, tries
   to touch other players. Once
   tagged, players hold body part
   tagged and help chase.

Avoid partner with quick twists
and turns, be alert and poised on
balls of feet.

Players must try to maintain balance
while dodging with hand in awkward
positions, try feint dodges to avoid
being touched.

3.4 SHOOTING

Additional rings located as shown
can be very useful, especially
in shooting practices.

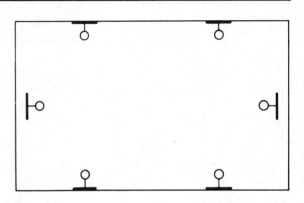

Skill 1   Two Handed Set Shot

Activities

1 Pairs • Take turns to shoot from
   different marked positions. Partner
   retrieves ball and has equivalent
   shots.

2 Pairs • Take turns to shoot from
   different marked positions. Partner acts as passive then active
   defender.

3 Pairs • Start away from ring, pass
   to each other until close enough
   for one player to shoot.

4 Fours • 3 v 1 passing and
   shooting using only two handed
   set shot.

Correct   Incorrect

Key points

Hold ball in front of chin, fingers
spread pointing upwards, thumbs
point at each other, right foot
slightly in front of left. Thrust
hands upward while stepping
further forward on to right foot.

Aim higher than the ring, not directly at it. Defender raises arm but
cannot move feet at first.

Gradually build up speed of passing
movement, alternate shooting
attempts.

Get free by passing and moving to
space, shoot when balanced and
within range.

Skill 2   One Handed Set Shot

1 Pairs • Take turns to shoot from
   different marked positions. Partner retrieves ball and has equivalent shots.

2 Pairs • Take turns to shoot from
   different positions, partner acts
   as passive then active defender.

3 Pairs • Take turns to shoot but
   player must 'feint' before actually
   making the shot.

4 Fours • 3 v 1 passing and shooting activity using one handed set
   shot.

Place one foot forward, knees bent,
shoulders square to basket, take
ball over head, fingers spread pointing back, elbow high, use other
hand to steady ball.

Straighten arm pushing ball towards
basket, shoot with strong wrist and
finger flick, straighten legs thrusting
upwards.

Always face target, hold ball in
front of body with both hands,
feint shot must appear like a real
attempt.

Look for the open space, if shot is
doubtful pass to team-mate in more
favourable shooting position.

Skill 3   Jump Shot

1 Pairs • Take turns to shoot from
   different positions. Gradually
   increase distance from basket and
   speed at which shot is made.

2 Pairs • Take turns to shoot from
   different positions, partner acts
   as passive then active defender.

Take ball above head with fingers
spread pointing back, use other
hand to steady. Jump high when
well balanced, shoot when at top
of jump.

Start close to basket, right foot
ahead of left, shoulders square to
basket.

3 Pairs • Defender passes ball out
   to shooter but then approaches
   to block the jump shot.

4 Fours • 3 v 1 passing and shooting activity using jump shot.

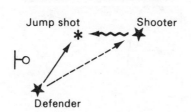

Jump shot   Shooter

Defender

Ball rests on the whole of the hand
and fingers, right elbow held high,
two footed jump, shooting over
defender.

A shot should be attempted on
every attack, try feint set shot
before jumping.

Skill 4   Lay Up Shot

1 Pairs • Take turns to perform
   lay up shot as demonstrated
   by teacher.

Practise footwork first, receive
pass in mid-air, take two steps and
jump high towards basket.

2 Sixes • Players arranged as in diagram, first in shooters' line attempts lay up, first in opposite line retrieves and passes to second player in shooters' line.

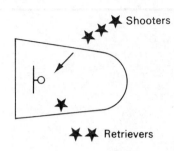

Catch ball in mid-air, count 'one, two', jump high near basket, both hands under ball, aim at vertical line of rectangle on backboard.

3 Sixes • As above except shooter dribbles in and attempts lay up shot. Shooters now start further away from basket. (Used only if dribbling skill has been taught).

Dribble until close to basket. With ball in hands take two steps and jump high to attempt lay-up shot.

4 Sixes • Lay up practices as above but approach from all angles, defenders chase or block approach.

Players should attempt lay-ups from all directions, dribbling or receiving pass, also dodging around a defender.

Examples of Competitive Challenges

(a)	Beat Your Own Record	How many consecutive goals can you shoot?
(b)	Time Challenges	Who can shoot most baskets in 3 min?
(c)	Partner Competitions	In pairs' activities above who can shoot most baskets with six shots each?
(d)	Group Competitions	In lay up activities which group can score most baskets?
(e)	Clock Golf Basketball	One or more shots taken from marked position. Move further back as skill improves. Point scored for every basket made.

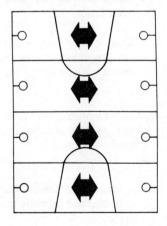

(f) 3 v 3 Basketball

• 1 Use two grid squares making 14m x 7m area. Play four games cross-court on full basketball court.

2 Use baskets if enough available or fix braids/coloured material to wall/fence at basket height: or use netball posts: or use skittles which have to be knocked over to score. (Defined areas should be chalked around skittles to prevent players overguarding.)

3 Two points now scored for basket made. One point if ball touches rim but does not go in.

4 Either team starts with possession, but when score has been made the team which did *not* score takes possession.

5 No dribbling allowed.

6 Play for 5 min. and change opponents.

7 Otherwise normal basketball rules.

3.5 DRIBBLING

Skill 1   Basic Dribble

Activities	Key points

Activities

1 Pairs • Take turns bouncing ball while stationary, right and left hand, high, low, close and far away from body.

2 Pairs • Take turns bouncing ball while stationary, right and left hand, changing speed and changing direction.

3 Class • Players with a ball dribble around other class members spaced out on playing area. On command change hands, direction or speed.

4 Threes • 'A' dribbles half way across area, stops, passes to 'B' who does the same passing to 'C'.

Key points

Shape hand to contours of ball, be flexible at the wrist to absorb pace of rising ball and avoid slapping ball, never use both hands together.

Bend over slightly, hold hand low to prevent ball rising too far, change hand position on ball to produce movement required.

Always make a clear change, e.g. jog to sprint, reverse direction. Never stop and then resume dribbling.

Try to look forward rather than at ball, when pass has been made take up position of player receiving pass.

C A ~~~~~~~~ - - - → B
           Pass

Skill 2   Dribbling and Pivoting

1 Class • With or without ball, shadow/copy demonstration of pivoting by teacher.

Come to stationary position, leave back foot firmly on floor, body can change direction by stepping with front foot.

2 Threes • Player dribbles and stops in front of imaginary opponent, pivots and passes to another player.

Keep activity lively with fast pivoting, quick passing and consistent backing up for the pass.

3 Fours • 'A' dribbles across to 'B', 'D' acts as passive opposition at first, becomes more active as skill improves.

C A ~~~~~~ D ↘ B

'B' returns, trying to dribble around 'D', use body to protect ball, change hands if necessary.

4 Fours • 3 v 1 dribbling, passing and shooting activity.

Draw opponent with dribble, pivot until pass can be made to player in space.

Examples of Competitive Challenges

(a) Races, Relay Races	Involving dribbling with either hand, around obstacles, including passing, etc.
(b) 1 v 1 Dribbling	Use grid square, player with ball tries to dribble over opponent's end-line, no contact.

(c) Steal-A-Ball	Half group with a ball each dribbling in confined area, those without ball try to steal one legitimately (i.e. no contact).
(d) Knockout Steal-A-Ball	As above except teacher stops activity every 20 secs, those without a ball drop out, take out one or more balls each round.
(e) Dribbling Chaos	One ball to each player who dribbles within confined area, players try to disturb other dribblers without losing control of their own ball. Those who lose control drop out.

3.6 BASIC DEFENCE TACTICS

Skill 1   Individual Defence Activities

Activities

1 Pairs ● Defence against opponent with the ball. Defender tries to prevent opponent from scoring.

2 Pairs ● Defence against the dribble. Defender tries to prevent opponent from advancing down the court.

3 Pairs ● Rebounding. Try to win ball from the rebound after partner has taken a shot.

Key points

One foot slightly in front of the other, knees bent, head up. Distract attacker with one arm whilst holding the other arm low to maintain balance.

Stay low and well balanced, hands low with palms up, watch ball intently and watch for opportunity to steal it.

Stay inside attacker, turn to face basket, time jump to catch ball at highest point possible.

Skill 2   Man-for-Man Defence

1 Fours ● 2 v 2 passing activity where each player marks a specified opponent all the time.

2 Sixes ● 3 v 3 games, each player marking specific opponent.

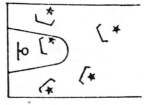

3 Full Game ● Emphasis upon picking up specified opponent in own team's defensive half of court.

Watch the player and ball as far as possible, stay in front of opponent, be alert to quick movements.

Try to intercept passes to your opponent, if unsuccessful stay close and harrass to force passing error.

Stay between basket and opponent, try to block any dribble or shot made by opponent.

3.7 BASIC ATTACKING TACTICS

Skill 1   Driving Past Defender

Activities

Key points

1 Pairs • Attacker dribbles around a fairly passive defender. Use both hands and increase speed.

Dribble with hand furthest from defender, turn away slightly to shield ball, dribble quite fast once action has started.

2 Pairs • Attacker tries to unbalance defender, dribble past and shoot.

Change the direction of the dribble, change pace by increasing speed quickly.

Skill 2   Wall Pass/Give and Go

1 Threes • 2 v 1 attacking situation emphasising use of wall pass. Defender passive at first.

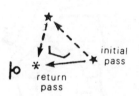

After passing to team-mate move immediately towards basket, signal and look for return pass, finish movement with a shot.

2 Threes • As above but team-mate receiving pass may shoot if defender holds off to watch first attacker.

Encourage quick, sharp wall passes to confuse defender. Attacker must look for shooting opportunity if wall pass covered.

3 Fours • 2 v 2 game as described earlier emphasising wall pass.

Players must keep moving when partner has ball, a stationary player is easy to mark.

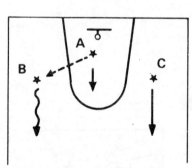

Skill 3   Fast Break

1 Threes • Fast break by three players once possession gained under own basket. No defenders at first.

Player A passes ball to either B or C. All three players move quickly down court using the full width. Shot attempted at far end.

2 Threes • Fast break by three players. Try some simple variations: players change lanes of attack, crisp passing to advance ball down court.

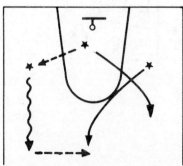

Stay at least 4 metres apart, transfer ball to middle lane at end of break to give more options, gradually increase speed.

3 Fours • Fast break by three players with one defender. Defender tries to harrass and intercept.

Pass only if defender prevents any further progress or if team mate is in a good position ahead of dribbler.

4. PROFICIENCY AWARDS

1 Award Scheme Title   Basketball Proficiency Award Scheme

2 Organising Body   English Basket Ball Association

3 Aim   To encourage children to improve their own standard and give each child recognition of his or her success.

4 Award Details

Test 1 — Quickfire Shooting
The player starts from any position, and as close to the basket as he wishes, with the ball held in two hands. On the signal 'Go' he scores as many baskets as quickly as he can, using any type of shot he wishes. The player gathers the ball himself after each shot.
Record the number scored in 30 seconds.

Test 2 — Repetition Passing
On the signal 'Go', the player passes the ball from a standing position at a line 9 feet (2.75m) from a solid wall, so that it rebounds from the wall to him. He then catches the ball, and repeats. For the passes to score they must be made from behind the 9 foot line and passed from above waist level. For the Mini Basketball Awards, the distance from the wall is 6 feet (1.80m).
Record the number of times the ball hits the wall in 30 seconds.

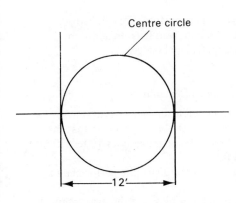

Centre circle

Test 3 — Dribbling
Use two parallel lines 12 feet (3.60m) apart, e.g. as shown in diagram. The player stands behind one line. On the signal 'Go', he dribbles across the space between the lines. After bouncing the ball outside the line on the opposite side, and having taken both feet across the line, the player changes the hand being used to bounce the ball and dribbles back to the starting point. Repeat, without stopping, dribbling with alternate hands on each trip, and stepping across the line with both feet before making the return trip.

One point is scored for each one way trip across the space.
One point deducted for each 'illegal' dribble (e.g. a double dribble).
Record the number scored in 30 seconds.

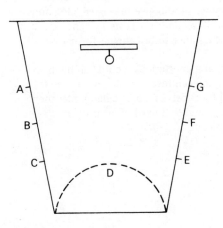

Test 4 — Shooting from Set Positions
The player starts at the spot on the court marked 'A' in the diagram. The ball is held in two hands. On the signal 'Go', using any shot, the player shoots for basket. He moves in, gathers the ball and moves to the next spot (marked 'B' in the diagram). He again shoots for basket, etc. The player moves round the key, shooting from each spot in turn. The shot shall be taken from the designated spot, and the player shall not move forward until the ball has been released. The player goes round the seven spots twice.
Record the number scored out of fourteen.
For the One Star Award, on this test the player is required to score four lay up shots, using a one bounce and 1-2 footwork, within 30 seconds.

MINI BASKETBALL	Mini Player	Mini 1*	Mini 2*
1. Quickfire Shooting	2–5	6–8	9 or more
2. Passing	12–22	23–24	25 or more
3. Dribbling	4–9	10–11	12 or more
4. Set Shooting	1 Lay-up Shot	7	8 or more
5. Free Shooting	–	–	–

FULL SIZE EQUIPMENT	1*	2*	3*	4*	5*
1. Quickfire Shooting	5–6	7	8	9	10 or more
2. Passing	17–19	20–22	23–24	25	26 or more
3. Dribbling	13	14	15	16	17 or more
4. Set Shooting	7	8	9	10	11 or more
5. Free Shooting	–	–	–	1	2–4

5 Applications

Must be made upon official application forms obtainable from:
The E.B.B.A. (Proficiency Awards)
Calomax House, Lupton House, Leeds 9.

6 General Details

General

The Mini Basketball Awards are open to children (boys or girls) under 13 years of age.

The award scheme tests proficiency in the basic skills of shooting, passing and dribbling. A person qualifies for the award that corresponds with the lowest standard reached in any test. The examination can be conducted by club coach, youth leader or teacher.

Successful candidates pay a test fee and are awarded a cloth badge and certificate. No fee is payable by a candidate who fails. In addition, successful candidates may purchase metal lapel badges.

Examining

The following notes are for the guidance of examiners:

1 The performer is not required to complete all four tests at one session.
2 Before undertaking Tests 3 and 4, a check should be made that the court is correctly marked. For Test 3, two parallel lines 12 feet (3.6m) apart should be marked on the floor.
3 Prior to taking the test, the examiner should give the performer an opportunity to warm up.
4 The examiner will require a stop watch. Following the instructions for each test carefully, the examiner should give the signal 'Go', and stop the performer at the end of 30 seconds on Tests 1, 2 and 3.
5 It is not necessary for the same examiner to test the performer on each item.
6 A progress chart is supplied so that a continuous record can be maintained of the performer's record on each test.
7 On gaining the 'pass' level on all four tests at a particular grade, the performer is considered to have gained that level of award.
8 For Mini Awards use Mini Equipment.

5. TEACHING/COACHING QUALIFICATIONS

5.1 MINI BASKETBALL OFFICIATING AWARD

1 Organising Body	English Mini Basket Ball Association
2 Aim	To encourage more children to officiate and to provide advice upon the art of officiating.
3 Assessment	To pass the award, children must prove to the teacher or coach that they are capable of carrying out each of the official's duties. (a) Answer questions about the rules of the game. (b) Referee a whole match. (c) Act as timekeeper for the whole of a game. (d) Act as scorer for the whole of the game and send this scoresheet in with the application.
4 Applications	Kenneth G. Charles, Headmaster, The Greneway School, Royston, Herts, SG8 7JF

5.2 PRELIMINARY TEACHERS' AWARD

1 Organising Body	English Basket Ball Association.
2 Aim	To provide information upon teaching and coaching in the normal school situation and in Youth Clubs. Advice will be given on the organisation of teaching/training sessions and organising a group on a court with two baskets.
3 Course Content	(a) Introducing the game to beginners. (b) Development of basic skills. (c) Cooperative skills. (d) Simple team offence and defence. (e) Class organisation and the organisation of group practice.
4 Duration of Course	8 hours.
5 Assessment	This is a non-examination award, and gaining the award is conditional upon satisfactory attendance at an approved course of instruction.
6 Applications	Brian E. Coleman, Senior Technical Officer, E.B.B.A., Calomax House, Lupton Avenue, Leeds, LS9 7EE.

6. REFERENCE INFORMATION

6.1 USEFUL ADDRESSES

Headquarters: *English Basket Ball Association*
Calomax House
Lupton Avenue
Leeds 9
LS9 7EE

Secretary: K.K. Mitchell,
Department of Physical Education
The University
Leeds LS2 9JT

English Mini-Basket Ball Association
Secretary: K.G. Charles
The Greneway School
Garden Walk
Royston
Herts SG8 7JF

English Schools' Basket Ball Association
Secretary: A. Mawson
8 Gosford Gdns
Ilford
Essex.

6.2 BASKETBALL REFERENCES

Publication				Description of Mini Game	Skill Descriptions	Practices	Tactics	Senior Rules
Banks G. 1974	Basketball	Schoolmaster Pub. Co.	Book			*	*	
Barnes M.J. 1973	Girl's Basketball	Sterling Pub. Co.	Book		*		*	Summary
Berry W.J.D. 1970	Basketball for Schools	Pelham	Book	Earlier Version	*		*	*
Coleman B. 1979	Better Basketball	Kaye & Ward	Book		*	*	*	
Coleman B. Ray P. 1976	Basketball	E.P. Pub. Ltd.	Book		*	*	*	
E.B.B.A.	Teachers Guides	E.B.B.A.	Booklet	*	*	*	*	
E.B.B.A.	Referees' Manual	E.B.B.A.	Booklet					Inter-pretations
E.B.B.A.	Official Basketball Rules	E.B.B.A.	Booklet					*
E.M.B.A.	Mini Basketball	E.M.B.A.	Booklet	*				
Hoy L. Carter C.A.	Tackle Basketball	Stanley Paul	Book		*	*	*	
Know the Game	Basketball	E.P. Pub. Ltd.	Booklet					*
Mumford K. Wordsworth M.A. 1974	Beginner's Guide to Basketball	Pelham	Book		*	*	*	
Thomas V. 1972	Basketball Techniques and Tactics	Faber & Faber	Book		*		*	
E.M.B.A.	Mini Basketball	Sports Films	Film	*	*			

MINI CRICKET

CONTENTS

1. PLAYING AREA

1.1 THE PITCH

Fielding positions
for right
handed batter

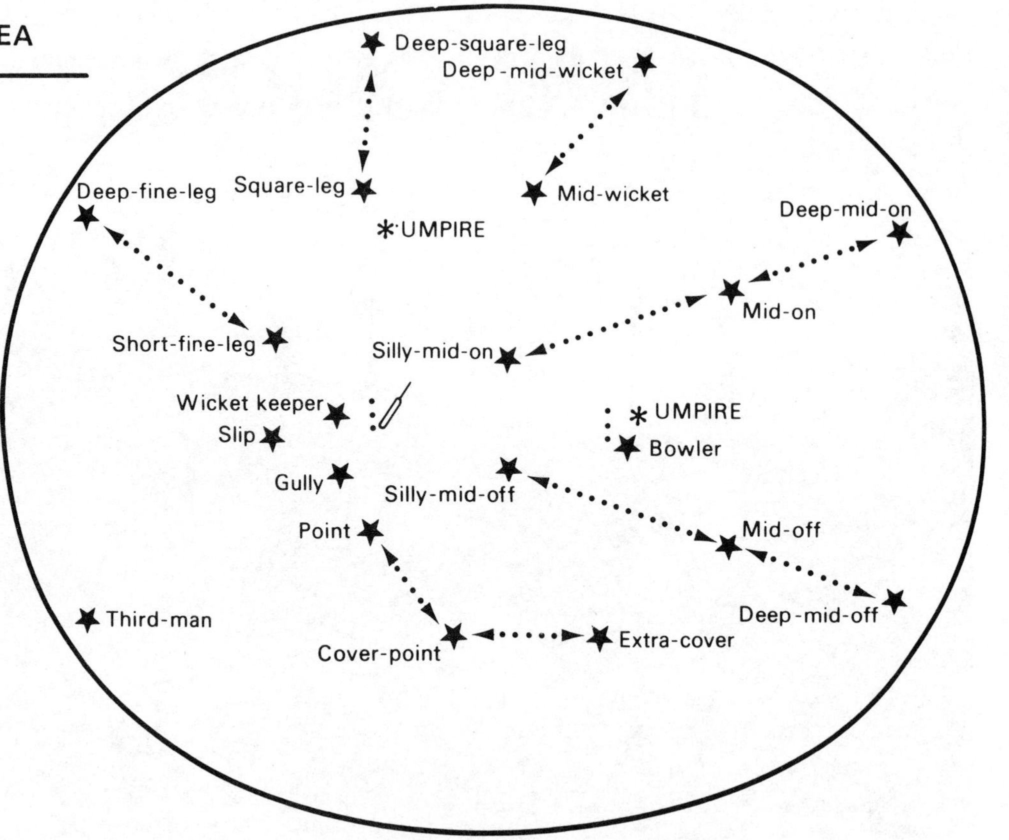

Deep-square-leg
Deep-mid-wicket
Square-leg
Deep-fine-leg
Mid-wicket
*UMPIRE
Deep-mid-on
Short-fine-leg
Mid-on
Silly-mid-on
Wicket keeper
*UMPIRE
Slip
Bowler
Gully
Silly-mid-off
Point
Mid-off
Third-man
Cover-point
Extra-cover
Deep-mid-off

Fielding zones

It is recommended
that children should
not field closer to
the bat than 10m
(in front of wicket).

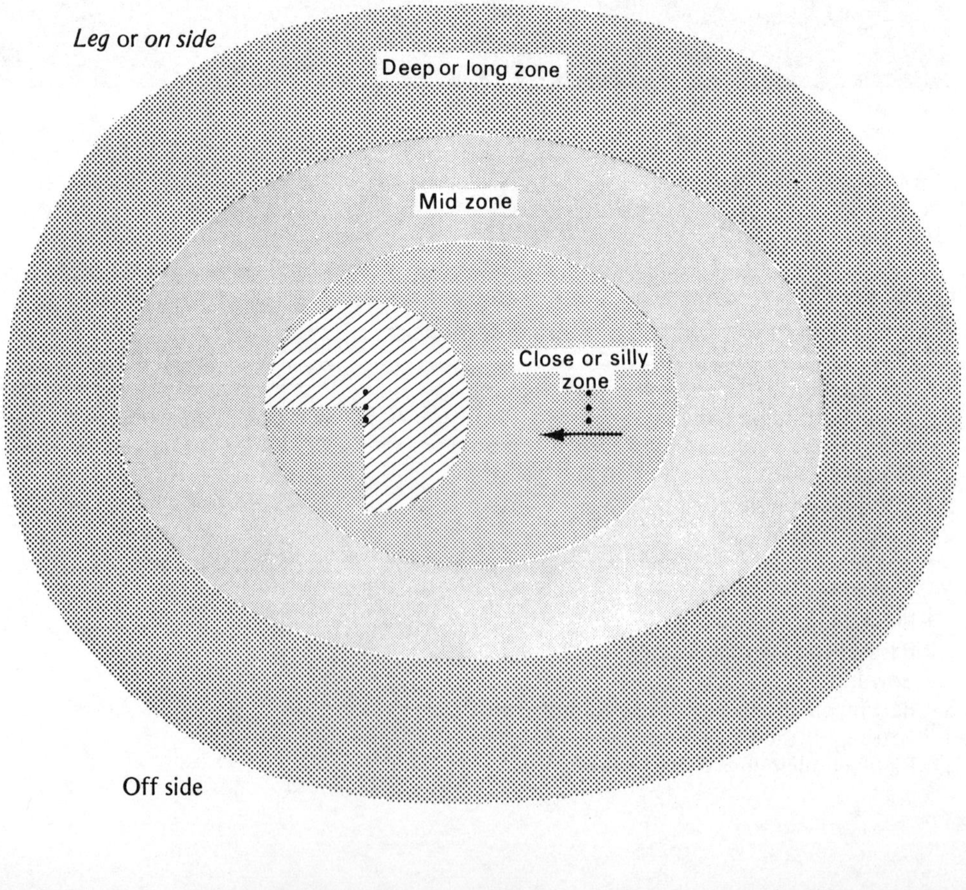

Leg or *on side*

Deep or long zone

Mid zone

Close or silly
zone

Off side

Boundary Distances:

Boundaries may well be determined by the extent of land available. The following are suggested boundary distances:—

Under 11 years	Radius 30m
11-13 years	Radius 35m
Over 13 years	Radius 40m

Pitch Lengths:

Under 11 years	15-16m
11-13 years	17-18m
Over 13 years	20m

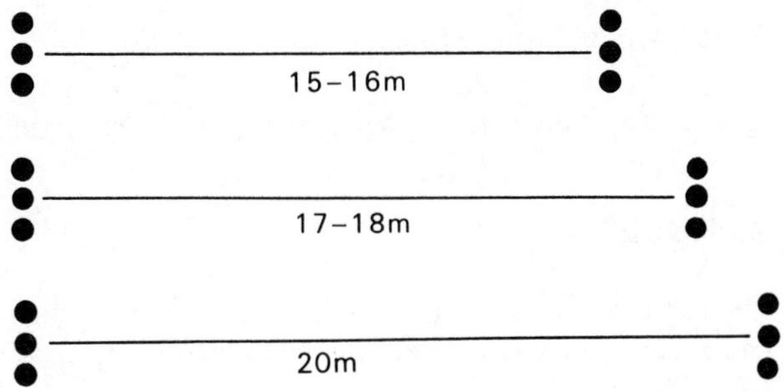

15–16m

17–18m

20m

1.2 ANCILLARY EQUIPMENT

(a) Ball:

1 Start with soft ball until skill develops e.g. tennis ball, rubber ball, lacrosse ball.

2 Synthetic balls are cheaper and more durable than leather.

Under 11 years	4 oz
11-13 years	4¾ oz
Over 13 years	5½ oz

(b) Bat:

1 Start with bat 'shapes' cheaply constructed in woodwork department.

2 If purchasing bats, buy those with an impervious plastic coating to give extra protection and durability.

Under 11 years	Size 4	Length 30"
11-13 years	Size 5	Length 31½"
Over 13 years	Size 6	Length 33"

(c) Stumps:

1 Chalk stumps on walls surrounding play areas.

2 Tie coloured braids/material on to wire fences.

3 Utilize chairs as portable wickets.

4 Make up portable wickets in handicraft department e.g. metal or wood.

5 Make up individual wooden stumps in woodwork department.

All ages   28" high   9" wide.

(d) Pads:

Under 11 years   Boys' size.

(e) Batting Gloves:

Over 11 years   Youths' size.

(f) Wicket Keeping Gloves:

Wear over thin, cotton inner gloves. Junior size for all ages.

2. RULES

The following rules pertain to a mini cricket game which can provide maximum activity and enjoyment for every child. The full laws of cricket can be found in *The Laws of Cricket* (see 6.2).

2.1 INTERPRETATION OF RULES

Rules

Notes

Object
(1) The object of the game is to score a higher *average* number of runs per wicket lost than that • scored by the opposing team.

(1) As will be seen later a player may lose his wicket more than once and these wickets will determine the overall average achieved.

The Teams
(2) Each team has *8 players*.

(2) These 8 players will be divided into 4 pairs for batting purposes.

Duration of Game
(3) Each game shall consist of *one innings* per side. Each innings to consist of 16, 20, 24 overs according to time available.

(3) 16 overs take approximately 45 min.
     20 overs take approximately 1 hr.
     24 overs take approximately 1 hr. 15 min.

Batting
(4) Batting side is divided into 4 pairs. Each pair batting for *4 overs* in a 16 overs innings. Pairs therefore change at end of 4th, 8th, and 12th overs.

(5) During the game the batting side pairs shall organize themselves as follows:

    1 pair batting
    1 pair padding up

If neutral umpires and scorers are not available the remaining pairs should undertake these duties.

(4) Pairs bat proportionally longer if more overs played.

e.g. 5 overs per pair in 20 over match.

(5) Pairs should rotate each time the batting pair finishes its innings.

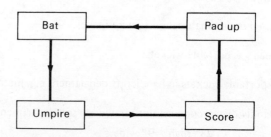

(6) Batters have *unlimited lives*, but each 'life' is recorded on the score sheet as a wicket lost.

If a pair of batters complete their innings without losing a wicket a bonus of *5 runs* is added to their score.

Remember the winning team shall be the one scoring the *highest average* number of runs scored, per wicket lost.
Bonus runs and extras included in total.

(7) Each team starts its innings minus one wicket.

(8) No batter may face more than *6 consecutive balls*. Batters change ends if such a situation arises.
(9) If boundaries are being played their values are as *normal*.

Bowling
(10) With the exception of the wicket-keeper all the fielding side must bowl at least one over. The wicket-keeper normally remains unchanged and is therefore exempted from bowling. In the 16 over game no player may bowl more than *3 overs*: in 20 and 24 over games no player may bowl more than *4 overs*.

(11) Wides and no-balls count 4 runs against fielding side and are added to the opponents' score.
(12) Extras *not* counted towards bowler's 6 ball over.

(6) Specimen score sheet: batting.

names	overs	runs	wkts	avge
John	1 1 . 2 w .			
	. 3 . . 1 2	24	2	12
Susan	1 . 4 w . 3			
	. 2 2 1 . 1			
Peter	3 . 4 4 w .			
	. 1 . . 1 2	28	4	7
Terry	2 2 1 w 1 .			
	4 . w w . 3			
Brian	. . 2 1 . 2			20+5
	3 . . 1 1 1	20	–	25
Tony	. 2 2 . 2 1			
	. . . . 2 .			
Mary	. . . 1 2 2			
	. 1 . 1 4 w	30	2	15
Jimmy	. 1 1 4 3 2			
	1 w 3 2 . 2			
Extras	1 1 4 1 4 1			12
				71

(7) This prevents anomalies arising if neither side loses a wicket.
(8) This rule tries to prevent one player dominating the batting while the partner faces few, if any, balls.
(9) *4 runs* for a ball which touches ground before crossing boundary: *6 runs* if ball crosses boundary before touching ground.

(10) Specimen score sheet: bowling.

names	overs	runs	wkts	avge
John	. 1 . w 2 2			
	2 . . w 4 1	12	2	6
Susan	2 3 . w 1 1			
	w w . 2 1 2	12	3	4
Peter	4 . . . 1 1			
	1 . 1 1 2 .	18	1	18
	3 4 . . w .			
etc				

(11) Bowlers must therefore bowl accurately and correctly to avoid these heavy penalties.
(12) 'Byes', wides and no-balls added to batting score but not to bowler's figures.

2.2 UMPIRING MINI CRICKET

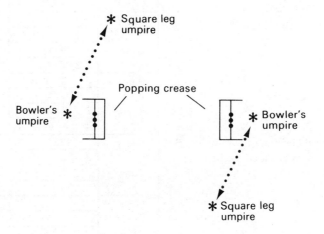

Brief Summary of Duties

Bowler's Umpire

(1) Stand 2m behind and in line with wkts.

(2) Watch the bowler's feet for no-balls.

(3) Watch the line and bounce of the ball (see Laws applying to L.B.W.)

(4) Watch the line of the ball after it has passed the batsman. Any slight deviation may indicate a touch.

(5) When the ball has been hit move to the same side of the pitch as the ball. Take up a position which gives a clear view of the popping crease.

(6) Count the balls (not including extras) and call 'over' when six have been bowled.

Square Leg Umpire

(1) Stand approximately 15m from, and in line with popping crease at batting end. If the view from square leg is obscured the umpire should move to a similar position on the off-side (i.e. point).

(2) Ensure that no fielders are positioned in the danger zone.

(3) Be alert for any possible stumpings.

(4) Watch carefully for any run-outs.

General Points

(1) Read the Laws of Cricket (see ref. 6.2) especially the Laws relating to the popping crease and to L.B.W.

(2) If in *doubt, not out.*

(3) Be consistent and decisive.

(4) Never rush a decision, always pause for thought.

(5) If necessary confer with the other umpire.

3. PRACTICES

3.1 BALL FAMILIARISATION

Activities	*Key points*
1 One ball each — underarm throwing approx. 1m into the air.	Emphasise simple underarm lob, cup hands together, elbows in to body when catching.
2 Underarm throwing into the air but vary height of throw.	Smooth upward movement of throwing arm, get into position quickly under dropping ball.
3 Same as above but catch with one hand, both left and right.	Watch ball carefully, try to catch above and below the head.
4 Now vary throwing hand and and catching hand.	How many different combinations can you find?
5 Underarm throw into the air slightly away from body to move and catch.	Not too far at first, watch out for other people.
6 Vary throwing and catching hands when throwing away from body.	Position yourself quickly under dropping ball.
7 Throw into the air with bowling action and catch.	Start with arm straight behind back, simply raise hand keeping arm straight.
8 Throw into the air and away from the body with bowling action.	Really challenge yourself to make the catch difficult.
9 Throw into the air in as many different ways as possible (e.g. javelin throw, arm under leg).	Try to catch every throw. Who can find the most ways and still catch the ball?
10 If the ball bounces — bounce low, high, very high, fast, slow, on a target (e.g. a line).	Bend your knees to catch low bounces, jump in the air to catch very high bounces.

Examples of Competitive Challenges

(a) Beat Your Own Record	How many consecutive catches can you make before the ball falls to the ground?
(b) Time Challenges	Who can bowl the ball into the air the most times in 20 sec?

(c) Race	Throwing ball into the air, walking or running over set distance.
(d) Relay Race	Small teams, standing in lines, a few metres apart. Which team can throw and catch down the line the quickest?

3.2 BASIC HITTING WITH A PARTNER

Activities

1 Shadow/copy the basic stance demonstrated by teacher.

2 5m apart, underarm throw by feeder aiming for bottom of bat. Ball hit on the full (before bouncing) straight back to feeder.

3 5m apart, underarm feed, ball hit on half-volley (i.e. just after it has bounced) straight back to feeder.

4 8m apart, underarm feed to bounce 2m in front of batter. Play the ball straight back to feeder.

Key points

Stand sideways to wicket, hands held close together. *Left* hand on *top*, stand up straight, keep eyes level.

Emphasize *straight* upright bat, stepping forward on to left leg, picking up bat behind body, left elbow kept high to angle bat downwards.

Feeder aims to bounce ball 1m in front of batter. Batter must pick correct time to step forward. Hit ball back along ground.

Batter now moves forward quickly to play stroke, otherwise same technique. Aim to get left foot close to bounce of ball.

Examples of Competitive Challenges

(a) Beat Your Own Record	How many consecutive hits can you make before missing your partner's feed?
(b) How Accurate Are You? 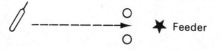	When feeding, partner stands behind target area (e.g. bricks, shoes), batter tries to hit ball through target.
(c) Target Competition 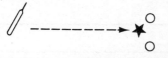 Fence, wall, etc. if available	Feeder stands in front of target and tries to stop batter hitting ball through target. Change opponents often.
(d) French Cricket	Groups of four. One batter, others try to hit batter below the knees with underarm throw. Batter defends legs with straight bat and hits ball away but cannot move feet at all. Ball is thrown from where it is retrieved. Catches count as 'out'. Fielder hitting legs or catching ball takes over as batter.

3.3 BOWLING

Skill 1   *Stationary Bowling Action*

Activities

1 All group • Shadow/copy bowling action demonstrated by teacher.

2 All group • Random practice of bowling action without ball.

3 Pairs • 20m apart, bowl ball to each other from 'coil' position (i.e. action at delivery).

Key points

Hold ball with fingers not palm, turn sideways, look at batter behind raised straight left arm.

As player steps on to left leg, right arm brought over straight.

No run up, back foot at right angles to bowling line, long step on to left leg, swing arm over in vertical plane, not around to side.

4 Pairs • 20m apart, bowl from coil position at target on ground (e.g. tile, hoop, chalked square).

Line up left arm in direction of target, keep all of action in the one plane, follow through stepping on to right leg.

5 Pairs • 20m apart, bowl from coil position at wickets (e.g. chairs, portable wickets).

Concentrate upon consistency trying to maintain true coil action, always step on to left leg at delivery.

Skill 2   *Bowling Action with Run Up*

1 All group • Shadow/copy run up and bowling action demonstrated by teacher.

2 All group • Random practice of bowling action without ball.

3 Pairs • 20m wicket distance, run up and bowl to partner.

4 Pairs • Bowl at targets on ground and at wickets.

Short, easy approach (no more than 8 steps) slight jump from left to right foot just before coil action as used in stationary action.

Right foot should be at right angles to bowling line after the jump, body leans slightly back.

Keep eyes fixed on wicket, keep bowling arm straight, natural follow-through.

Try to achieve a completely smooth action with no pauses, jerking or clumsy steps.

5 Pairs • Vary the type of bowling, e.g. bowl over and around wicket (i.e. left and right sides); short of a length, full toss; angling in to and away from wicket.

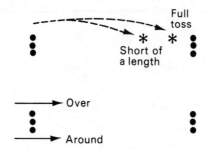

Notice the different demands of bowling different types of ball, e.g. turning the body slightly more, directing the arm in a different way, releasing the ball earlier or later.

Examples of Competitive Challenges

(a) Beat Your Own Record   How many times can you hit the target/wicket?

(b) Time Challenges   How many wickets can you bowl in 2 min?

(c) Partner Competitions   Who can bowl the most full tosses in one over (i.e. hitting a pre-determined target area on the ground)?

(d) Target Bowling

Bowler - - - - → (1(2(3)))   Fence, wall, etc.

Fours, 2 v 2, points scored according to where ball pitches (bounces).

(e) Challenge Bowling

Bowler - - - - →   1 m. [ ] 3 m.   Target area   Fence, wall, etc.

Fours, 2 v 2,
1 point scored if ball pitches in target
1 point scored if ball hits wicket
3 points if ball pitches in target and hits wicket.

(f) Non-stop Cricket

Batting team

←———10m———→ ★ Bowler

1 Teams of preferably not more than 8 players.
2 Players arranged as in diagram. Batting team must stay where positioned so as not to interfere with play. Fielding side may position themselves anywhere.
3 Ball may be bowled overarm or underarm from *stationary position*.
4 Batsman *must run* around obstacle every time he hits the ball in front of the wicket.
5 Runs may only be scored when ball hit *in front* of wicket.
6 Bowler may bowl as soon as fielders have returned ball, whether batter has returned to wicket or not.
7 Batter can be out bowled, caught or hit wicket.

3.4 BATTING OFF THE BACK FOOT (INCLUDING PAIRS CRICKET)

Skill 1   Pull Stroke

Activities

Key points

1 All group • Shadow/copy pull stroke as demonstrated by teacher.

Pick bat up high, step back and across with right foot, left foot comes back level with right, bat swung down and across body.

2 Pairs • Underarm feed for partner to play pull to leg. Position pairs so that ball is hit at fence/wall.

Feed short so that ball bounces up to hip height. Keep body square to line of ball, hit well in front of body.

3 Pairs • As above but batter attempts to hit targets on fence/wall.

Mark 3 targets:— Forward, square, and behind wicket, aim for particular target.

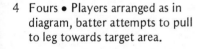

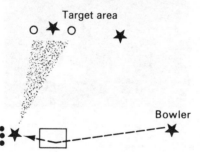

4 Fours • Players arranged as in diagram, batter attempts to pull to leg towards target area.

Stationary overarm bowling to pitch ball on target, use two balls so that one can be played while other is being returned to bowler, change often.

Skill 2   Attacking Drive off Back Foot

1 All group • Shadow/copy stroke as demonstrated by teacher.

Pick bat up high, step back on to right foot, swing bat down to hit ball just in front of body.

2 Pairs • 10m apart, underarm feed for partner to play attacking stroke.

Feed short. Batter keeps left elbow high, hit with bat vertical, follow through in line with stroke.

3 Pairs ● 20m wicket, overarm bowl for partner to play stroke, bowl between skittles/shoes etc.

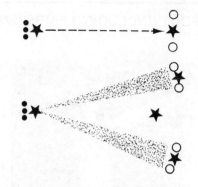

Pitch ball short. Batter tries to swing bat through in one vertical plane, always keep head down looking at ball.

4 Fours ● Players arranged as in diagram, batter attempts attacking stroke to target areas.

Pitch ball short. Ball on the off-side should be played out to off-side target area, on-side ball should be played out to on-side target area.

Skill 3 Backward Defensive

1 All group ● Shadow/copy stroke as demonstrated by teacher.

Pick bat up high, step back on to right foot, meet ball with full face of bat, bat kept still on impact.

2 Pairs ● 10m apart, underarm feed for partner to play defensive stroke.

Feed short. Batter steps back slightly in front of wicket. Keep left elbow high, angle bat down.

3 Pairs ● 20m wicket, overarm bowl for partner to play stroke.

Pitch ball short, try to make batter give a catch. Batter angles bat down to avoid giving a catch.

4 Fours ● Players as arranged in diagram, batter tries to avoid giving catch to fielders.

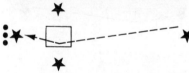

Play ball back in line with position received (i.e. to off-side if ball pitches on the off-side).

Examples of Competitive Challenges

(a) Make Activities Competitive

e.g. Skill 2 no. 3 Batter tries to force ball through target area. Run scored if successful.

(b) Pairs Cricket

1 Pitch size according to recommendations (see 1.1).
2 Game played between pairs. (Between 3 and 6 pairs optimum.)
3 Winning pair is the one with highest *average* number of runs per wicket lost.
4 Game organised as follows:

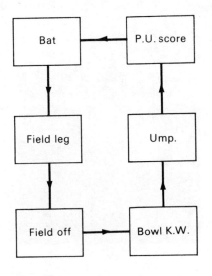

Pair 1 Bats 2 overs
Pair 2 Fields leg-side 2 overs
Pair 3 Fields off-side 2 overs
Pair 4 Bowl and keep wicket
   (1 over each)
Pair 5 Umpire — 2 overs
Pair 6 Pad up and score 2 overs

6 pairs @ 2 overs = 30 min approx.
Overs can be increased if more
time available.
If fewer pairs playing (e.g. 4),
padding up and umpiring can be
omitted.
5 Six ball overs delivered to
  alternate wickets.
6 Scoring as for Mini Cricket
  (see Rules).
7 Dismissals:

1 Bowled   3 Hit wicket
2 Caught   4 Run out

3.5 BATTING OFF THE FRONT FOOT

Skill 1   Attacking Drive off Front Foot

Activities

Key points

1 All group ● Shadow/copy drive
as demonstrated by teacher.

Pick bat up high, lean head and
shoulders forward while stepping
to the line of the approaching ball.

2 Pairs ● 10m apart. Underarm feed
for partner to play drive. Pitch
ball well up to batter.

Front foot placed just to left of
approaching ball, bat held down
very close to front foot.

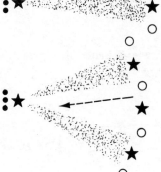

3 Pairs ● 20m wicket, overarm bowl
for partner to play drive, bowl
between skittles, shoes etc.

Pitch ball up. Batter tries to step
close to pitch of ball hitting on
half-volley with no gap between
bat and pad.

4 Fours ● Players arranged as in
diagram, batter attempts drive
to target areas.

Pitch ball up. Ball approaching on
the off-side should be played out to
off-side target area, on-side ball
should be played to on-side target
area.

Skill 2   Forward Defence

1 All group • Shadow/copy forward
   defence as demonstrated by
   teacher.

2 Pairs • 10m apart, underarm feed
   for partner to play forward defence stroke. Pitch ball well up
   to batter.

3 Pairs • 20m wicket, overarm bowl
   for partner to play forward
   defensive.

4 Fours • Players arranged as in
   diagram, batter plays forward
   defensive, fielders try to catch.

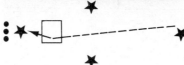

Pick bat up high, lean head and
shoulders forward while stepping
to the line of approaching ball.

Front foot placed just to left of
approaching ball, bat comes down
very close to front leg meeting ball
with full face of bat. No follow
through.

Pitch ball up. Batter tries to step
close to pitch of ball hitting on
half-volley with no gap between bat
and pad.

Pitch ball on target. Batter keeps
left elbow high to angle bat downwards and play ball into ground.

Examples of Competitive Challenges

(a) Make Activities Competitive

e.g. Skill 1 no. 4. Batter tries to force ball through target areas.
Run scored if successful.

(b) Rotation Cricket

1 Pitch size according to recommendations (see 1.1).
2 Players divided into 2 teams.
  Eight-a-side preferable.
3 Winning team is the one with
  highest *average* number of runs
  per wicket lost.
4 Game organised as follows:

(a) Players take up positions
    as shown on diagram.
(b) Batter receives one 12
    ball over. If batter
    finishes up at bowler's
    end he walks back down
    wicket when ball is
    dead.

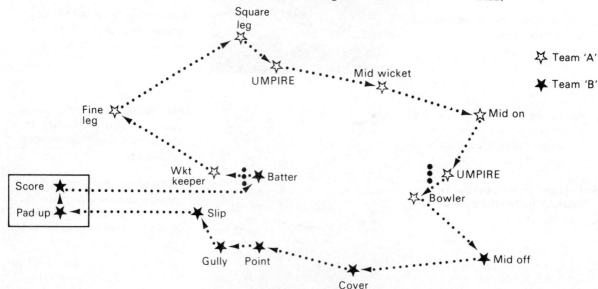

(c) At end of over all players move round one position clockwise.

(d) Players of the same team may not bowl to each other.

(Note positions of players from each team).

(e) Scoring: same principle as Mini Cricket (see Rules).

3.6 FIELDING (INCLUDING WICKET KEEPING)

Skill 1 Fielding Ball on the Ground

Activities

1 Pairs • 10m apart, roll ball to each other to practise stopping.

2 Pairs • 20m apart, same as above but over greater distance.

3 Pairs • 20m apart, same as above but make partner move to stop ball.

4 Pairs • 20m apart, A rolls ball to B who collects and throws back to A who now keeps wicket.

5 Pairs • 20m apart, as above except ball collected and returned on the move.

Skill 2 Catching

1 Pairs • 5m apart. Experiment with every kind of catch possible (e.g. 2 hands, 1 hand, low, fast, slow).

2 Pairs • 10m, 20m, 30m apart. Experiment as above.

Skill 3 Wicket Keeping

1 Pairs • Partner bowls down the wicket giving a variety of balls.

Key points

Get in line with approaching ball, kneel sideways on one leg, fingers point down, hands together to receive ball.

Make a long barrier with lower leg in kneeling position in case hands miss ball.

Aim a few metres to side of partner. Move quickly to get in line with ball.

When ball is safely collected turn sideways, point left hand at wicket and throw while stepping on to left leg.

Move towards line of approaching ball, bend down with hands together fingers pointing down; without pausing pick up and throw.

Anticipate flight of approaching ball, make a cup shape, little fingers together, elbows in to chest, hands and arms relaxed.

How many different types of throw and catch can you find?

Crouch down just behind and to the side of stumps, keep evenly balanced on toes.

2 Threes • One player bowls, second
   bats aiming just to miss ball.

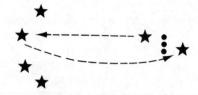

Wicket-keeper steps towards line of
ball, fingers point down, hands
together, palms face forward.

3 Sixes • One player hits ball out
   to fielders who collect and
   return to wicket-keeper.

Wicket-keeper stands behind
stumps, otherwise technique same
as 1 and 2.

Examples of Competitive Challenges

(a) Beat Your Own Record   How many consecutive catches can you make?

(b) Time Challenges   Who can collect and return most balls in 3 min?

(c) Competitive Collecting

←———— 20m ————→

In pairs, each player guards
specified area; partner tries to
roll ball through target area.

(d) Competitive Collecting

←———— 40–50m ————→

In fours, 3 players guard a large
target area (e.g. on boundary),
batter tries to hit ball through
target area.

(e) Circle Catching   Approximately 8 players in circle, throw difficult (but possible)
catches to anyone in an effort to force a dropped catch, penalty
if catch dropped.

(f) Howitzer

1 Two teams of 2 players. 100 x
  20m playing area.

2 Both teams start midway in
  own halves.

3 Object is to throw ball over
  opponents' end line.

4 If ball is caught, player may
  take 5 strides before throwing.
  If ball touches ground, throw
  from where stopped.

5 Ball must be thrown over head
  height.

6 Ball must stay in specified area
  (e.g. if ball thrown out of area,
  opponents may throw from
  where it crosses line and not
  where they stop it).

7 Point scored if ball crosses
  opponents' end line.

4. PROFICIENCY AWARDS

1 Award Scheme Title	'Test' Cricket
2 Organising Body	National Cricket Association
3 Aim	To provide a series of incentives that will encourage boys and girls to learn and enjoy the skills of cricket.
4 Award Details	Score needed to pass each Test:

1st Test	40 Points
2nd Test	60 Points
Final Test	75 Points

The Tests are passed by attempting the appropriate skills tests in each of the following:—

Fielding	30 Points max.
Batting	30 Points max.
Bowling/wicket-keeping	30 Points max.
Oral	10 Points max.
Possible total score	100 Points

5 Applications

Entry forms, record sheets and further information from The Administrator, N.C.A., Proficiency Awards Scheme, Lord's Cricket Ground, London, NW8 8QN.

Batting Tests

Strokes

1 Pull	To be played off	Back foot
2 On drive		Front foot
3 Straight drive		Front or Back foot
4 Off drive		Front foot
5 Cover drive		Front foot
6 Forcing shot		Back foot
7 Cut		Back foot
8 Lofted drive		Front foot

Strokes 1 to 7. The ball must be struck so that it bounces at least once before passing, with reasonable speed, between two markers 10 metres apart placed at a distance of 20 metres. Markers can be placed proportionally closer if space is restricted.

Stroke 8. The ball must pass between two markers, and carry beyond them before pitching. The markers are placed at the appropriate distance. It is recommended that a tennis ball is used for all tests.

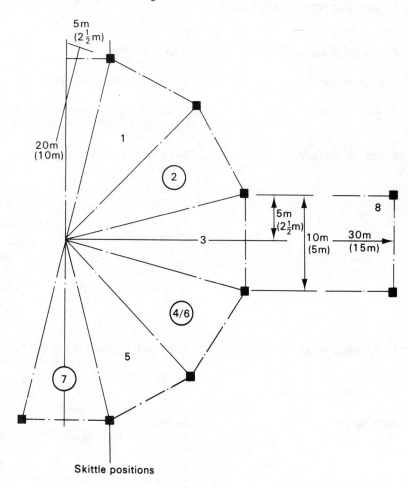

Lay-out for batting tests

Skittle positions

1st Test
Select three strokes, 10 attempts at each.
One point each successful attempt.
Possible score, 3 x 10 = 30 points.

2nd Test
Select five strokes, 6 attempts at each.
One point each successful attempt.
Possible score, 5 x 6 = 30 points.

Final Test
Select six strokes, 5 attempts at each
One point each successful attempt.
Possible score, 6 x 5 = 30 points.

Service
Front foot strokes, ball dropped vertically onto a target, one stride in front of the batsman and hit on the second bounce. Back foot strokes, ball thrown from a distance of approx. 10 metres onto a target approx. 5 metres away from the batsman.

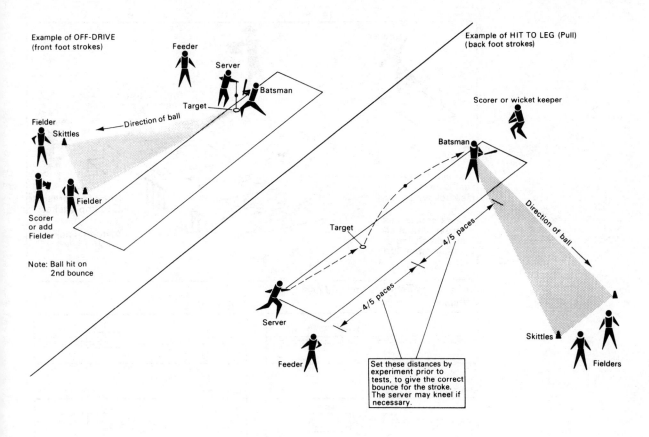

Example of OFF-DRIVE (front foot strokes)

Feeder
Server
Batsman
Target
Direction of ball
Fielder
Skittles
Fielder
Scorer or add Fielder

Note: Ball hit on 2nd bounce

Example of HIT TO LEG (Pull) (back foot strokes)

Scorer or wicket keeper
Batsman
Target
4/5 paces
4/5 paces
Direction of ball
Server
Feeder
Skittles
Fielders
4/5 paces

Set these distances by experiment prior to tests, to give the correct bounce for the stroke. The server may kneel if necessary.

Bowling Tests

Pitch

11 years of age and under	18 yards	*Distances should*
12 and 13 years of age	20 yards	*be measured*
14 years of age and over	22 yards	*for tests*

Ball for Boys

13 years of age and under	4¾oz
14 years of age and over	5½oz

Ball for Girls

18 years of age and under	4¾oz

Plastic type for swing
Leather for spin   *(recommendation only)*

All Tests

Two overs to be bowled, best over to count. The bowler may bowl over or round the wicket with an overarm action.
An over is 6 consecutive deliveries.
Possible score per ball 5 points.
Possible score per over 6 x 5 = 30 points.

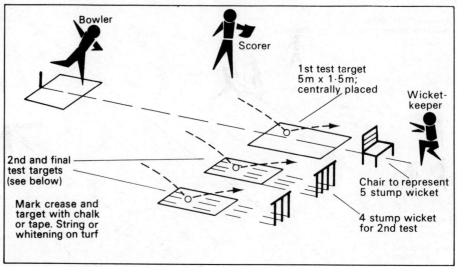

Target measurements 2nd and final tests

Off-spin

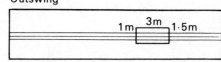

Outswing

Leg-spin

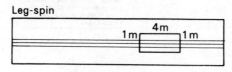

Inswing

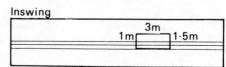

1st Test

Wicket, 5 stumps wide. (i.e. School chair or similar will suffice).
Target, 5m x 1.5m, in front of popping crease and centrally placed.
Score: 3 points for hitting target, 2 points for hitting wicket.

2nd Test

Wicket, 4 stumps wide or board to represent.
Target,

    Offspin 3m x 1m
    Legspin 4m x 1m   placed as
    Outswing 3m x 1m   indicated
    Inswing 3m x 1m

Score: 2 points for hitting target, 2 points for hitting wicket, 1 point for swing or spin.

Final Test

Wicket, normal 3 stumps.
Target

    Offspin 3m x 1m
    Legspin 4m x 1m   placed as
    Outswing 3m x 1m   indicated
    Inswing 3m x 1m

Score as for 2nd Test.

Wicket Keeping Tests

Equipment — Pads, gloves and inners, protector.

1st Test

1 Standing up — take 5 consecutive deliveries from a slow bowler.

Each delivery to be returned to the bowler at easily catchable height. 2 points for each clean 'take'. Deduct one (1) point for each inaccurate return. Maximum points 10.

2 Standing back, take 5 consecutive deliveries from a pace bowler, the ball should not be allowed to bounce after passing the wicket. *In this test a batsman should 'shadow' strokes.*

2 points for each clean 'take'. Maximum points 10.

2nd Test

1 Standing up — take 5 consecutive deliveries from a slow bowler. Each delivery to be returned to the bowler at easily catchable height. *In this test a batsman should 'shadow' defensive strokes.* Score as in 1st Test.

2 Standing back, take 5 consecutive deliveries from a pace bowler. The ball should not be allowed to bounce after passing the wicket. *In this test a batsman should play at all deliveries missing occasionally until the wicket-keeper has had the opportunity of taking 5 deliveries.*

2 points for each clean 'take'. Score as in 1st Test.

Final Test

1 Standing up — take 5 consecutive deliveries from a slow bowler as 1 and 2. *In this test a batsman should play at all deliveries missing occasionally until the wicket keeper has had the opportunity of taking 5 deliveries.*
Score as in 1st and 2nd Tests.

2 Standing back, take 5 consecutive deliveries from a pace bowler as in 2nd Test.
Two of the 5 deliveries must be taken in one hand only.
2 points for each clean 'take'.
Score as in 1st and 2nd Tests.

Chalk or ad. tape-
wickets, two markers.
Catching area.

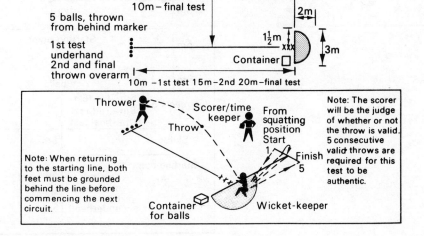

Maximum points per Test: 30. 10(1) 10(2) 10(3)

Where possible, wicket-keeping tests to be taken with bowling tests,
i.e. balls same as for bowling tests.

All Tests

3 From a measured distance behind the wicket run up to the wicket and
take 5 consecutive throws from a measured distance square with the
wicket. After each 'take', return to the starting point before running to
the wicket again. Throws should be made only when the wicket-keeper
is in the marked area, alongside the wicket. As soon as a throw has been
'taken' it must be dropped into the container before starting the next
circuit. Maximum points 10.

*A deductable time allowance of
3 sec is made for each clean
'take', e.g. Time taken from
start to finish 34 sec., 4 clean
takes (4 x 3) less 12 = 22.
8 points scored.*

Time Taken	Points
20	10
20.1 – 25	8
25.1 – 30	6
30.1 – 35	4
35.1 – 40	2

Fielding Tests

Use tennis balls for 1st Test, Cricket balls for 2nd and Final Tests.

Catching

Six consecutive attempts to catch a ball thrown or hit the appropriate
distance. 1 point for each catch. Maximum 6 points.

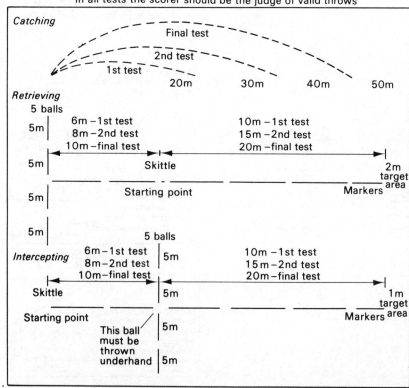

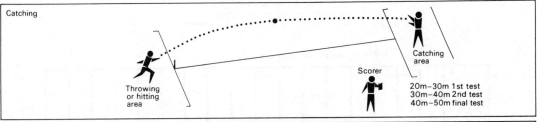

Catching

Throwing or hitting area

Scorer

Catching area

20m–30m 1st test
30m–40m 2nd test
40m–50m final test

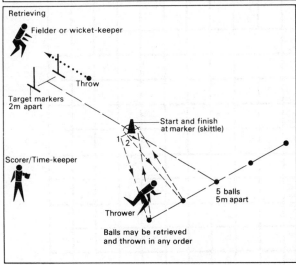

Retrieving

Fielder or wicket-keeper

Throw

Target markers
2m apart

Start and finish
at marker (skittle)

Scorer/Time-keeper

Thrower

5 balls
5m apart

Balls may be retrieved
and thrown in any order

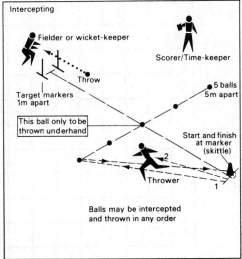

Intercepting

Fielder or wicket-keeper

Scorer/Time-keeper

Throw

Target markers
1m apart

5 balls
5m apart

This ball only to be
thrown underhand

Start and finish
at marker
(skittle)

Thrower

Balls may be intercepted
and thrown in any order

Retrieving

A consecutive effort to retrieve and throw 5 balls through a 2m target.
After each throw the fielder must return to the starting point. A deductable time allowance of *3 secs is allowed* for each throw that passes
through the target with reasonable speed and has not bounced before the
target.

Time (secs)	Points
20	12
20.1–25	10
25.1–30	8
30.1–35	6
35.1–40	4
40.1–45	2
45	0

Time taken is recorded from
when the fielder leaves the starting point to when the fielder
passes that point after the final
throw. 12 points maximum.

Intercepting

A consecutive effort to intercept and throw 5 balls through a 1m target.
After each throw the fielder must return to the starting point. A deductable time allowance of *3 secs is allowed* for each throw that passes
through the target with reasonable speed and has not bounced before the
target.

Note: The middle ball must be thrown underhand. Time taken as 2.
12 points maximum.

e.g. scoring 2 and 3:
Time taken: 35 sec.
Valid Throws: 4.
Points: 35 − (4 x 3) = 23 = 10 points.
Maximum Points per Test: 30
      6 − Catching
    12 − Retrieving
    12 − Intercepting

National Cricket Association
Award Scheme for Proficiency in the Skills of Cricket
With the support of the Wrigley Cricket Foundation

RECORD SHEET

(this record sheet is for the convenience of examiners, not to be returned)

NAME																				
TEST																				
FIELDING C																				
FIELDING R																				
FIELDING I																				
TOTAL																				
BATTING 1																				
BATTING 2																				
BATTING 3																				
BATTING 4																				
BATTING 5																				
BATTING 6																				
BATTING 7																				
BATTING 8																				
TOTAL																				
BOWLING 1–6																				
TOTAL																				
WICKET KEEPING a																				
WICKET KEEPING b																				
WICKET KEEPING c																				
TOTAL																				
ORAL																				
GRAND TOTAL																				

6 General Details

1 All children are eligible for the Awards. A youngster may enter at 1st or 2nd Test level, according to ability.
2 Successful candidates receive badges and inscribed certificates.
3 A small fee is charged to cover costs.
4 Schools, clubs, recognised bodies (e.g. Youth Clubs) and individuals may organise Test Cricket.
5 Any teacher or adult member of the organising body may examine the 1st and 2nd Tests.

The Final Test may be examined by:

(a) Any holder of an N.C.A. or M.C.C. Coaching or Teaching Award.
(b) Anyone nominated by the Local C.C. or Schools C.C.A. or the L.E.A.

6 Tests may be continued over a number of sessions.
7 'Proficiency Award', a film guide to Test Cricket for coaches may be hired from the N.C.A.

5. TEACHING/COACHING QUALIFICATIONS

5.1 RANGE OF COURSES

1 Introductory Course for clubs and schools (6 hrs).

2 Teaching Award Course (12 hrs); Certificated.

3 Teaching Award (12 hrs); Certificated.

4 Coaching Award Course (20 hrs); Certificated.

5 Senior Coaching Award (20 hrs); Regional Certificate.

6 Advanced Course (national 7-day residential course); Certificated.

Applications

Courses organised by:

Colleges of Education
Local Education Authorities
County Cricket Associations.

Information regarding local courses can be obtained from:

The Director of Coaching
National Cricket Association
Lord's Cricket Ground
London NW8 8QN

6. REFERENCE INFORMATION

6.1 USEFUL ADDRESSES

English Schools' Cricket Association
Secretary: C.J. Cooper
68 Hatherley Road
Winchester
Hampshire

National Association for Young Cricketers
Secretary: C. Smith
Benton Cottage
Springstone Avenue
Ossett
West Yorkshire

National Cricket Association
Secretary: B.J. Aspital
Lord's Cricket Ground
London NW8 8QN

National Cricket Association Film Library
N.C.A.
Lord's Cricket Ground
London NW8 8QN

Women's Cricket Association
Administrative Officer
16 Upper Woburn Place
London WC1H 0QP

6.2 CRICKET REFERENCES

Publication				Description of Mini Game	Skill Descriptions	Practices	Tactics	Senior Rules
Andrew K. Carter B. Lenham L. 1978	Cricket – the techniques of the game	E.P. Pub. Co.	Book	*	*		*	*
Chappell G. 1974	Successful Cricket	Pelham	Book		*			
Cowdray C. 1974	Tackle Cricket	Stanley Paul	Book		*		*	
Creek F.N.S. 1973	Cricket	English Univ. Press	Book		*			*
Duff A. Chesterton G. 1974	Your Book of Cricket	Faber & Faber	Book		*			
Greig T. 1974	Greig on Cricket	Stanley Paul	Book		*		*	
Illingworth R. 1972	The Young Cricketer	Stanley Paul	Book		*		*	
Know the Game	Cricket	E.P. Pub. Co.	Booklet					*
M.C.C. 1972	M.C.C. Cricket Coaching Book	Heinemann	Book		*	*		
N.C.A.	Various Instructional Films in Film Library				*	*		
N.C.A.	The Laws of Cricket							*
N.C.A. 1977	Test Cricket in Clubs and Schools	N.C.A.	Booklet	*	*	*		
Oakman A.S.M. 1980	Games for Cricket Training	Pelham	Book			*		
Richards B. 1975	Cricket	Pelham	Book		*			
Sutcliffe P. 1976	Teaching Cricket Simply	Lepus	Book	*	*			
Women's Cricket Assoc. 1970	Mini-Cricket	W.C.A.	Booklet	*		*		

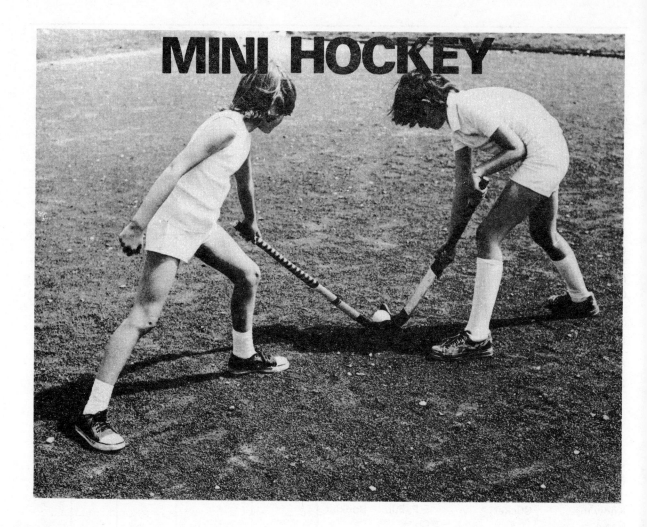

CONTENTS

1. PLAYING AREA

1.1 THE PITCH

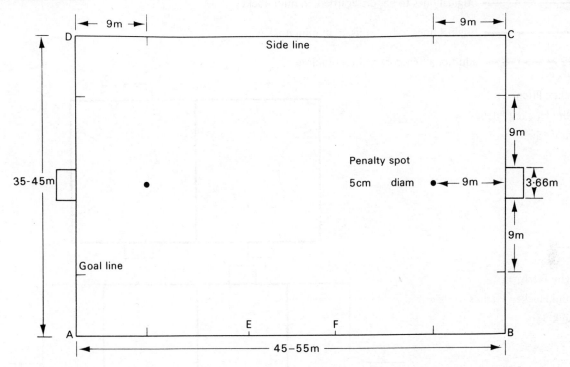

Note: There is *no* striking circle.

Marking Instructions (For 50 x 40m pitch)

1 Use two lengths of string:

   (a) 50m with a knot tied at 20m and 30m.
   (b) 40m with a knot tied at 9m.

2 Fix one end of 50m string at A, hold string taut and mark B. Also mark points E and F (20m and 30m from A).

3 Fix one end of 40m string at A and fix one end of 50m string at F. Holding the free end of both strings walk away until they are taut. Point D may then be marked.

4 Now fix one end of 40m string at B and fix one end of 50m string at E. Holding the free end of both strings walk away until they are taut. Point C may then be marked.

5 Mark exterior lines joining ABCD. All 9m points may also be marked with the 40m string knotted at 9m.

1.2 ADAPTATIONS OF OTHER PLAYING AREAS

─────────────── original lines to be 'disregarded' in mini hockey

━━━━━━━━━━━━━━━ original lines to be 'utilised' in mini hockey

━ ━ ━ ━ ━ ━ additional temporary lines required

Hockey Pitch
2 Mini Hockey Pitches
60m x 45m

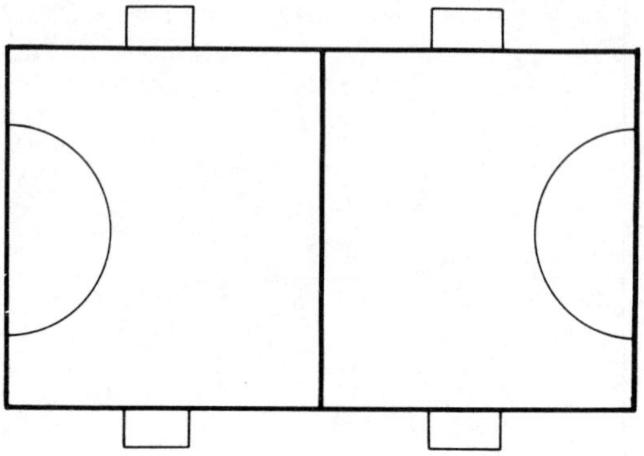

Rugby Pitch
2 Mini Hockey Pitches
70m x 33m

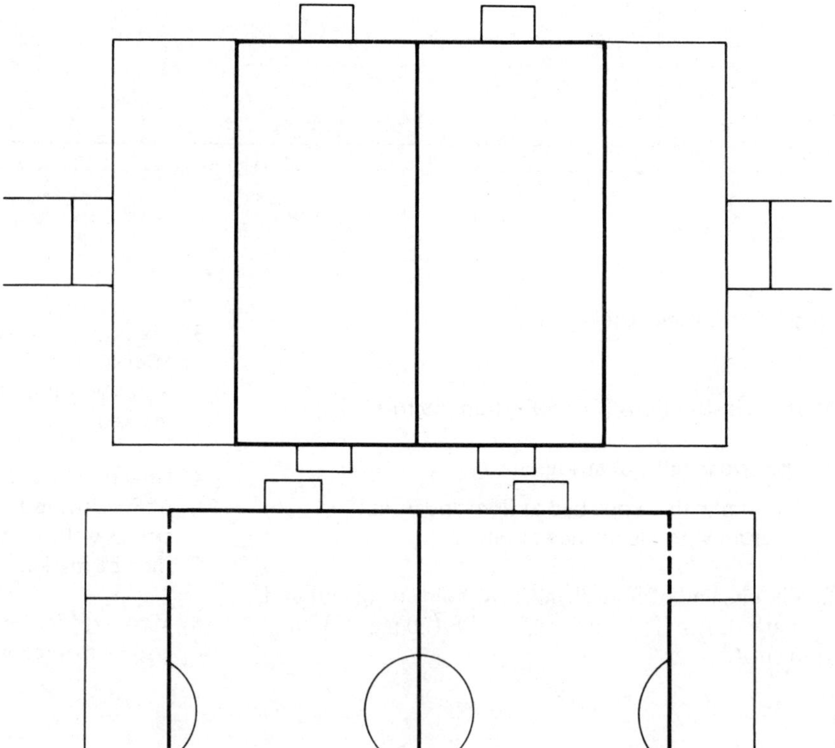

Soccer Pitch
2 Mini Hockey Pitches
70m x 40m

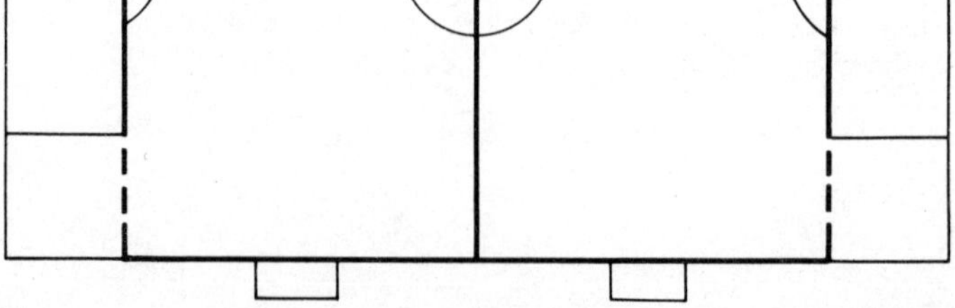

1.3 ANCILLARY EQUIPMENT

(a) Goal Posts:

1 Senior goals may be utilised as they are of the same dimensions.

2 Portable posts of light tubular metal are also effective and durable. Some means of attaching goal-boards would need to be found however.

3 Coloured plastic marker cones make ideal goal posts. Especially useful for small-sided games.

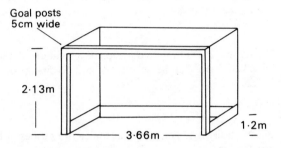

(b) Stick:

Sticks may not exceed 28 oz, nor be less than 12 oz in weight; for mini hockey children will probably need sticks of less than 18 oz. There is no restriction on length and 30-34'' is probably most suitable.

(c) Ball:

1 Inner core of cork and twine, outer cover of white leather. Weight 5½ oz, circumference 9''.

2 Composition balls and plastic balls are cheaper and suitable for practice.

3 A soft-core ball of similar weight to a hockey ball can be used in the early introductory stages.

(d) Shin Pads:

Essential for the protection of the shins. Those with foam lining, plastic covering and tie ups are most efficient.

2. RULES

The full rules of senior hockey can be found in *Rules of the Game of Hockey* (see 6.2).

2.1 INTERPRETATION OF RULES

Rules

Notes

Object

(1) The main object of the game is to push, hit or flick the ball with the stick into the goal of the opposing team.

(1) As there is no circle a goal may be scored from *anywhere* on the pitch, provided the stroke is legal.

The Teams

(2) A team has *7 players*: 6 field players and 1 goal-keeper. The goalkeeper may wear regulation pads, kickers and gloves.

(2) A team may elect to play without an equipped goal-keeper, in which case they may nominate a kicking-defender who must wear some distinguishable clothing to indicate this fact.

Time in Play

(3) Playing time shall be two halves of a maximum of, *10 minutes* and a minimum of *6 minutes* with an interval of not more than 2 minutes.

(3) Where the minimum duration of a total of 12 minutes is taken there shall be no interval and no change of ends.

Ball in Play

(4) At the commencement of play in each half and after each goal a *hit/push back* shall be taken from the centre spot.

(4) No bully-off. The player at the centre pushes or hits the ball back to one of his or her team members.

(5) The ball *may* be raised off the ground in normal play providing it is not dangerous.

(6) There is *no off-side*.

(5) If the ball lands amongst other players it is constituted as dangerous.

(6) Players are thus free to move anywhere on the pitch during play.

(7) When the ball passes over the *side-line* a player opposed to the team who last touched the ball will take a *hit* or *push-in* from the point where the ball crossed the line.

(7) Ensure players of both teams are at least 5 metres from the ball.

(8) A *free hit* shall be awarded to the defending team if the attacking team plays the ball over defenders' goal-line. Hit to be taken up to 9 metres from goal-line opposite where ball went out of play.

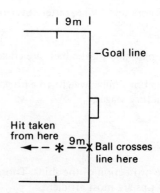

| 9m |

—Goal line

Hit taken
from here
←— * —9m—x Ball crosses
line here

(9) When a ball is played by a defender over his *own* goal-line the attacking team takes a *hit/push-in*

(a) from the point where the ball crossed the line
(b) but not within 9m of the goal.

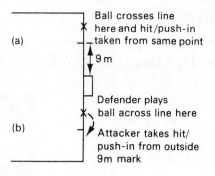

Ball crosses line here and hit/push-in taken from same point

9 m

(a)

(b)

Defender plays ball across line here

Attacker takes hit/push-in from outside 9m mark

(10) A *free hit* is awarded for any breach of the rules as in Senior Hockey (e.g. kicking, dangerous play, obstruction).
(11) For all free hits and free pushes players of *both* teams must be *5 metres* from the ball.
(12) For all free hits and free pushes the ball must travel *along the ground*. All free hits, except the penalty hit, will be *indirect*.

(10) The hit is taken from where the breach occurred but not within 9 metres of the goal.

(11) This rule should be strictly applied to prevent congested and muddled play.
(12) This rule should be closely observed to prevent dangerous play.

Penalty Hit
(13) For any breach of the rules which prevents a goal being scored a *penalty hit* is awarded. This shall take the form of a hit from a spot 9 metres from the centre of the opposing team's goal, with only the goalkeeper defending this hit.
(14) Unless a goal has been scored or awarded the game shall be re-started by a *free hit* to be taken by a defender from a spot 9 metres from the centre of the goal.

(13) The player taking the hit is allowed only one stride forward, only one touch of the ball and thereafter must not approach either the ball or the goalkeeper. Otherwise all the usual rules of a penalty stroke in Senior Hockey apply.
(14) All time taken between the award of a penalty hit and resumption of play shall be added to the time of play.

Umpire
(15) There shall be *one* umpire who shall take sole charge of the game.

(15) With no off-side one umpire can adequately control a game of mini hockey.

2.2 UMPIRING MINI HOCKEY

1 In Mini Hockey the referee should be a 'friend' and should not be too severe.

2 The umpire should be conversant with all the rules of hockey and the appropriate signals (see *Rules of the Game of Hockey*, 6.2).

3 Be positive and cooperative, helping the players to observe the rules rather than seeming to treat them as criminals.

4 The umpire should always keep up with the play *on the field* (not on the side-line) to ensure a clear view of all events.

5 Use the whistle sparingly and try to keep the game flowing by allowing the advantage where feasible.

6 Penalise any dangerous play immediately (e.g. undercutting, raising the stick very high, lifting the ball into a player).

7 To prevent crowding and congested play ensure that both teams are 5m from the ball on all free hits and pushes.

8 Take special note of Rule 9 where a defender plays the ball over his own goal line. This rule differs from that of Senior Hockey.

9 Do not allow players to question any decision.

3. PRACTICES

3.1 BALL FAMILIARISATION (INCLUDING DRIBBLE)

Activities		*Key points*

1 Move the ball at walking pace about 1m ahead of body.

Left hand at top of stick, right hand 15-30 cm below left. Tap ball with flat side of stick.

2 Move at walking pace keeping the ball in contact with stick at all times.

Place ball just ahead of right foot, body bent forward, head and shoulders over ball, right hand turns stick to direction required.

3 Practise both methods at walking pace but weaving amongst other players in specified area.

Watch out for other players, footwork most important at this stage, lightly tap ball keeping it very close to stick.

4 Practise all three activities but gradually increase speed without losing control.

Emphasize a *gradual* increase in pace. Try to avoid dribbling on reverse side of stick.

5 Practise all activities but teacher changes pace, stops and starts players.

Whistle command could be used, try to look up as much as possible.

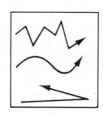

6 Practise all activities but teacher varies direction and line of movement. (e.g. angular, rounded, reverse).

Body must be moved quickly to new positions, twist right hand sharply to change direction.

7 Half group stand with legs apart, remainder dribble through and around legs without touching them.

Push ball lightly through legs and collect on other side, gradually close legs to make it more difficult.

8 Use any objects to act as obstacles which have to be successfully negotiated (e.g. shoes, satchels, bricks).

Always keep ball close to stick while watching for obstacles and other players.

Examples of Competitive Challenges

(a) Control Challenges — Who can dribble over specified route without losing control: walking, jogging, running.

(b) Ball Control Races — Around obstacle and back to starting line.

(c) Ball Control Relay	Simple 'there and back' principles at first, gradually introduce obstacle relays. Small teams for maximum activity.
(d) Steal-A-Ball	Half group with a ball each dribbling in confined area, those without ball try to steal one legitimately.
(e) Knockout Steal-A-Ball	As above except teacher stops activity every 30 seconds, those without a ball drop out, take out one or more balls each round.
(f) Make Activities Competitive	e.g. In 5 and 6 impose penalty points on players who lose control or are slow to change.

3.2 THE PUSH AND STOP

Skill 1   The Push

1 Class • Players form semi-circle around teacher. Demonstrate grip and body position for imaginary push.

2 Class • Push without a ball, using right hand only (right hand and shoulder give the force behind push).

3 Pairs • 10m apart, push and stop.

4 Pairs • 10m apart, push and stop. Vary pace and make partner move slightly to one side to stop.

5 Pairs • 10m apart, push through a target gate (e.g. shoes, skittles).

6 Individuals • Push ball against a wall from 1-2m. Build up a rhythm and aim at a mark on the wall.

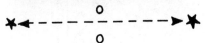

Right hand now taken further down stick, feet placed well apart, left shoulder facing direction required.

Feel the force being applied by the right side of the body. Ensure stick does not rise above shoulder level.

Put ball level with left shoulder and about ½m away from body.

Push firmly with right hand and guide with left, transfering body weight to front foot on impact.

Left shoulder points in direction of target, try not to lift ball off ground.

Stand sideways, try to 'absorb' ball on stick to avoid any slapping on impact.

Skill 2   The Stop

Activities

1 Class • Players form semi-circle around teacher. Stop imaginary balls from direction called by teacher.

Key points

Grip similar to that for dribble. Stick held *vertically*. Handle held away from body, head close to feet.

2 Pairs • Partner rolls ball along
   ground to player who
   attempts stop.

3 Pairs • Partner pushes ball and now
   varies pace and direction.

4 Pairs • Each player defends a goal,
   2m wide (e.g. track suits, shoes).
   Try to push ball into partner's goal.

Body directly behind stick and
approaching ball, feet slightly apart.

Move to get stick in line with
approaching ball, as it makes contact
let stick 'give' to absorb impact.

Emphasise pushing ball along
ground at 'reasonable' pace. Ensure
head of stick is touching ground
when stopping ball.

Skill 3   Pushing and Stopping (more advanced)

1 Pairs • 5m apart, pushing and
   stopping whilst moving across
   playing area, walking, jogging
   running.

Very tiring on the back so intersperse with coaching pauses. Ensure
stick is in firm contact with ball
when push is made.

2 Pairs • Same as 1 but vary
   distance and direction.

Watch ball carefully when stopping
and controlling, dribble a short
distance before passing.

3 Pairs • Ball passed by A to B and
   B to A_1. A moves across to A_1,
   controls, passes ball to B and
   returns to original position.

B must stop carefully, turn and
push pass with the correct amount
of pace to allow A to collect.

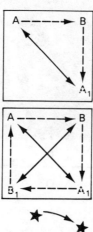

4 Pairs • As 3 except B also moves
   across diagonal once pass has been
   made, ball should travel around
   square.

Walk through exercise first. Accuracy of push pass must be maintained, move off immediately pass
has been made.

5 Sixes • In circle formation, push
   and stop around circle, alternate
   direction and increase speed.

Always stop the ball and turn to
pass, ball must not be deflected on
to next player.

6 Sixes • Players as in diagram.
   Centre player passes out continuously whilst others move
   around circle.

Progress from stationary passing to
walking and running, centre person
aims just in front of running player.

7 Threes • Pressure on one player
   (A), ball being pushed rapidly
   from a wide angle.

Turn and get body behind stick,
maintain consistency for as long as
possible, change positions often.

Examples of Competitive Challenges

(a)	Time Challenges	How many passes can you make in 30 sec?
(b)	Beat Your Own Record	How many consecutive passes can you make without a mistake?
(c)	Relay Races	Push passing, 5m apart, across playing area.

(d)	Circle Pass Out		Players pair off and form circle with one partner standing in front of other. Player in middle with ball tries to pass to a player on outer ring. Inner ring defenders try to intercept. Each team has 3-5 min.

(e) Individual Retrieve Ball

Two equal teams, 20m apart, ball equidistant from each team; each team member numbered diagonally. When teacher calls a number the two players assigned that number compete to dribble ball to opposite side. Later two or three numbers may be called at one time.

(f) Group Retrieve Ball

As above but place a ball equidistant between each pair. On whistle each pair competes to dribble ball to opposite side. Variations include players competing for any ball or for more than one ball.

(g) 2 v 2 Hockey

1 Use 10m x 10m grid square.
2 Goal scored by *stopping* ball on opponents' end line.
3 Push pass only. No hitting or lifting the ball.
4 If ball crosses side-line, non-offending team simply takes possession at point where ball crossed line.
5 If ball crosses end-line, defending team takes possession at point where ball crossed line.
6 Play for 5 min. and change opponents.
7 Otherwise normal hockey rules.

3.3 HITTING (INCLUDING SHOOTING)

Skill 1   Basic Hitting

Activities

1 Class • Players space out. Practise grip, swing and weight transfer by trying to shave grass with stick.

2 Pairs • 20m apart, practise hitting and stopping.

3 Pairs • 20m apart, hitting and stopping, aim 1m to side of partner.

4 Pairs • 20m apart, hit through a target gate.

5 Pairs • Try to force a plastic football over an opponent's end line by hitting hockey ball at it.

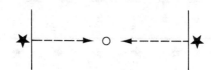

Key points

Left shoulder facing in direction of hit, stand one step behind ball, feet together, hands together (left above right) near end of stick.

Simultaneously step forward and begin backlift. Ball is struck just in front of left foot.

Eyes on ball, hold wrists firm to prevent raising stick above shoulder, follow through in the direction of hit.

If stick hits ground then ball may be too close, if ball is 'topped' head may be up or ball too far away.

Accuracy vital, line up left shoulder, swing through in one plane with no veering off to one side.

Skill 2   Hitting and Stopping (more advanced)

1 Pairs • 20m apart, A hits to B and moves 5m in any direction. B stops and hits back as soon as possible to find A in the new position.

2 Pairs • 20m apart, try to drive partner back by forcing an error on the stop. Hit must be within 1m of partner or it is disallowed.

3 Threes • Hitting at different angles. A hits across body to B and away from body to C.

4 Fours • Hit ball around triangle, follow ball to take up position of player (e.g. A hits and goes to take up B's position, B hits and takes C's position).

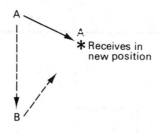

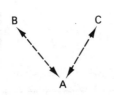

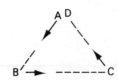

B must be very accurate with direction and pace (e.g. partner may move 5m closer). Always hit crisply and never push through slowly.

Score a point each time the ball crosses a player's defensive line (e.g. goal line). Temper power with accuracy. 60 m.p.h. but 10m wide is poor practice.

Turn the wrists and upper part of body in direction required rather than turning whole body.

Explain task carefully, always start where the two players stand, concentrate hard on hitting accurately and stopping consistently or breakdown will occur.

Skill 3   Shooting

1 Pairs • Each player defends a goal. Size of goal and distance between players dependent upon ability and type of shot.

Concentrate on accuracy, aiming for a specific spot in the goal. First to 5 goals and change opponents.

2 Fours • One goal per group. Dribble towards goal and shoot from at least 10m. Use wall, fence, etc. if available.

Encourage different types of shot (e.g. push, hit) from different directions. Use goalkeepers or player to retrieve balls.

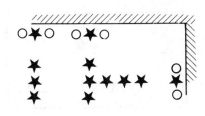

3 Sixes • One goal per group. One of group passes to attacker who shoots. Ball to be passed from behind, square and in front.

Pass must be timed well and passed accurately (no 60 m.p.h. centres). Attacker should control ball but then shoot quickly. Change to different angles.

4 Eights • One goal per group. 2 attackers take on 1 defender (and goalkeeper if available). Play continues until ball is cleared or goal scored.

Attackers try to draw defender and pass to unmarked player who shoots. When ball is dead players move out wide to avoid next pair.

Examples of Competitive Challenges

(a) Beat Your Own Record   How many consecutive balls can you hit through target gate?

(b) Howitzer

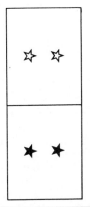

1 Two teams of 2 players: 50m x 20m playing area.
2 Both teams start midway in own halves.
3 Object is to hit ball over opponents' end line.
4 Ball must stay in specified area (i.e. if ball is hit out of area, opponents may hit from where it went out and not where they stop it).
5 Ball must be hit along ground.
6 Point scored if ball crosses opponents' end line.

(c) Clock Golf Hockey

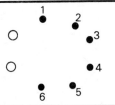

One or more shots taken from each marked position. Move further back as skill improves. Point awarded for every goal scored.

(d) 4 v 4 Hockey

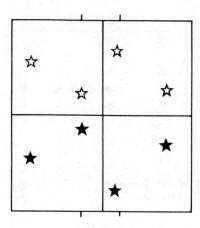

1 Use 4 grid squares
   i.e. Total = 20m x 20m.
2 Narrow goals (1-2m) may now
   be used.
3 Conditions (e.g. 3 touches and
   pass) may be imposed to improve particular aspects of play.
4 When ball passes over the side-
   lines or goal-lines push-ins
   taken by players opposed to
   team which last touched ball
   at the point where the ball
   crossed the line.
5 Other rules as in Mini Hockey
   should be encouraged, (e.g.
   players of both teams 5m from
   ball for free pushes).
6 Play for 5 mins. and change
   opponents.

3.4 TACKLING

Skill 1 Open Side Tackle (opponent's right side)

Activities

Key points

1 Class • Teacher stands in front of players who shadow/copy a variety of tackling attempts.

Stick held with left hand high up on grip, tackler steps well forward onto left leg jabbing stick at the ball.

2 Pairs • One player dribbles slowly, partner attempts tackle on open side. Speed up and vary direction of dribble.

Tackler approaches on an angle rather than from directly in front, never rush in but make a sudden lunge when sure of winning the ball.

3 Pairs • One player dribbles, partner attempts tackle. Start beside or slightly behind player with ball.

When tackling in retreat as here, defender shadows until an opportunity arises to dispossess dribbler.

Skill 2 Reverse Side Tackle (opponent's left side)

1 Class • Practise grip and tackling action at imaginary ball or object on ground (e.g. weeds, stones).

Stick held with left hand high up on grip but with head pointing down, step well forward on to left leg and aim head of stick at ball.

2 Pairs • One player dribbles, partner attempts tackle on reverse side. Speed up and vary direction.

Try to stop or slow ball so that attacker overruns it, try to get low and well balanced, watching ball all the time.

Skill 3 Jab or Lunge Tackle (from the front)

1 Class • Practise grip and tackling action trying to shave objects on ground. Place ball 2m away, lunge forward and try to lift ball off ground.

Stick held in left hand (flat side up) step well forward on to left foot and jab suddenly, trying to lift ball over opponent's stick.

2 Pairs • One player dribbles slowly forward, partner attempts tackle from front.

Timing is most important, never lunge unless absolutely sure of winning ball.

3 Threes • Two attackers with ball, defender tries to dispossess them with lunge tackle.

Defender must approach carefully keeping well balanced, try to tackle before attacker can make pass.

Examples of Competitive Challenges

(a) Possession Ball

4 players, 3 trying to keep possession while fourth attempts tackle to win ball.
Player losing possession (i.e. making the pass) goes into middle.
Use a grid square approx. 10m x 10m. Count consecutive passes.

(b) Funnel Ball

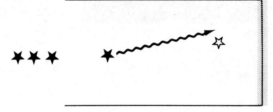

Groups of 4 or 5. Funnel approx. 5m wide 10m in length. Defender tries to tackle attacker to prevent him reaching end of funnel. Attacker must not run outside sidelines. Second attacker starts when defender has recovered.

(c) 2 v 1 Funnel Ball

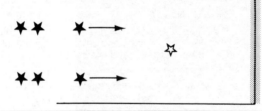

Same as above except two players attempt to take ball through funnel. Defender must tackle or intercept pass. Change defender often.

3.5 TACTICAL PLAY

Players should be encouraged to play in all positions so that they can find the one for which they are best suited. The following two formations are suggested to lay the foundation for positional play.

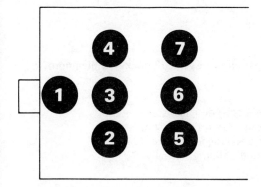

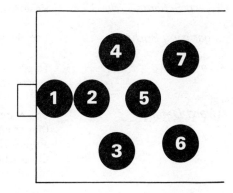

1 Goalkeeper	5 Right Attacker
2 Right Defender	6 Centre Attacker
3 Centre Defender	7 Left Attacker
4 Left Defender	

1 Goalkeeper	5 Midfield Link
2 Sweeper	6 Right Attacker
3 Right Defender	7 Left Attacker
4 Left Defender	

Eight Principles to Follow:

1 Successful hockey involves a blend of good skills and an understanding of the principles of play.

2 *All* 7 players must be involved all the time, even the goalkeeper.

3 Use *all* the playing area. If players herd around the ball then set territorial limits (e.g. restrict defenders to their own half for a short time until positional play is appreciated).

4 Play the ball *wide* out of defence, not up the middle.

5 Always *support* the player with the ball. Be available for a pass or ready to tackle if the ball is lost.

6 Always look for *safe* passes in midfield to maintain possession and build up attack.

7 Try to be *creative* in attack (e.g. run on the diagonal instead of straight).

8 Listen carefully to all the suggestions of your *coach*.

4. PROFICIENCY AWARDS

BOYS

1 Award Scheme Title	Rose Award Scheme
2 Organising Body	The Hockey Association
3 Aim	To promote interest and participation in the game of hockey while improving overall standards of play.
4 Award Details	There are **6 tests**. The scheme has been designed so that groups of 5 or 6 children can work on one test at a time. The timing of the scheme is designed so that the teacher or coach can operate the timing centrally for all tests.
	For children under the age of 14 years the time allowed for each test is **30 seconds**.
	The tests are as follows:

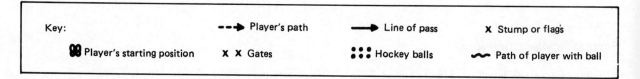

Key:

- ⇢ Player's path
- ⟶ Line of pass
- X Stump or flags
- ●● Player's starting position
- X X Gates
- ⋮⋮ Hockey balls
- ∿ Path of player with ball

Test 1 — Shooting

The player starts in circle — six balls are placed behind a line 3 yards outside the circle. On the command "GO" the player collects the first ball, dribbles it into the circle and shoots at goal.

Shots must be made before the player reaches the penalty stroke spot.

The player scores the points shown in the diagram for each shot. If he misses the goal or hits the goal post and the ball rebounds out of goal, no score is given for that shot. If the stump is hit and the ball rebounds out of the goal, one point is scored.

Maximum 12 points

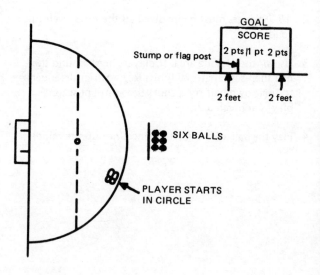

GOAL
SCORE

Stump or flag post

2 pts /1 pt 2 pts

2 feet   2 feet

SIX BALLS

PLAYER STARTS
IN CIRCLE

Test 2 — Push

The player has to push six balls through a gate one yard in width, 14 yards from a line. the player must have the ball on the line before pushing it.

Rules for Penalty Corner, when pushing, apply, i.e. ball along the ground.

2 points are scored each time the ball passes through the gate. No points if the ball misses the gate.

Maximum 12 points

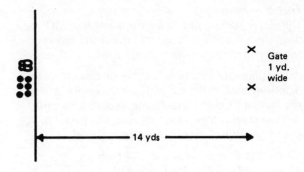

Test 3 — Hitting

The player stands inside the line of the pitch. He must then draw the ball in from his left with stick in the reverse position *using the left hand only*.

When the ball crosses the side line, adopt the hitting position and hit two balls through each gate.

The ball must be hit at the gates from within the two-yard square.

2 points each time a ball passes through a gate. No points if the gate is missed.

Maximum 12 points

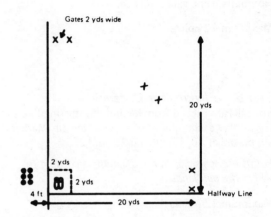

Test 4 — Dribble

Stumps or flags are placed as shown in the diagram, each offset from a centre line by 1 yard.

From the starting point the player takes the ball outside each of the markers, as shown by the dotted line, round the post at the end and back outside each marker, to the starting point. If he returns to the starting point within the time allowed, he continues to do the course a second time.

The number of markers rounded counts as the player's score for this test.

No maximum score

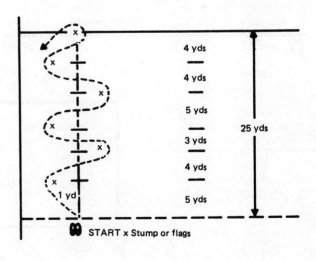

Test 5 — Passing

The player starts at line A. On the command "GO" he takes the ball to the left and past the centre marker and plays it through Gate 1 using a reverse stick push.

He continues forward to collect the first ball from line B, moving back to the left and past the centre marker, and plays it through Gate 2 using an open stick push. He then moves on to collect the next ball from line A, and so on until all the balls have been played.

All shots at Gate 1 — Reverse stick push
All shots at Gate 2 — Open stick push

2 points each time a ball passes through a gate.
No points if the gate is missed.

Maximum 12 points

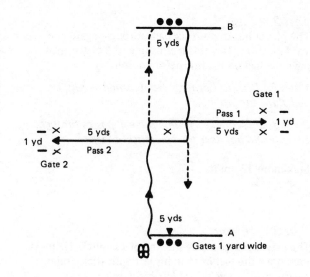

Test 6 — Flicking for Distance

Six balls are flicked from behind the starting line to try to play each as far as possible in the air. Markers are placed at 10, 15, 20 and 25 yards.

Points are scored as in the diagram, according to where the ball lands.

Maximum 12 points

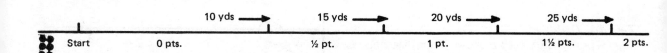

Score Table	
1 Rose	24–30 points
2 Rose	31–36 points
3 Rose	37–48 points
4 Rose	49–54 points
5 Rose	55 plus points

5 Applications

Further details from:
The H.A. Co-ordinator, The Red House,
Great Horkesley, Colchester, Essex

6 General Details

1 The scheme is organised at two levels:
Under 14 (i.e. on 1st January in the year of the competition)
Under 20 (i.e. on 1st January in the year of the competition)

2 Successful candidates receive a certificate and a badge and can progress from the elementary 1 Rose standard to the difficult top award of the 5 Rose standard.

3 Award winners also compete for individual and team National Awards for the highest test scores in the country.

GIRLS

The Award Scheme organised by the All England Women's Hockey Association has been discontinued and has not been replaced as yet. Teachers and coaches wishing to provide a skills challenge could utilise the following tests which are based on the old scheme.

Test 1 — Dribble
Dribble the ball on the run without losing control of it around the skittles travelling from A to B. Score /10 according to time.

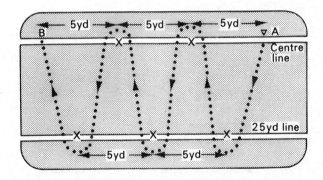

Test 2 — Dribble and Drive on the run
Place four skittles around the edge of the goal circle, one opposite each goal post, and the others opposite the penalty corner mark. Dribble on the run from the centre of the 25yd line through each lettered space and shoot within one yard of the circle edge; two tries only through each gap. Score /10.

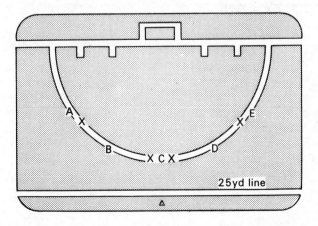

Test 3 — Push in

Place one skittle on each 25yd line two yards from the side line, and two skittles two yards apart five yards from the side line, halfway between each 25yd line and the centre line. Player starts from A and aims to push the ball through the gaps created by the skittles. Ten attempts only with at least two through each gap. Score /10.

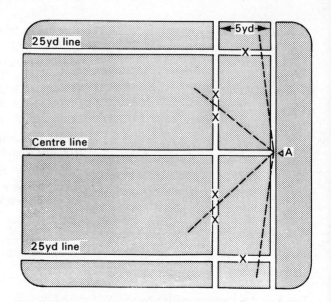

Test 4 — Kick

Soft balls may be used for this test.
Use skittles as Test 2. Dribble from the centre of 25yd line, using feet only, through each lettered space and kick for goal within one yard of circle edge. Two tries only through each gap. Score /10.

Test 5 — Receive and Pass

A ball is rolled at the skittles from A. Player being tested runs to collect the ball and passes it through the gate before reaching the skittle. Five attempts. Repeat test from the other side of the pitch. Score /10.

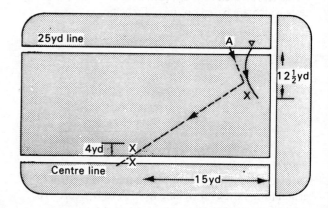

Method of Scoring

Each test will be scored /10.
Each award will be scored /50.

1 Where a test has ten attempts, 1 point is awarded for each successful attempt.

2 **Time Tests**

Points Preliminary
          Test 1

Points	Test 1
10	below 30 sec.
9	35
8	40
7	45
6	50
5	55
4	60
3	65
2	70
1	75

3 Standards
based on an accumulative score

5	45/50
4	40/44
3	35/39
2	20/34
1	25/29

4 Candidates must achieve at least one point in each
test to qualify for an award.

Key to Diagrams

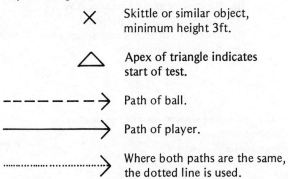

✕	Skittle or similar object, minimum height 3ft.
△	Apex of triangle indicates start of test.
– – – – – →	Path of ball.
⟶	Path of player.
·············⟩	Where both paths are the same, the dotted line is used.

Where possible the tests have been set out in relation to
a pitch making extra marking unnecessary. The relationship of the skittles, etc., to these markings should be
carefully observed in order that the regulations are
adhered to. Please note that the stick shall not be taken
over the top of a skittle.

5 Applications

Further information from:

c/o A.E.W.H.A.,
160 Great Portland Street,
London, W1N 5TB

5. TEACHING/COACHING QUALIFICATIONS

5.1 PRELIMINARY COACHING CERTIFICATE

1 Organising Body — The Hockey Association

2 Aim — The award is designed for those wanting an introduction to coaching, in particular teachers who are new to hockey. Holders of this award would be capable of covering the introduction of hockey at school.

3 Syllabus

(a) Individual ball control
(b) Methods of passing
(c) Types of pass
(d) Movement off the ball
(e) Receiving the ball
(f) Beating an opponent
(g) Shooting

(h) Tackling
(i) Marking
(j) Basic principles of tactical play
(k) Losing and gaining possession
(l) Set pieces in attack and defence
(m) Basics of goalkeeping

4 Duration of Course — Minimum of 12 hours

5 Assessment

Part I. 2-hour written paper including section on rules of hockey.
Part II. 30-minute coaching session.
Part III. Assessment during course.

6 Applications

Open to men and women
Applications to Director of Coaching (address below).

6. REFERENCE INFORMATION

6.1 USEFUL ADDRESSES

All England Women's Hockey Association
Secretary: Miss T. Morris
160 Great Portland Street
London W1N 5TB

National Coach for Women
Miss E. Stuart Smith
3 Priestwood Close
Thornhill
Southampton
SO2 5RN

English Schoolboys' Hockey Association
Secretary: D.J. Newton
Kennedy's House
Aldenham School
Elstree, Herts.

Director of Coaching, Hockey Association
J. Cadman
The Red House
Great Horkesley
Colchester, Essex.

Deputy Director of Coaching
T.H.E. Clarke
Hunters Lodge
Broadmore Green
Rushwick
Worcester, WR2 5TE

Hockey Association
Secretary General: Colonel D.M.R. Eagan
16 Upper Woburn Place
London WC1H 0QD.

6.2 HOCKEY REFERENCES

Publication				Description of Mini Game	Skill Descriptions	Teaching Practices	Tactics	Senior Rules
Brandrick A.H.		Hockey for Junior Secondary Age Group	A.E.W.H.A. Booklet	*	*	*	*	
Cadman J.	1979	Hockey Rules Illustrated	Pelham Book					*
Glencross D.H.	1973	Hockey	Seal Books Book		*	*		*
Heyhoe Flint R.	1976	Women's Hockey	Pelham Book		*		*	Summary
International Hockey Rules Board	1976	Rules of the Game of Hockey	Internat. Hockey Rules Board Booklet	Junior Hockey				*
Know the Game		Men's Hockey	E.P. Pub. Co. Booklet					*
Know the Game		Women's Hockey	E.P. Pub. Co. Booklet					*
Podesta T.	1977	Hockey for Men and Women	E.P. Pub. Co. Book		*	*	*	
Poole G.	1972	Better Hockey For Boys	Kaye & Ward Book		*	*	*	
Read B.	1971	Better Hockey For Girls	Kaye & Ward Book		*		*	
Wein H.	1973	The Science of Hockey	Pelham Book		*	*	*	
Weir M.	1974	Women's Hockey For the 70's	Kaye & Ward Book		*	*	*	
West B.W.	1972	Hockey in the Primary School	A.E.W.H.A. Booklet	Junior Hockey		*		

MINI NETBALL

MINI NETBALL CONTENTS

1. PLAYING AREA

1.1 THE COURT

Ring should be 3m from the ground; 2.60m for younger children (e.g. under 11).

On a smaller court the shooting circle should still be kept as near to 5m as possible.

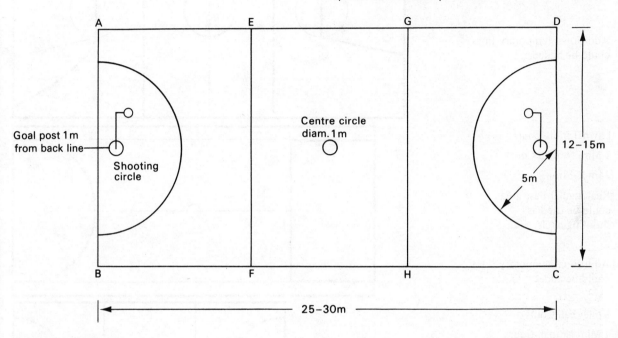

Marking Instructions

1 Use two lengths of string:

   (a) 30m with a knot tied at 15m.
   (b) 18m with a knot tied at 5m.

2 Lay down the 30m string and mark line AD and the point E (10m from A in this case).

3 Fix one end of 30m string at A. Fix one end of 18m string at E. Hold 30m string at 15m knot and free end of 18m string. B is marked where both strings meet when taut.

4 Using D as the fixed point for the 30m string and G as the fixed point for the 18m string, mark C.

5 Mark lines AB, BC, CD, EF and GH.

6 Fix one end of the 18m string at the mid-point of line AB. Holding the string at the 5m knot walk round and mark in the shooting circle.

7 Repeat at the other end.

1.2 ADAPTATIONS OF OTHER PLAYING AREAS

———————— original lines to be 'disregarded' in mini netball

———————— original lines to be 'utilised' in mini netball

– – – – – – – additional temporary lines required

Basketball Court

1 Mini Netball Court

26m x 14m

Basketball zone could
be used as shooting
circle

or

Additional temporary lines
could be added.

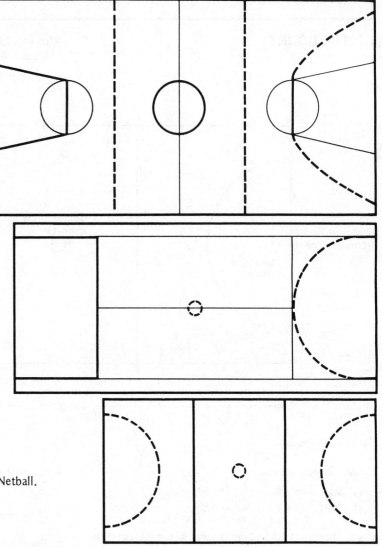

Lawn Tennis Court

1 Mini Netball Court

24m x 11m

Rectangular base area
could be used as
shooting circle

or

Additional temporary lines
could be added.

Volleyball Court

1 Mini Netball Court

18m x 9m

A small court perhaps suitable for 5-a-side Netball.

1.3 ANCILLARY EQUIPMENT

(a) Goal Posts:

1 For safety reasons posts with circular bases are preferable to those with
   angular projections.

2 Posts with adjustable rings are most suitable since they can be raised for
   Senior Netball.

3 Dual use of volleyball posts if available. Attach rings at appropriate height.

4 Utilise Mini Basketball posts.

(b) Ball:

May be made of sewn or moulded leather, rubber or synthetic material.

   Circumference: 0.64m (25'')
   Weight: 340-397gm (12-14 oz).

2. RULES

The following rules are suggested for Mini Netball.

2.1 INTERPRETATION OF RULES

Rules

Object
(1) The object of the game is to throw the ball into the opponents' ring and to prevent the opponents from scoring in one's own basket.

The Teams
(2) Each team has *7 players*.
(3) Players may go anywhere in the court except:—

Centre players may not enter either circle.
Shooters and *defence* may not enter the circle at the opposite end. If a player is offside (moves into a prohibited area) a free pass is given to an opponent where the foul occurred.

Notes

(1) Each score (goal) counts 1 point.

(2) 2 shooters, 2 defence, 3 centres.
(3) In order to prevent crowding when learning the game, coaches may wish temporarily to limit the areas of play and to encourage two of the centres to use the space near the side lines.

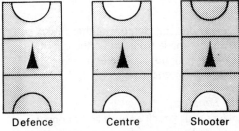

Defence · Centre · Shooter

(Shaded portion = permitted areas on court.)

Time in Play
(4) *15 minutes* each way, with not more than 5 minutes interval for half time.

(4) This is flexible and shorter time may be played.

Ball in Play
(5) Play is started by a *pass* from a centre player standing with both feet in centre circle. On the whistle the player must pass within *3 seconds*. Alternate sides make the pass after each goal or after half-time. Centre pass must be received in centre third.

(5) There are no fixed positions at the start of play, except that players must be in their correct *third*. Players may move freely within their own area and should be encouraged to use the whole width of court.

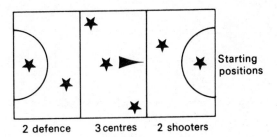

Starting positions

2 defence · 3 centres · 2 shooters

(6) A ball is *out of court* when it, or a player holding it, touches the ground outside the court. Throw-in awarded to opposing team.

(7) *Throw-in* taken at point where ball crossed line (feet must be behind line). Umpire should call *'play'* before play is restarted.

(8) When a player has the ball she must pass or shoot within *3 seconds*.

(9) A player may *not* roll or kick the ball, play the ball to himself/herself, hand the ball to another player or touch a ball held by an opponent.

Footwork

(10) A player with the ball may move her feet on the spot but may not travel except under the impetus of her run, jump or throw.

(11) After receiving the ball in the shooting circle the player may not take *deliberate steps* towards the goal to bring her nearer though she may step in any direction with one foot to give her balance or control or as part of her natural shooting action.

Goals

(12) A goal may only be scored by either of the two shooters by a shot made from within the circle. A defending player may not impede or intercept *in any way* a shot for goal.

Fouls and Penalties

(13) No player shall knock or push an opponent, or interfere with her play, either accidentally or deliberately.

(14) A player may not *obstruct* with her arms or body the movement of an opponent with or without the ball.

Throw-up

(15) Two players stand 1 metre apart, arms to sides, facing each other and the goal into which their team is shooting. Umpire flicks the ball not more than ½ metre into the air from a point midway between the players.

(6) If the umpire is uncertain which team last touched the ball, she must take a *throw-up* just inside the court (see 15).

(7) Throw-ins must be taken from behind the line banding the player's own area (e.g. a defence player cannot throw-in from behind the shooting circle in her team's attacking third).

(8) This applies to the throw-in and free pass.

(9) A *free pass* to the opposing team is awarded if such an infringement should occur.

(10) Children need not be made self-conscious of footwork by restricting their natural movement. Taking a step or two while catching on the run should not be penalised; but where an advantage is gained by taking deliberate steps in a particular direction a free pass should be given to the opposing team.

(11) The comments in 10 apply here although the umpire may need to be more strict in this vital zone. All deliberate stepping should be penalised by a free pass to the opposing side.

(12) Both feet must be inside the circle. The line counts as part of the circle.

(13) Rough play should be penalised immediately with a free pass. If defence fouls in circle the shooter may choose to shoot instead of pass.

(14) No particular distance is stated but umpires should ensure that players are not handicapped in throwing or shooting.

(15) All other players may stand or move anywhere. Whistle is blown as ball is released. Ball is in play once it has been touched by one of the two players concerned.

2.2 UMPIRING MINI NETBALL

A Brief Summary of Duties

2 Umpires per match

The following responsibilities are advised:

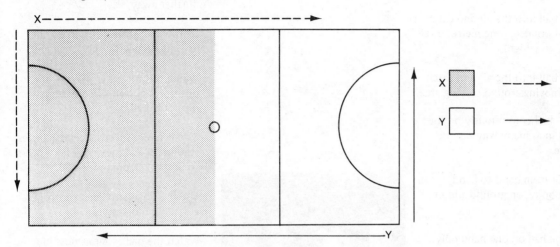

1 Keep moving in order to secure a clear view.

2 Each umpire should take responsibility for timing one of the halves.

3 The umpire in whose half the goal has been scored, restarts the game with the centre pass, after having called the score.

4 The umpire should indicate on the score card which team has first centre pass. In the first half this team will continue to have the centre pass when the total aggregate of goals scored is an *even* number.

5 In Mini Netball the umpire should be a 'friend' and should not be too severe.

When to Use the Whistle

1 To start game and for every centre pass.

2 When a goal is scored.

3 At the throw up when the ball has been released.

4 To indicate ball is out of play.

5 When a foul occurs and when an accident occurs.

3. PRACTICES

3.1 BALL FAMILIARISATION

Activities	*Key points*
1 Throw ball into the air and catch after it has bounced once.	Watch ball carefully, catch with two hands, gradually throw ball further away.
2 Throw ball into the air and catch without bounce, (one metre, three metres, very high).	Throw ball straight up in the air. try catching with only one hand.
3 Throw ball into the air and catch whilst moving around playing area.	Watch out for other players, try to position yourself directly under dropping ball.
4 Bounce ball continuously on the ground in as many ways as possible.	Try different speeds, heights, angles: stationary and moving. Flex fingers to prevent slapping the ball.
5 Pass ball from hand to hand around body, on ground and in the air.	Use the fingers to keep control, gradually build up speed.
6 Hold the ball on one hand only. Move the arm continuously around the body trying not to drop ball.	Watch the ball as far as possible, angle the hand to prevent ball falling, try to circle body.
7 Throw ball against wall and catch. With bounce, without bounce, high, low, fast, slow, with a turn, at a target.	Throw ball high at first to give more time, gradually increase the difficulty of the throws.

Examples of Competitive Challenges

(a) Beat Your Own Record	How many times can you catch rebound off wall before dropping ball?
(b) Time Challenges	How many times can you bounce ball on ground in 30 sec?
(c) Races, Relay Races	Encouraging different ball skills.

3.2 CATCHING AND THROWING

Skill 1   Catching with a Partner

Activities

1 2-3m apart, try a variety of passes and catches.

2 As 1 but gradually increase distance to 5m.

3 2-3m apart, pass and catch whilst moving along playing area.

4 Catch softly trying to make no sound with the hands as they contact ball.

5 Any of 1 to 4 but now throw ball slightly wide of partner.

6 All pairs intermingle in playing area. Make a pass when clear.

7 Pass and catch whilst moving but vary direction, speed and distance apart.

Key points

Watch ball carefully, keep hands and wrists relaxed, try to judge speed and direction of ball flight.

Stretch arms to reach out for ball, keep fingers widely spread and flexed when receiving ball.

Take pace off ball by bringing hands and arms quickly in to body.

Ball brought close to body at speed similar to that of flight of ball.

Stretch with one hand to start catching action, then other hand is placed quickly on ball to control it.

Keep moving in and out of others, only pass when certain of reaching partner.

Prescribe route to prevent pairs colliding, encourage great variety.

Skill 2   One Handed Throw

1 Pairs ● 3m apart, catcher stands with arm outstretched at any level, thrower aims to hit catcher's hand.

2 Pairs ● 3-5m apart, catcher calls body part, thrower aims for this area.

3 Pairs ● 5-8m apart, as above but now throwing over greater distance.

4 Pairs ● Any of 1 to 3 but concentrate upon underarm throw and bounce pass.

Stand sideways, feet slightly apart, ball in two hands, just above waist level. Take both arms back, ball transferred to right hand.

As ball is released, push arm through turning right shoulder forward.

Place left foot in direction of throw, transfer weight on to it.

Arm swung back and released below waist level. Overarm still used for bounce pass.

5 Pairs • Vary angle of throw by practising with target on wall.

6 Threes • Pressure on one player to move quickly to new position. Players A and B throw straight, C runs back and forth catching and returning throw.

7 Fours • Pass and follow ball taking up catcher's position. Always start where the two players stand.

Skill 3   Two Handed Throw

1 Threes • 3m apart, two handed throw around triangle, gradually increasing distance.

2 Sixes • In two lines facing each other, pass back and forth along line.

3 Threes • Two handed passing whilst moving across playing area. Avoid running in a straight line.

4 Threes • Pressure on one player to pass quickly in different directions.

5 Threes • In grid square, two pass to each other trying to keep possession, other player tries to intercept.
(Use 3 v 1 if skill level is low).

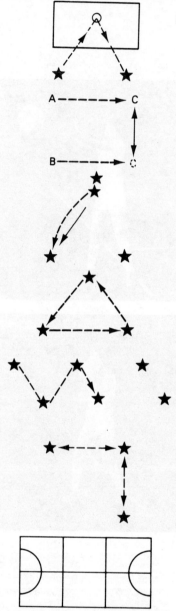

Six 10x7m (approx.) grid squares

Skill 4   Where and When to Throw

1 Pairs • B moves to pre-determined place, A aims to pass ball so that it reaches B at this spot.

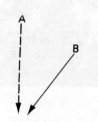

Point left shoulder and place left foot in direction of throw, make the whole action continuous.

A and B throw quickly but within reason. C stops and turns to face direction of intended pass, crisp throwing makes interception difficult.

Walk through the activity first, move immediately the pass has been made, gradually increase speed.

Hold ball in front of chest, fingers spread pointing upwards, thumbs point at each other, elbows away from body.

Thrust hands away from body whilst stepping on to left foot. Step in direction of pass.

Explain route and boundaries carefully, two handed passing only, try not to take more than two steps with the ball.

Turn to face direction of pass, try to maintain accuracy as speed increases.

'Pig in the middle' idea, pass and *move to space*, pass only if partner is free, defender tries to mark receiver.

Throw ball in direction of moving player, but ahead of them so that it can be caught with extended arms.

2 Threes • When A gives signal B moves to get free from opponent C. A must pass to B without C intercepting.

B must move quickly and indicate with hand where pass is wanted. A should experiment with a variety of throws.

3 Small groups • Players form circle with one in middle. Pass across circle below head height. Player in middle tries to intercept.

No passing *over* player in middle. Throw crisply and watch for safe pass, quick preparation and fast action reduces chance of interception. Player causing interception goes into middle.

4 Fours • D marks C, A feeds to B, C moves to get free from D and B times accurate pass to C.

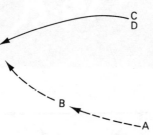

Ball thrown when C's final movement to get free is *clear*. Watch for: a sudden break, receiver increasing speed, receiver changing direction.

Examples of Competitive Challenges

(a)	Time Challenges	How many two handed passes in 30 sec?
(b)	Beat Your Own Record	How many accurate, consecutive passes can you make over a set distance?
(c)	Relay Races	e.g. Skill 1 no. 7. Pass and catch over set distance.
(d)	Dodge Ball	Threes in grid square, middle player dodging to avoid being hit below knee by ball.

(e) Circle Pass Out

Children pair off, form circle with one person standing in front of the other. Player in middle with ball tries to pass to a player on outer ring. Inner ring defenders try to intercept. Emphasis on 'getting free' by dodging. Each team has 3-5 min.

(f) 2 v 2 Netball

A_1 A_2

v

B_1 B_2

1 10m x 7m area: divide court into six areas with a line from goal post to goal post.
2 Score by catching ball while standing on opponents' end line.
3 Either team starts with possession, but when score has been made, the team which did *not* score takes possession.
4 Play for 5 min. and change opponents.
5 Otherwise normal netball rules (e.g. no deliberate steps with ball).

3.3 FOOTWORK

Skill 1   Achieving Balance When Stopping

| *Activities* | | *Key points* |

1 Class • Sprint, stop on whistle.

Thrust leading foot towards ground to act as brake.

2 Class • Sprint, jump and stop on whistle.

Emphasise bending of knee on landing.

3 Class • Sprint, jump and stop on whistle, move off in new direction.

Take smaller steps to slow down, thrust off hard from back leg.

4 Class • Throw ball high and forward. Sprint towards it, jump to catch and land on right foot.

Right leg acts as stabiliser so that left can be used to help subsequent throw.

5 Pairs • A stands on straight line, B 5m away. B throws to side of A who sprints, jumps to catch and stops. A steps towards B to throw back.

Land from jump on one leg, but stop by taking a long stride with other leg bending hard at the knee. Pivot to step in direction of throw.

6 Pairs • Same as 5 but A now moves off at different angles.

Stop as in 5 but always pivot round towards B when returning throw.

7 Threes • Stand on three corners of square. A runs to vacant corner, C throws to this vacant corner, A jumps, catches, pivots and passes to B. B throws to vacant corner (where A was originally), A returns, catches and passes to C.

Walk through activity at first. Keep the pressure on A but throw must be accurate and challenging. Change A frequently.

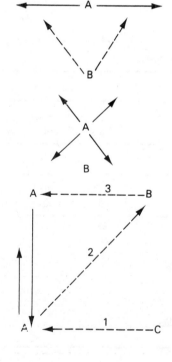

Skill 2   Jumping for Ball

1 Class • Stand on two feet, step quickly on to one foot and thrust upward, repeat on other foot.

Rapid bending of knees, arm swing may be used at first but later arms need to be free to catch ball.

2 Class • Player tosses ball to right and leaps from right foot to catch, repeat on left.

Practise leaping from *both* feet, flex ankles and push off hard from foot, catch ball as high as possible.

3 Pairs • One player holds ball very high, partner sprints and leaps upwards to take ball off the hand.

Achieve maximum speed before leaping, try to take the ball upwards off the hand.

Skill 3   Pivoting

1 Class • Using any objects available (e.g. posts, jumpers, lines) run at random, stop and pivot when meeting an object.

2 Pairs • Same as 1 but pass to each other. Still use objects as imaginary opponents.

Come to rest on the foot which is on the same side as throwing arm. Use this foot to pivot, make imaginary throw and move off again.

If direction of passing movement is prevented by object, stop, hold ball, pivot and pass to partner who should have moved off in new direction.

3 Pairs • Two players in two corners of square. Pass to each other always moving to free corner to catch, e.g. B passes to A where arrows meet and then moves to vacant corner X.

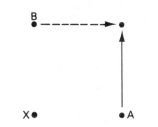

Walk through activity at first. Raise heel and turn on the ball of pivoting foot. Transfer body weight from pivoting foot to other as throw is made.

Skill 4   Dodging and Marking

1 Class • All types of tag.

Stay in a restricted area, emphasise dodging, not running away.

2 Pairs • Random shadowing and dodging away from partner.

Use quick turns and twists. Be alert and poised on balls of feet.

3 Pairs • Stay within 2m of partner. Stop on whistle to check distance apart.

Make to move one way and then sprint away in new direction.

4 Fours • Fox and Geese game. Three players line up holding waist of person in front. Fourth tries to touch back of last player in line.

Line of geese keep dodging away but must stay in contact. Change Fox if last player is touched.

5 Class • Hunter and Dogs game. Hunter and 2 Dogs stand in centre of playing area. Rest of class try to get to other end without being touched by Hunter.

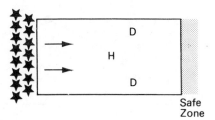

Dogs cannot tag players but assist by catching players for Hunter. When touched by Hunter other players become Dogs.

3.4 SHOOTING

Skill 1   Standing Shot

Activities

1 Pairs • Take turns to shoot from different marked positions. Partner retrieves ball and has equivalent shots. (Use wall targets at goal height if not enough goals available).

Key points

Put hand under and behind ball, point elbow forward, support with other hand. Concentrate on spot just over front of ring.

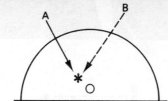

2 Pairs • B throws ball into circle. A runs to catch, stops and places feet correctly before shooting.

Feet placed apart to give adequate balance. Body weight stays over feet until just before ball is released.

3 Pairs • Shooter takes several shots, starting from a different position each time and taking a step towards the goal.

Before releasing ball check that body is evenly balanced over foot on which weight has been taken.

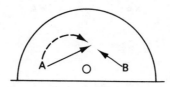

4 Pairs • A tosses ball in any direction and moves to catch, taking balanced position to shoot. B moves to defend shot.

When shooting bend elbows and wrists slightly, then extend smoothly with final push from fingers.

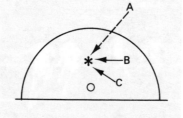

5 Threes • A throws to B from outside circle. B lands and pivots to face goal. C defends and retrieves.

B signals where pass is to be made. Shoot very high to avoid defender. C fairly passive at first.

Skill 2   Running Shot

1 Pairs • Shooter starts in circle with ball, takes two steps and shoots. Partner retrieves at first, may defend later.

Jump upward from left foot while aiming ball at goal. Use less force than in standing shot.

2 Pairs • As Skill 1 no. 2 with B throwing ball into circle for A to catch. Here the action is continuous with A running in to shoot.

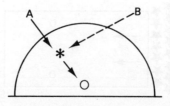

Catch ball in mid-air, land on right foot and concentrate on ring. Continue on to left foot bringing ball towards body before thrusting upwards.

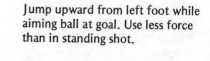

Skill 3   Forward Step Shot

1 Pairs • Shoot 5 times from different positions in circle using forward step shot. Partner tries to score more goals.

Encourage good balance throughout the skill to achieve consistency. Lean back on last stride, jump upwards not forwards.

2 Pairs • Forward step shot 1m from goal. If goal scored move back ½m for next shot. Keep moving back until shot missed. Partner tries to get further back.

Step forward on to one foot before lifting other. After this step immediately spring upward releasing ball at height of jump.

Examples of Competitive Challenges

(a)	Beat Your Own Record	How many consecutive goals can you shoot?
(b)	Time Challenges	Who can shoot most goals in 3 min.?
(c)	Group Competitions	Any of the activities above. Form small teams and see which team can score most goals.

(d) Clock Golf Netball

One or more shots taken from each marked position. Move further back as skill improves. Point scored for every goal scored.

(e) Skittle Ball

1 Use 20m x 15m playing area. Play across Netball court if space available.
2 5-7 a-side, one player defending skittle outside circle, change after every score.
3 Hit opponents' skittle to score point.
4 Game started by throw up at centre.
5 To prevent crowding around ball players keep to own side of dividing line.
6 Players entering circles penalised by free pass to opponents.
7 Otherwise normal netball rules as far as possible.

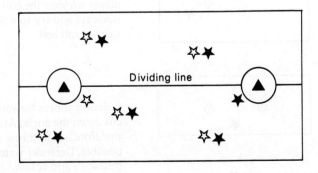

(f) 3 v 3, 4 v 4
   Netball

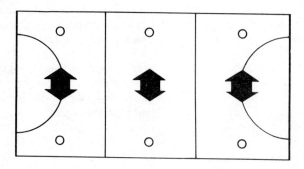

1 Use 15m x 10m playing area.
   Play cross court on each third.
2 Use goal posts if enough
   available or utilise mini-basket-
   ball goals or fix braids/coloured
   material to wall/fence at goal
   post height.
3 Either team starts with possession, but when score has been
   made the team which did *not*
   score takes possession.
4 Play for 5 min. and change
   opponents.
5 Otherwise normal netball rules.

3.5 DEFENDING SKILLS

Skill 1   Intercepting the Catch

Activities

1 Class • Catch the rebound off the
   wall. Throw ball to left and right
   sides.

2 Class • As above but increase the
   angle, speed and height. Partner
   could give quick reaction catches
   if no wall available.

3 Threes • A and B pass to each
   other while stationary. C starts
   in position shown and only moves
   to intercept once pass is made.

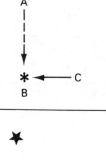

4 Threes • Pig in the Middle game
   emphasising crisp interceptions.
   Use grid to restrict playing area.

Key points

Throw underarm. Give easy catches
at first, gradually throw harder.

Body weight slightly forward ready
to spring and catch. Use small,
quick steps before leaping sideways.

C must keep alert on toes with legs
bent. Thrust off quickly as ball
leaves A.

Person in middle keeps close to
player *without* the ball. Stand
sideways and try to watch both
catcher and ball.

Skill 2   Intercepting the Throw

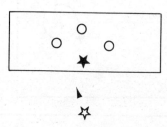

1 Pairs • Targets on wall as in diagram. Defender stands at wall,
   attacker stands 3m back, ball at
   feet. On signal attacker picks up
   ball, shoots at targets. Defender
   runs forward to intercept.

Defender moves forward quickly to
cut down the angle. Attacker
therefore has to throw as soon as
possible. Defender watches
thrower's arm action.

2 Threes • As above except third player takes place of wall. Defender C stands in front of B. On signal C runs forward to intercept, B moves to receive pass.

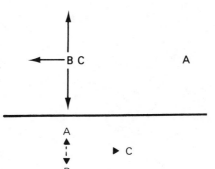

Start with ball on ground, A stationary. Encourage C to move forward to cut down angle. Attempt to intercept by thrusting out arm and jumping upwards or sideways.

3 Threes • Funnel marked as shown. A and B try to reach end of funnel passing continuously. C tries to intercept.

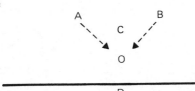

Be strict on players going outside funnel. Encourage C to work back if beaten once.

4 Fours • A and B pass to each other. C and D try to intercept throws.

Coach for interceptions, try to watch player and ball. Change pairs frequently.

Skill 3 Intercepting the Shot

1 Pairs • Shooter stands with ball in shooting position. Defender stands 1m back and tries to intercept shot.

Place right foot forward and turn body slightly. Flex ankles and knees keeping body weight forward.

2 Pairs • Shooter varies type of shot, defender tries to anticipate and intercept.

Time jump to make contact with ball as soon as it leaves shooter's hands.

3 Fours • Pressure on defender. A and B shoot alternately at a rapid pace. C defends and D retrieves ball.

Ensure jump is made before shooter releases ball. If jumping forward avoid personal contact.

3.6 ATTACKING SKILLS

Skill 1 Getting Free

Activities

Key Points

1 Class • Run 5m with a sudden sprint start on the whistle.

Keep alert, weight on balls of feet, knees bent, thrust hard with trailing leg.

2 Class • Races over very short distances.

Take short strides, drive with arms.

3 Class • On the whistle make a sudden dodge and then run 5m.

Make an emphatic movement of the body or step to one side. As rapidly as possible move off in opposite direction.

4   Pairs • As 3 but partner tries to shadow movement.

5   Pairs • As 4 but attacker may spring straight off or feint more than once.

6   Threes • Try to get free as in activities above but third person C passes ball once attacker is free.

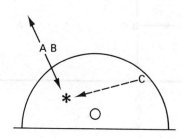

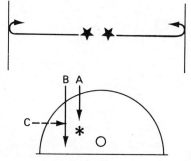

7   Class • Practise sprinting and stopping quickly on whistle.

8   Pairs • Spring and stop races, e.g. start back to back centre of court, sprint to side-line and back.

9   Threes • Attacker A marked by defender B runs goalward and stops suddenly to receive pass from C. A can then shoot.

10 Class • While running around playing area change speed or direction on different whistle signal.

11 Threes • Attacker uses any of methods already described to get free from defender and receive pass in shooting position.

Feint dodge must be realistic, try to catch partner off balance.

Attacker should mix it up to confuse defender, fast acceleration always vital.

B stays fairly passive at first, then tries to stick with attacker. Try from different positions.

When stopping take a long, last stride, bending leg sharply at knee.

Take body low when stopping, turn and thrust away sharply.

Ensure that there is no slowing down before stopping or else surprise element is lost.

Ensure there is a distinct change of pace which would surprise an opponent.

Use sudden sprint start, dodge and sprint, sprint and stop, change of speed and direction.

4. PROFICIENCY AWARDS

1 Award Scheme Title   Netball Shooting Badge Scheme.

2 Organising Body   All England Netball Association.

3 Aim   To improve the standard of shooting in netball.

4 Award Details

Rules:

1 A regulation goalpost (i.e. 10ft high) and a regulation ball (i.e. size 5 football) shall be used.

2 20 consecutive shots at goal shall be taken at one session as described in these rules, but they can be taken in any order.

3 The goal circle shall be divided into four areas by three semi-circles, with radii 4ft, 8ft and 12ft respectively (see diagram below). All lines are part of adjacent areas and shall not be more than 2" wide.

4 Five shots must be taken from within each area, one taken from immediately in front of the goal (as spot X in diagram below), and two on either side, but all from different positions.

5 If the footwork rule is infringed, any goal scored shall be disallowed.

6 During her shooting action, the shooter must have both feet wholly within the correct area until the ball has left her hands.

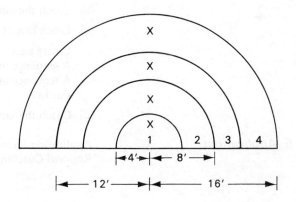

Awards:

Cloth badges will be awarded as follows:—

3rd Class (Green)   10-14 goals scored from 20 shots.
2nd Class (Blue)   15-19 goals scored from 20 shots.
1st Class (Red)   20 goals scored from 20 shots.

5 Applications   Forms supplied by County Associations or A.E.N.A. (Requests should include S.A.E.)

Forms and fees should be sent to:
Hon. Secretary of appropriate County Committee,
or Mrs L Haldenby, 35 Yarborough Close, Godshill, Isle of Wight.

6 General Details
1 Awards open to all age groups.
2 Small fee charged for each test.
3 Testers:

    (a) Any specialist teacher of physical education.
    (b) A.E.N.A. coaching or umpiring award holder.
    (c) Any responsible person approved by County Association.

5. TEACHING/COACHING QUALIFICATIONS

5.1 REGIONAL COACHING AWARD

1 Organising Body	All England Netball Association.

2 Aim
To provide a preliminary coaching qualification which hopefully will lead to improved teaching and coaching standards.

3 Requirements
(a) A working knowledge of the rules of the game.
(b) To take a practical test, coaching two club or school teams for at least 30 min.

4 Assessment
Practical Test:

(a) Coach in small groups a skill from one of the following:

Footwork.
Throwing and catching.
Getting free.
Methods of passing.

(b) Coach the same skill in a game.

(c) Coach one of the following tactics:

Centre pass.
A sequence of passes from the centre to the shooting circle.
A sequence of passes down the court either from the back line or the side line.

(d) Coach the same tactic in a game.

5 Applications
Application forms obtainable from:
Regional Coaching Secretaries.

6. REFERENCE INFORMATION

6.1 USEFUL ADDRESSES

All England Netball Association
The Director:
For queries concerning the game of Netball.

The National Technical Officer:
For interpretation of rules.

A.E.N.A. Publications

All c/o   16 Upper Woburn Place
               London WC1H 0QP

English Schools Netball Association
Secretary: Mrs G. McGarvie
               34 Partridge Flatt Road
               Bessacarr
               Doncaster
               South Yorkshire DN4 65D

6.2 NETBALL REFERENCES

Publication					Description of Mini Game	Skill Descriptions	Practices	Tactics	Senior Rules
A.E.N.A.		Junior Netball	A.E.N.A.	Booklet	*	*	*		
A.E.N.A.		Netball Skills	A.E.N.A.	Booklet		*	*		
A.E.N.A.		Official Netball Rules	A.E.N.A.	Booklet					*
Baggallay J.	1972	Netball for Schools	Pelham	Book		*	*	*	
Butcher D.W.	1970	Netball, Do It This Way	John Murray	Book		*			
Know the Game		Netball	E.P. Pub. Co.	Booklet					*
Miles A.	1981	Success in Netball	John Murray	Book		*	*	*	*
Pritchard O.H.		Pick a Practice Netball	Candidum Press	Practice Cards		*	*		
Stratford R.B.	1976	Netball	E.P. Pub. Co.	Book		*		*	
Wheeler J.	1969	Better Netball	Kaye & Ward	Book		*		*	
Wheeler J.	1980	Games for Netball Training	Pelham	Book			*		
A.E.N.A.		Coaching Charts	Sports Posters	Posters		*		*	

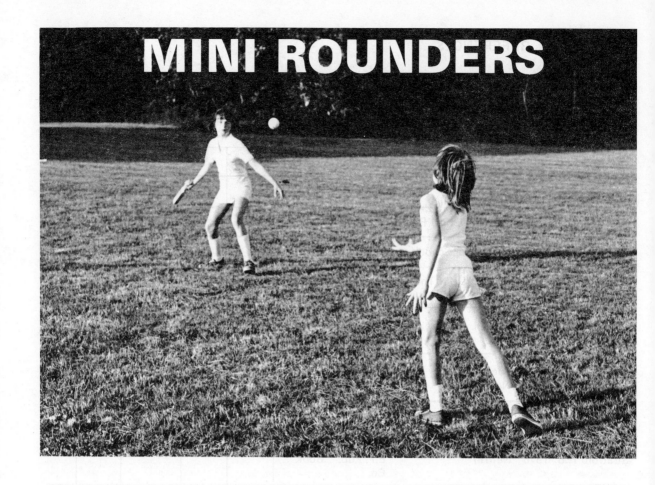

MINI ROUNDERS

CONTENTS

1. PLAYING AREA

1.1 THE PITCH

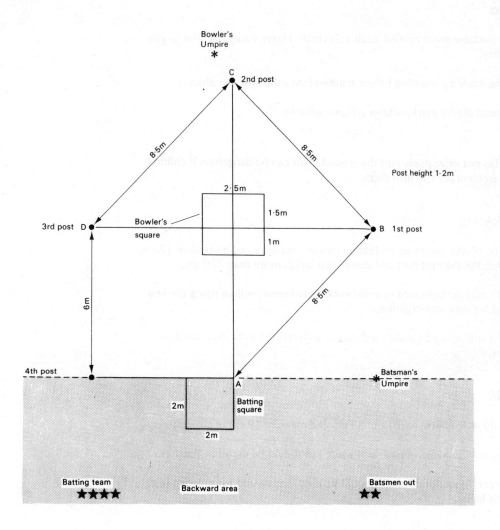

Marking Instructions

1 Use two lengths of string:

(a) 17 metres with a knot tied at its mid-point.
(b) 12 metres with a knot tied at its mid-point.

2 Fix one end of 12 metre string at A where the right front corner of the batting square will be. Fix the other end of the string at C. This gives the position of 2nd post.

3 Fix one end of 17 metre string to each of points A and C and carry the centre knot out to the right until the string is taut. This gives the position of the 1st post B.

4 Leave the ends of this string fixed, carry the centre knot out to the left until the string is taut. This gives the position of the 3rd post D.

5 Fix one end of the 12 metre string at D and fix the other end at A. Carry the knot to the left until the string is taut. This gives the position of the 4th post E.

1.2 ANCILLARY EQUIPMENT

(a) Posts:

1 Four portable posts needed, each 1.2m high. Heavy bases essential to give stability.

2 Can be made by inserting broom handles into solid wooden blocks.

3 Coloured plastic marker cones are also suitable.

Note: Do not drive posts into the ground. This can be dangerous if children accidentally run into them.

(b) Stick:

1 Can be of any length up to 46cm. It should measure not more than 17cm around the thickest part and should not weigh more than 370 gm.

2 Sticks may be fashioned in woodwork department; willow being the best wood for their construction.

3 Sticks with spliced handles and bound with string can be purchased in shops.

(c) Ball:

1 Should weigh between 70 and 85 gm and measure 19 cm in circumference.

2 Good quality balls covered with white kid should be used for matches.

3 Cheaper, more durable balls should be used in class and for practice (e.g. tennis balls).

2. RULES

The following rules outline the game of Mini Rounders. The full rules of Senior Rounders can be found in the N.R.A. *Rules Book* (see 6.2).

2.1 INTERPRETATION OF RULES

Rules

Notes

Object

(1) The object of the game is to score rounders, the team scoring the greater number shall win the game.

(1) Note the rules for scoring in later section.

The Teams

(2) Each side has *6 players*. (Up to 3 additional players may play, e.g. to fit all class members into a game, to increase number of fielders.)

(2) Suggested fielding positions are outlined in the section on positional play 3.5.

Duration of Game

(3) Each game shall consist of *one innings* per side.

(3) An innings is terminated when all the batters are declared 'out'.

(4) A team shall keep the same batting order throughout an innings.

(4) No changing positions for tactical reasons.

Scoring

(5) If a batter stops at 1st, 2nd or 3rd post but reaches 4th post without being declared 'out' *1 rounder* is scored.

(6) If a batter reaches 4th post without stopping at any others *3 rounders* are scored.

(7) *1 rounder* can also be awarded if

    (a) the bowler delivers 3 consecutive no-balls to the same batsman.

    (b) Without hitting the ball the batter reaches 4th post (without stopping).

    (c) There is obstruction by the fielding side.

(5) A batter could stop at every base, (while other team members are batting), but still score 1 rounder if 4th post is reached safely.

(6) Extra weighted value of 3 rounders given to the full circuit achieved with no stopping.

(7) Specimen Score Sheet: Batting

BATTING ORDER		SCORE	HOW OUT	BOWLER	TOTAL
1	Jane	1, 1,	caught	Jill	2
2	Tom	1, 3, 1, 1,	caught	Jill	6
3	Carol	1,	stumped	Jenny	1
4	Mark	3, 1, 3, 3, 1,	stumped	Phil	11
5	Bill	3,	caught	John	3
6	Louise	1, 1, 3, 1,	bounced out	John	6

Three Consecutive No-balls 2

Obstruction . . . . –

                  Total Score   31

Batting

(8) The batter must run after having hit, attempted to hit, or let pass the *first good ball* delivered by the bowler. Thus the batter shall receive only one good ball. The batter may stay at any post on the way round. When further balls are bowled the batter may run on to the next post or further.

(9) The batter may take a no-ball and score in the usual way.

(10) If the ball is hit into the backward area the batter may go no further than *1st post*. This rule does not apply if the ball lands *first* in the forward area and afterwards goes behind (e.g. swings or spins into backward area).

(8) Definition of a *good ball:* the ball must be bowled within the reach of the batter. It should pass no higher than the top of the batter's head and no lower than the batter's knees.

(9) A ball is considered taken if 1st post is reached.

(10)

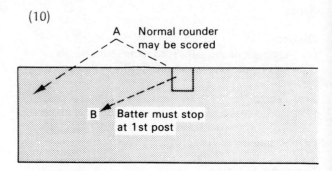

A   Normal rounder may be scored

B   Batter must stop at 1st post

(11) When running around the track the batter must pass *outside* the posts.

(12) When at a post the batter must remain in contact either with hand or bat.

(13) If the batter stops at a post but some misfielding occurs the batter may continue and is *not* penalised.

(14) There can never be *two batters* at one post.

(15) The batter must touch *4th post*.

(16) The last batter has the option of *3 good balls*.

(17) When there is no batter waiting to bat all batters may be put out by any fielder throwing the ball *full pitch* into the batting square.

(11) The batter is not out if he passes inside the post when obstructed from going outside by a fielder.

(12) If contact is lost he can be put out by a fielder touching the next post with ball in hand.

(13) If however the batter stops, and a fielder touches the post immediately ahead of the one with which he is in contact, (and then misfields), the batter can run on but he *cannot score*.

(14) Batters should not overtake other batters.

(15) Hand or bat may be used.

(16) Once a ball is taken however the batter forfeits the right to any that are remaining.

(17) Backstop usually steps into batting square, receives ball from the fielder and drops it in the square.

Fielding

(18) After every *6 good balls* bowled the fielders rotate *one place* around the field (see diagram). Bowler's umpire indicates when 6 good balls have been bowled.

(18)

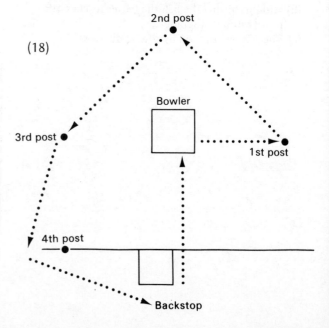

2nd post

Bowler

3rd post

1st post

4th post

Backstop

(19) The ball must be bowled *underarm*.

(20) The main methods of putting a batter out are:

  (a) catching a hit.

  (b) stumping a batter running for a post.

  (c) bouncing out the last batter.

(19) From inside bowling square.

(20)

  (b) A batter can also be put out if touched by the ball in the fielder's hand when running towards 'any' post.

  (c) i.e. When there are no batters waiting.

2.2 UMPIRING MINI ROUNDERS

(For more extensive advice see *Hints to Umpires* published by the N.R.A.)

Batsman's Umpire

1 Stand in area as shown on diagram for pitch markings (1.1)

2 Watch that the bowler does not come out of the front of bowling square when bowling.

3 Watch for balls which drop short of the batter: these are no-balls.

Bowler's Umpire

1 Stand in area as shown on diagram for pitch markings (1.1) but ensure that the ball can be seen when the batter is about to hit it.

2 This umpire normally (but not exclusively) calls any no-balls bowled.

General points

1 A batter should be put out who steps forward out of the square in attempting to hit the ball. Stepping out sideways or backwards is permitted.

2 A batter should be put out when the bowler has possession of the ball in his square:

  (a) if he loses contact with the post before the bowler starts his action and the post immediately ahead is touched with the ball.

  (b) if he loses contact during the bowler's action but before the ball is released.

3 In the obstruction rule both fielders and batters may be guilty. The umpire must decide who is to blame. Also the umpires should ensure that the team waiting to bat in no way interferes with the fielders.

4 Note that stopping within reach of a post (provided the post immediately ahead has not been touched after the batter's arrival) does *not* prevent a rounder being scored.

5 If the ball is hit into the backward area the umpire should call 'behind'. Remember a rounder may be scored if the batter runs on when the ball has returned from the backward area.

6 Remember that it is not a no-ball if the batter moves into the line of flight of a good ball. A 'body ball' occurs when the ball is bowled straight at the body of the batter when in his original waiting stance.

3. PRACTICES

3.1 BALL FAMILIARISATION

Activities

Key points

1 Underarm throwing approx. 1m into the air.

Emphasise simple underarm lob, cup hands together, elbows in to body when catching.

2 Underarm throwing into the air using the other hand.

Watch ball all the time, let hands and arms give as ball arrives.

3 Underarm throwing into the air but vary height and direction of throws.

Smooth upward movement of throwing arm, move into position quickly for the dropping ball.

4 As 1 to 3 but catch with one hand.

Try to catch above and below head height, use both hands to catch.

5 Underarm throw slightly away from body, needing some movement to catch.

Not too far at first, watch out for other people, move quickly and be stationary when catching.

6 Vary throwing and catching hands when attempting activity 5.

Try to swing arm upwards smoothly, throw with one hand, catch with another.

7 Throw into the air in as many different ways as possible (e.g. javelin throw, arm under leg).

Try to catch every throw, who can find the most ways of throwing the ball into the air?

8 When ball is in the air do some action before catching, e.g. clap three times, turn a circle, sit down.

Start with easy tasks and get more ambitious, who can think of a new action?

Examples of Competitive Challenges

(a) Beat Your Own Record	How many consecutive catches can you make before the ball falls to the ground?
(b) Time Challenges	How many one-handed catches can you make in 20 sec?
(c) Races, Relay Races	Throwing the ball to a partner while running over a set distance.

3.2 BATTING

Skill 1 Hitting with hand feed from partner (Mini Tennis bat may be used in early stages)

Activities

Key points

1 6m apart, underarm throw to left of partner (looking from feeder). Hit ball back to partner.

Emphasise accurate feeding, stand sideways, left shoulder forward, hold right arm lifted backward ready to strike ball.

2 As above but give slightly more difficult feeds e.g. faster.

Support stick with left hand, now move feet to hit more effectively, weight moves from back to front foot during action.

3 As above but to test accuracy striker aims at target goal defended by feeder.

Keep stick horizontal when striking ball, try to turn shoulders when hitting, follow through after impact.

Skill 2   Hitting in different directions

1 Threes ● Players as in diagram, striker attempts hit to left through targets (e.g. shoes, skittles, rocks).

Emphasise accurate feeding, on impact try to turn hand so that knuckle faces ground, hit ball slightly earlier (further forward) to direct it to the left side.

2 Threes ● As above but move targets further round.

Slightly more open stance i.e. left shoulder towards 3rd post, swing comes across front of body, ball hit early.

3 Threes ● As above but move targets to right.

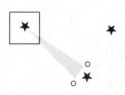

Left shoulder and foot towards bowler, hit ball late, keep wrist open i.e. hand bent well back.

4 Fours ● Players as in diagram, striker attempts to hit ball along the ground to beat the fielders.

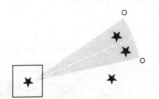

Ball must be hit between targets, aim to the side of the fielders, try not to hit under the ball thus lofting it in air.

5 Fours ● As above but move fielders and targets to right side.

Move the feet quickly, lean slightly away when striking ball.

6 Fours ● As above but place fielders very deep. Striker tries to loft ball over their heads.

As an alternative to ball hit along ground, try to hit deep into a space over the fielders.

7 Sixes ● Players as in diagram. Striker attempts to hit through field of 4 players. Change places after 6 attempts.

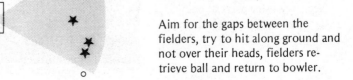

Aim for the gaps between the fielders, try to hit along ground and not over their heads, fielders retrieve ball and return to bowler.

Examples of Competitive Challenges

(a)	Make Activities Competitive	Points scored every time ball is hit through targets.
(b)	Beat Your Own Record	Count number of 'consecutive' hits through targets.
(c)	Time Challenges	How many points scored in 1 min?
(d)	How Far Can You Hit The Ball?	Nominate a direction (e.g. over 1st post) and see who can hit the ball furthest in that direction.

(e) 3 v 3 Rounders •

1 Players arranged as in diagram. Players from opposing teams need to be placed next to each other. (Players from same side will then not be bowling at each other.)

2 Batter may only score when ball is hit into playing area. Score by touching 1st post and returning to touch bat in batting square.

3 Fielders attempt to throw ball to backstop who tries to drop ball in batting square before batter returns.

4 Players rotate one place each time batter is out.

5 Players can be put out if:

    (a) run out (as in 3)
    (b) caught
    (c) touched (whilst running) by fielder holding ball
    (d) 2 consecutive good balls missed
    (e) 2 consecutive balls hit into 'out of bounds' area.

6 Ball simply replayed if hit once into 'out of bounds' area by mistake.

7 When all players have had a turn in each position team scores are totalled.

★ Team A
☆ Team B

Fielders

PLAYING AREA

Batter   Bowler

Backstop   6m

OUT OF BOUNDS

● 1st post

3.3 BOWLING

Skill 1   Underarm Bowling

Activities

1 Pairs • 6m apart. Bowling practice to each other.

2 Pairs • 6m apart. Bowling for accuracy using parts of body as targets (e.g. outstretched arm, shoulder).

Key points

Stand sideways, swing arm back close to body, step on to left foot as arm swings forward and ball is released.

Line up the target with the left shoulder, turn the shoulders, release ball and follow through with throwing arm.

3 Pairs • 6m apart. Bowling practice with stepping action to increase speed.

4 Pairs • 6m apart. Experiment
   with different types of bowling
   action e.g. use different approaches, bowl fast and slow, try
   spin and swerve.

Step sideways with left foot, lift
throwing arm behind, close right
foot up to left, step forward with
left foot, bend left knee, swing
throwing arm forward.

Use all the space in imaginary
bowling square approaching from
different angles, vary speed and
height within rules, try varying
grip for spin.

Examples of Competitive Challenges

(a) Beat Your Own Record	• How many consecutive 'good' balls can you bowl to partner?
(b) Creative Bowling	• How many different ways can you bowl at your partner?
(c) Target Bowling	• Aim for (i) Targets marked on wall. (ii) Free standing targets (e.g. stoolball posts). (iii) Open targets (e.g. hoops attached to skittles).

All targets should resemble height and size of imaginary
rectangle for 'good' ball. (see rule 8)

3.4 FIELDING

Skill 1   Underarm Throwing and Catching

Activities

Key points

1 Pairs • 3m apart. Underarm throw
   to partner who catches with 2
   hands.

Swing arm back close to body,
release ball as arm swings forward.
Make a cup shape with hands
when catching.

2 Pairs • 3m apart. Underarm throw
   high in the air, close to the ground,
   waist high.

Transfer weight on to left foot as
ball is released. When catching
anticipate flight of ball, stretch
hands out. Bring elbows in to body
as catch is made.

3 Pairs • 3m apart. Underarm
   medium height throw. Try
   catching with one hand. Both
   right and left.

Concentrate hard on flight of ball,
let hand 'give' as ball arrives, close
fingers around ball quickly.

4   Pairs • 3m apart. Experiment
with all types of underarm throw
(e.g. hard, soft, high, low) and
all types of catching.

Can you surprise your partner with
your throw? Keep alert all the time,
find as many different ways as
possible.

5   Fours • Form a square 3m apart.
All types of underarm throw and
all types of catching. Pass to
anyone.

Try swinging arm in varied ways
but still releasing ball underarm
be alert for throw from any player.

6   Fours • Move about within con-
fined area, throw ball to anyone
else in the group.

Try to throw and catch while moving, throw just in front of moving
player, anticipate flight of approaching ball.

Skill 2   *Overarm Throwing and Catching*

1   Pairs • 5m apart. Overarm throw
to partner who catches with 2
hands.

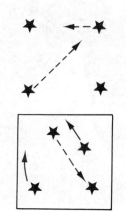

Stand sideways, weight on back
foot, throwing arm bent behind
head, throw made by turning shoulders and straightening arm as it is
brought quickly forward.

2   Pairs • 5m apart. Vary the flight
of the throws (e.g. high, very
high, low, hard, soft).

Non-throwing arm lifted to aid
balance, front shoulder points in
direction of throw, weight trans-
fers forward during throw.

3   Pairs • Experiment with greater
distances, different types of
throw and catching with 1 or 2
hands.

Elbow leads as throwing arm
brought forward, strong wrist
flick and sharper straightening
of arm increases distance.

4   Pairs • Throwing for accuracy.
Each player aims for target (e.g.
rock, shoe, mark on ground).

Players stand directly in line with
target to retrieve throw of partner.
Gradually increase distance.

5   Pairs • Throwing for accuracy.
Aim at targets on wall/fence.

Aim just above target to allow for
distance ball is travelling.

6   Pairs • Throw to predetermined
spot, partner must move to
attempt catch on the run.

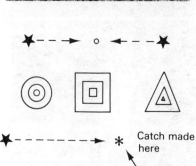

Throw must be sensible to give
partner a chance, catcher must
run quickly to dropping ball, try
to catch with two hands.

7   Pairs • Make throw difficult for
partner to catch — make him
leap high and lunge sideways.

Mix up the catches to keep partner alert, be prepared to catch wide
balls one handed.

Examples of Competitive Challenges

(a)	Make Activities Competitive	Score penalty points for every catch dropped.
(b)	Speed Challenges	Who can make most catches in 30 sec?
(c)	Beat Your Own Record	How many consecutive left-handed catches can you make?
(d)	Circle Catching	Approx. 8 players in circle, throw difficult (but possible) catches to anyone in an effort to force a dropped catch, penalty if ball dropped.

Skill 3 Collecting and Returning

1 Pairs • 10m apart, roll ball to each other to practise stopping.

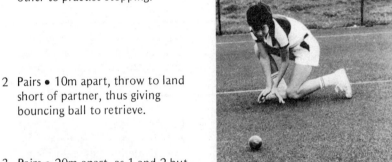

Get in line with approaching ball, kneel sideways on one leg, fingers point down, hands together to receive ball.

2 Pairs • 10m apart, throw to land short of partner, thus giving bouncing ball to retrieve.

Get in line with approaching ball, bend knees and get low to retrieve.

3 Pairs • 20m apart, as 1 and 2 but over greater distance.

Make long barrier with lower leg in case hands miss ball.

4 Pairs • 20m apart, same as above but make partner move to stop ball.

Aim a few metres to side of partner, retriever moves quickly to get in line with ball.

5 Pairs • 20m apart, A rolls ball to B who collects and throws back to A who takes up post position.

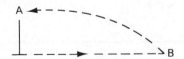

When ball safely collected turn sideways, point left hand at post and throw while stepping on to left leg.

6   Pairs • 20m apart, as above except
    ball collected and returned on the
    move.

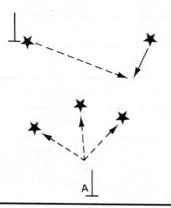

Move towards line of approaching ball, bend down with hands
together, fingers pointing down,
without pausing pick up and
throw.

7   Fours • Players arranged as in
    diagram. Player A hits ball to give
    fielders collecting practice.
    Fielders return ball to A now in
    post position.

Player A aims for gaps to test
fielders. He drops stick to take
return from fielders. Fielders
should back each other up to
cover misfields.

Examples of Competitive Challenges

(a) Competitive
    Collecting 'A'

In pairs each player guards
specified area, partner tries to
roll ball through target area.
(Also 2 or 3 aside with bigger
target areas).

(b) Competitive
    Collecting 'B'

In fours, competitive version of
(7) above. 3 players guard target
area, batter scores point each
time field is pierced.

(c) Beat the Field

1 3 or 4 a-side.
2 Pitch as for Mini Rounders
  or adapted to suit ability (e.g.
  only 3 posts). Players arranged
  as on diagram.
3 Batter throws 3 balls anywhere
  in front of backward area and
  attempts to reach 4th post
  before all balls are collected and
  returned to bowler's square.
4 Players rotate one position
  after every attempt.
5 When all players have had a
  turn in each position scores
  are totalled.

3.5 POSITIONAL PLAY

Skill 1   Backstop

Activities

1   Pairs • 6m apart. Bowl to each
    other. Receiver experimenting
    with the 3 suggested stances
    for backstop.

Key points

(a) Crouching stance, knees fully
    bent.
(b) One foot forward, body slightly
    bent forward.
(c) Legs together, stooping over.

2 Pairs ● 6m apart. As 1 but inten-
tionally mix up bowling, (e.g.
high, low, wide, close).

Always have hands out in front and
together in readiness for catching,
always watch the flight of the ball
carefully.

3 Threes ● Bowler, player holding
hoop in batting position and
backstop.

Bowler aims for hoop, backstop
must catch before ball drops
to ground.

Bowler **1st post**

4 Threes ● Players as in diagram,
backstop practises fast throw to
1st post.

Backstop throws to 1st post fielder
immediately ball is caught. Once
ball is bowled can bowler reach 1st
post before the ball?

Backstop

Skill 2   Post Play

1 Fives ● Backstop and 4 post
players. Throw ball from backstop
to all posts.

Stand on inside of post, touch post
with ball and throw on quickly to
next post.

2 Sevens ● As above with runner at
1st post. Runner tries to reach 4th
post before ball can be bowled and
thrown to all posts.

Stand close to post but be ready to
move for inaccurate throw, touch
post with ball, accurate throw to
next post, touch runner if possible.

**Deep
field**

3 Sevens ● Player in bowling square
throws to deep fielders who retrieve and throw in. Runner starts
in batting square and tries to reach
4th post before ball is returned.

No player needed at 1st base, runner
starts when ball thrown to deep
fielders. Change positions often:
Fielders must quickly decide at
which post to aim.

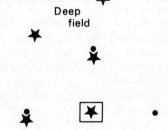

  Runner

Skill 3   Deep Fielders

1   Pairs • 20-30m apart. Give high
catches to each other.

2   Pairs • 20-30m apart. Throw ball
for partner to field, partner
returns as fast as possible.

3   Fours • Players as in diagram.
Batter hits towards fielders who
return to bowler.

Move quickly to dropping ball,
hands cupped, elbows in to body,
'give' with hands.

Always use two hands where
possible, pick up and throw quickly,
aim for chest area of partner.

Fielders back each other up in case
of a mis-field, throw to bowler to
put out imaginary runner.

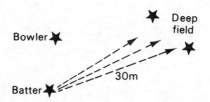

Examples of Competitive Challenges

(a) Speed Challenges	Which group can be first to throw the ball around the four posts twice?
(b) Beat Your Own Record	How many consecutive high catches can you make?
(c) Make Activities Competitive	Points scored in Skill 2 activities.

Suggested Positional Roles

Bowler:
Once the ball has been bowled this player should be
alert to as much close fielding as possible in order that
the post players may concentrate upon post play. He
should quickly return to the Bowler's Square, however,
since the batting team must remain at their posts once
the bowler has possession of the ball in the Square.

Backstop:
The backstop should always be ready to throw the
ball immediately to 1st post although there may be
situations when it is more advisable to throw the ball
to one of the other posts (e.g. A strong batter running
to 4th post). Backstop may also back up throws to
4th post and even take over the post if the 4th post
player has to field the ball. If there is no batter home
backstop should be ready to put out the whole team
by throwing the ball full pitch into the batting square.

1st Post Fielder:
Initially this player should stay close to the post in
order to stump out batters who fail to hit a good ball
bowled at them. If a long hit is made 1st post fielder
can back up throws to 2nd and 3rd posts.

2nd Post Fielder:
This fielder should stand fairly deep in anticipation of
long hits but be ready to move in quickly to the 2nd
post if necessary.

3rd Post Fielder:
3rd post fielder is in the line of the most natural hit
for right handers and should field deep initially. This
player should also be ready to move in quickly to take
up the post position.

4th Post Fielder:
As there is a possibility of a short catch and a quick
ball from the backstop this fielder should stay fairly
close to the post. Also when the batting team are
running on a hit 4th post remains a vital position
and should be guarded closely.

4. PROFICIENCY AWARDS

1 Award Scheme Title   National Rounders Award for Schools

2 Organising Body   National Rounders Association

3 Aim   To foster all round ability in the game of rounders

4 Award Details

Gold Award	— Above 60 marks and no less than 7 in any one test.
Silver Award	— Above 45 marks and no less than 5 in any one test.
Bronze Award	— Above 30 marks and no less than 3 in any one test.

The tests are as follows:— 1 mark for each successful attempt.

1 Demonstrate the ability to:

    (a) Catch balls in outfield (5 attempts).
    (b) Field ball hit (thrown) hard along the ground (5 attempts).

    Coach should throw balls to fielder from batting square.

2 Return ball from the deep to bowler (5 times) and 4th post (5 times) '1st bounce' or direct.

3 Back stop position. Demonstrate the ability to stop (catch) ball and throw accurately to 1st post. The bowler should bowl 5 balls to a right handed batsman and 5 balls to a left hander, the batsman should play and *miss*.

3 Demonstrate a good bowling action using the 'whole' square. Bowl to right and left handers 5 times each.

4 At 1st post catch and stump base, show some ability to handle 'bad' balls from back stop, (10 times).

5 At 4th post catch and stump base, 5 balls from deep and 5 from close fielders.

6 Hit 'friendly' balls beyond imaginary lines between posts into the forward area (10 times).

5 Applications   No application forms. Test results and fees, together with the name, sex, age of child, name of tester and where tested should be submitted to:

    Hon. Award Secretary
    Miss M. Edmondson
    Sheena Simon College
    Whitworth Street
    Manchester M1 3HB

6 General Details   (a) Children should be under 16 on 1st September.
    (b) Small fee charged for each child.
    (c) Cloth embroidered badge awarded to each successful child.

5. TEACHING/COACHING QUALIFICATIONS

5.1 QUALIFIED UMPIRE AWARD

1 Organising Body National Rounders Association

2 Test Requirements
(a) To umpire a game or games (girls', boys' or mixed team).
(b) To answer verbally questions bearing on the Rules of Play, pitch dimensions, equipment, duties of umpires, etc.

3 General Details
(a) Candidates must be over 17 years of age and be recommended by an experienced coach.
(b) A successful candidate will have his or her name entered on the Umpires' Panel of the N.R.A. and will be awarded a certificate and badge.
(c) In the event of failure, a candidate may not apply for re-examination until the following season.

4 Applications
To Hon. Umpire Test Secretary of the N.R.A.
Mr. L. Willoughby
Maerlea
Boyne Mead Road
Kingsworthy
Winchester
Hants

5.2 QUALIFIED COACH AWARD

Candidates for this award must first have become a qualified umpire.

1 Organising Body National Rounders Association

2 Syllabus
(a) Be able to mark out a rounders' pitch.
(b) Devise a lesson in games skills showing groups practising batting, bowling and fielding. (Group of more than 40 players, 9 years and over.)
(c) Coach a game and improve standard of play.

3 Standard
Candidates will be required to show a thorough knowledge of the game and a high standard of leadership and coaching skill. They must show ability to control large numbers, to coach by group methods, to maintain the interest of the group, to ensure that everyone is actively employed throughout the period and to establish readily a good relationship with the group.

4 Applications
To Hon. Coaching Secretary of the N.R.A.
Miss M. Lee
34 Stamford Road
Kettering
Northants

6. REFERENCE INFORMATION

6.1 USEFUL ADDRESSES

National Rounders Association

Secretary:	Mrs. S. Fixter
	4 Gloucester Close
	Desford
	Leics

Sales	Miss F.A. Banks
Secretary:	23 Colworth Road
	Leytonstone
	London E11 1JA

Affiliations	Mr. T. Woolhouse
Secretary:	26 Folds Crescent
	Sheffield S8 0EQ

6.2 ROUNDERS REFERENCES

Publication				Description of Mini Game	Skill Descriptions	Teaching Practices	Tactics	Senior Rules
Know the game	Rounders	E.P. Pub. Co.	Booklet		*			*
N.R.A.	Hints to Umpires	N.R.A.	Booklet					interpretations
N.R.A.	Rules	N.R.A.	Booklet					*
N.R.A.	The Coaching of the Game of Rounders	N.R.A.	Booklet		*	*	*	

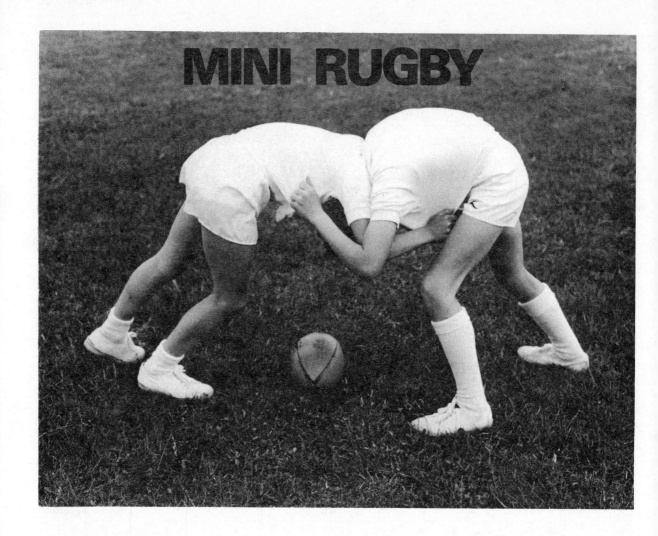

MINI RUGBY

CONTENTS

1. PLAYING AREA

1.1 THE PITCH

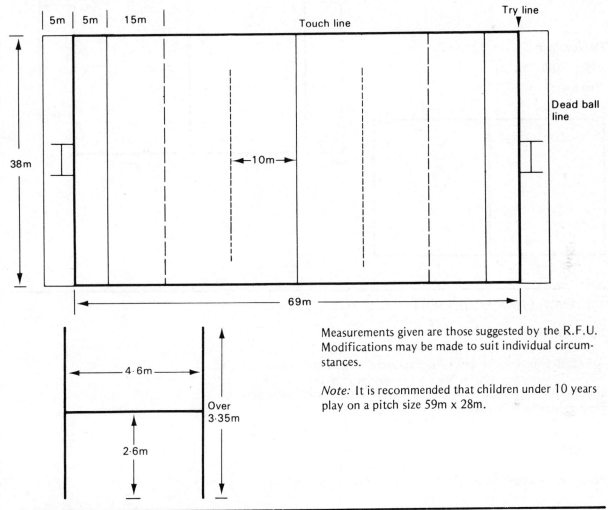

Measurements given are those suggested by the R.F.U. Modifications may be made to suit individual circumstances.

Note: It is recommended that children under 10 years play on a pitch size 59m x 28m.

1.2 ADAPTATIONS OF OTHER PLAYING AREAS

—— original lines to be 'disregarded' in mini rugby

—— original lines to be 'utilised' in mini rugby

- - - additional temporary lines required

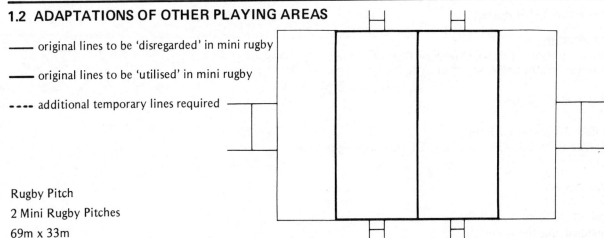

Rugby Pitch
2 Mini Rugby Pitches
69m x 33m

Soccer Pitch
2 Mini Rugby Pitches
70m x 40m

Hockey Pitch
2 Mini Rugby Pitches
60m x 45m

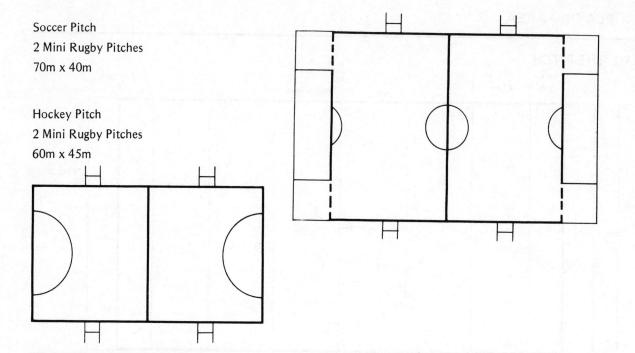

1.3 ANCILLARY EQUIPMENT

(a) Goal Posts:

Can be made up quite simply. Obtain adequate lengths of 4'' diameter wood
from local timber merchants. Mark off height for cross-bar (i.e. 2.6m) and
attach with sturdy angle brackets. Apply a primer and finish off with white
paint. Posts should be padded.

(b) Ball:

Plastic and moulded rugby balls, sizes 3 and 4 from local suppliers.

(c) First Aid Supplies:

Available from:
Medisport Ltd., Freepost, Ottershaw, Chertsey, Surrey, KT16 0BR.
Sports Systems, 5 High St., Windsor, Berks.

(d) Mouth Guards:

Information available from:
Sport Safety Ltd., 139 Jesmond Road, Newcastle-upon-Tyne.

(e) Boots:

Encourage multi-studded moulded rubber soled rugby or soccer boots to
eliminate the risk of cuts.

2. RULES

The following are the official rules of mini rugby as suggested by the Rugby Football Union. However the Union emphasises that they are 'not so much rules as guidelines' — variations being acceptable to meet particular needs. The complete rules of Rugby Union are available in *The Laws of the Game* (see 6.2).

2.1 INTERPRETATION OF RULES

Rules	*Notes*
Object (1) The main object is to touch the ball down with the hands over the opponents' try line to score a try.	(1) The emphasis should be upon scoring tries.
The Teams (2) A team has 9 players: 5 backs and 4 forwards. At scrums 2 boys form the front row and 2 the second, with the flanker packing down on the *same* side that the ball is put in.	(2) Scrum formation.

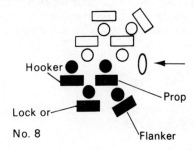

(3) Behind the scrum there is a scrum half, outside half, centre, wing and attacking full back.

Time in Play
(4) Playing time depends upon circumstances. *15 minutes each way* is suggested.

(4) Class time may well dictate the duration of a match but 15-20 mins. each way should prove sufficient for 9-11 yrs., 20-25 min for 11-13 yrs.

Ball in Play
(5) The rules of mini-rugby follow those of the 15-a-side game with a few important exceptions.

(5) For example all the laws of off-side, on-side, knock-on, throw-forward, etc. apply as usual. Also tackling is unrestricted.

(6) The kick-off is from the centre and drop-outs are taken on or behind the *15 metre line*. (This will need to be marked if the mini pitch is not placed across a senior pitch). Under 8's can use a place kick.

(6) Remember: place kick after a converted try, drop kick after an unconverted try: both at the centre.

(7) There are *no line-outs*, if the ball goes into touch, play re-starts with a scrum ten metres in from side-line.

(7) This rule keeps the game simple, avoiding the complex laws regarding line-outs.

(8) During play, direct touch-kicking is allowed *only* from within the defensive 15m area.

(8) As in 15-a-side rugby this law aims to restrict defensive touch-kicking. If the ball is kicked directly into touch from outside the 15m area a tapped penalty is taken at the point where the kick was made.

(9) The scrum-half must *not* follow his opposite number round the scrum until the ball is out.

(9) Thus giving the scrum half a better chance to get the ball away cleanly. Penalty — tapped penalty.

(10) Penalty kicks can be taken direct to touch, but *not* at goal. At all penalties the opposition must be at least *7 metres* away or stand on their own goal-line if it is nearer than 7 metres.

(10) Thus the emphasis is on scoring tries and not penalty kicks for points.

(11) 'Fly-kicking' is illegal at any age level and from any place on the field of play.

(11) The opposition is awarded a scrum at the point of the kick. (Fly-Kick is an indiscriminate and uncontrolled kick at the ball, usually on the ground.)

Scoring

(12) Scoring is conventional, except that conversion kicks are always taken *in front of goal* for children under 10. For older groups the conversion is taken on a line through the place where the try was scored.

(12)

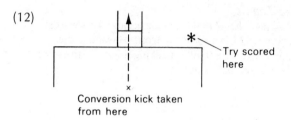

Try scored here

Conversion kick taken from here

(13) A try scores *4 points*. If the conversion is successful another *2 points* are added.

(13) Drop kicks taken in play score 3 points as usual if successful.

2.2 REFEREEING MINI RUGBY

1   In addition to learning the rules obtain a copy of *The Art of Refereeing*, a Handbook for Rugby Football Referees published by the R.F.U. (see 6.2).

2   Observe the positioning and general handling of the game by a senior referee.

3   Be positive and co-operative, helping the players observe the laws.

4   Ensure that the players are clear as to why the whistle has gone.

5   Be consistent and decisive.

6   Maintain the continuity and rhythm of the game by sensible usage of the advantage law.

7   Always keep up with the play and move up and down the field in the middle area of the pitch.

8   For set pieces vary your positioning but ensure you have a clear view of the tunnel at a scrummage.

9   A replacement player is allowed to join the game if an injured player has to leave the pitch. Remember no player may join the game without the referee's permission.

10   Discourage any high tackling and apply the law on dangerous play rigorously.

11   The dead ball area is at the discretion of the referee if not marked.

3. PRACTICES

3.1 SCORING A TRY

Maximum activity game emphasising main aim of rugby (i.e. scoring a try).

(a) Utilise playing area 35m x 20m (i.e. half mini-rugby pitch).
(b) 4 or 5 a-side.
(c) Score a try in normal way (demonstrate).
(d) Running and passing, with no limitations on method or direction of pass.
(e) Release ball if touched by opposition.
(f) No kicking.
(g) For ball out of play free ball to non-offending team where ball crossed line.
(h) When try scored free ball to defending team from centre.
(i) Change opponents often.

3.2 BASIC HANDLING

Skill 1   Ball Familiarisation

Activities

1 Fours ● Ball passed around square of players, 3-5 m apart. Face inwards then change to facing outwards.

2 Fours ● Moving around grid square or across pitch. Pass ball in as many ways as possible.

3 Fours ● Roll ball along ground to any group member. Try to make it bounce as awkwardly as possible.

4 Fours ● Mix up the passes. In the air, on the ground, one hand, two hands.

Skill 2   Basic Pass and Catch

1 Fours ● Ball passed around square of players, 5m apart. Face inwards then change to facing outwards.

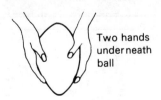
Two hands underneath ball

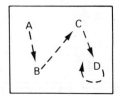

2 Fours ● Zig-zag passing. A to B, B to C, C to D, D turns and passes back to C and so on.

Key points

Use one or two hands to pass but always two to catch. Try passing with spin, without spin, high and low.

Try to get used to the shape of the ball. Notice how the flight changes with the different kinds of pass.

Try to collect ball cleanly by watching its gyrations, e.g. skewing in an arc, popping up, rolling sideways.

Be alert to sudden changes of bounce and flight. Try not to let the ball touch the ground. How many different ways can you pass the ball?

Look before passing, hold ball upright, hands behind ball, swing from shoulders, pass to partner's hip area.

Try not to face direction of approaching ball. When catching turn upper body, stretch arms out, draw ball into body.

3   Fours • On signal players run in
    all directions around grid giving
    quick two handed passes.

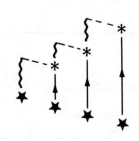

Intersperse short running bursts
with teaching points, e.g. look for
player, twist upper body as you
swing the arms.

4   Fours • Chain passing across
    pitch, ball must now be passed
    backwards, change middle
    players frequently.

Hold ball with two hands in front
of hips, aim just in front of player,
stay close together (3-4m), run
straight.

5   Fours • Passing across pitch but
    interchange positions, be creative,
    switch direction of pass.

Run in different directions but stay
close, go towards (back up) player
with ball. When passing turn towards
receiver.

Skill 3   Screen Pass

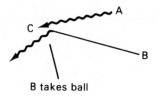

B takes ball

1   Threes • A runs forward to C,
    drives into him with shoulder,
    B supports and takes ball from
    A.

Get low, strong position by dropping
shoulder as you drive through, do
not back into opponent, try to keep
driving forward.

2   Fives • Same as 1 but use 3 attack-
    ers and 2 defenders. A drives at D,
    passes to B, B drives at E passes
    to C.

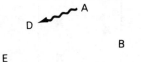

Protect possession by pushing ball
back to opposite hip from driving
shoulder with 'two' hands.

Examples of Competitive Challenges

(a) Beat Your Own Record	Who can make most consecutive passes before ball falls to ground? (e.g. Skill 2 no. 2)
(b) Time Challenges	Who can score most passes in 30 sec? (e.g. Skill 1 no. 3).
(c) Funnel Ball 	3 v 1, passing across playing area, defender tries to intercept attacker's pass.
(d) Skittle Ball with Rugby Ball 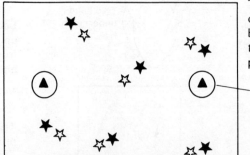	Two targets set up at each end of playing area. Two teams pass ball and try to hit opponents' target. Ball must be passed when player touched.

3 m diameter
no-entry zone

(e) Folk Rugby

1 Pitch size proportionate to number playing.
2 Spread all available balls on mid-line of playing area.
3 Two teams lined up 10m from rugby balls.
4 On signal each team scores as many tries as possible.
5 Once a try is scored that ball goes out of circulation.
6 *No* kicking allowed.

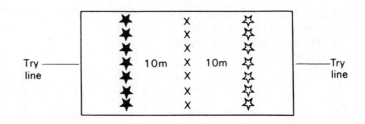

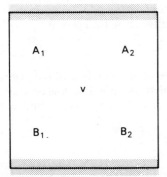

(f) 2 v 2 rugby

1 Use a grid square approximately 10m x 10m.
2 Tries scored over opponents' end line.
   or
   Highest number of consecutive passes made.
3 No passing forward.
4 No kicking.
5 Ball must be passed when player touched.
6 If ball crosses side-line, non-offending team simply takes possession at point where ball crossed line.
7 If ball crosses end-line, defending team simply takes possession at point where ball crossed line.
8 Play for 5 min. and change opponents.

3.3 TACKLING

Skill 1   Side Tackle: (Take equal turns at tackling. Tackle on left and right sides.)

Activities

1 Pairs • Tackler kneels beside standing partner, performs tackle.

2 Pairs • Tackler kneels, partner walks in to be tackled.

3 Pairs • Tackler standing, partner walks in to be tackled.

4 Pairs • Both players jog towards each other, tackle is made.

5 Pairs • Both players run towards each other, tackle is made.

6 Pairs • If tackling bag available utilise to build up diving confidence.

Key points

Arms envelope player just above knees, shoulder thrusts into player's thigh.

Grasp tightly with arms, ensure head is *on top* of tackled player's body.

Tackler approaches as low as possible, coupled with powerful drive from legs.

Pin legs together tightly and hold on until partner has fallen and released ball.

Approach low, aim for thighs, drive in with shoulder, land on top.

All previous teaching points, drive from further away slowly building up confidence.

7 Pairs • In grid area player A tries to score try while B tries to tackle. Start with ball on ground and A 3m back.

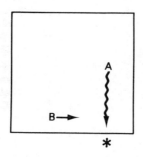

*

Player A must stay within grid or specified area. In competitive situation B must allow for changes of direction by A.

Skill 2   Front Tackle

1 Pairs • Same progressions as for side tackle except players face each other to start.

Get low, aim for thigh with shoulder, drive into opponent to make sure of firm grip. Try to twist attacker to land on top.

Skill 3   Smother Tackle (to prevent the pass)

1 Pairs • Same progressions as for side tackle except players face each other to start.

Shoulder goes in hard but higher, defender tries bear hug on attacker, try to twist attacker to land on top.

Skill 4   Rear Tackle

1 Pairs • Same progressions as for side tackle except one player now stands behind the other.

Defender accelerates and drives in, wrapping arms round at thigh level, aim to one side to leave head clear.

Examples of Competitive Challenges

(a) Funnel
    Tackling

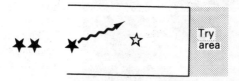

Groups of 4 or 5. Funnel approximately 5m wide 10m in length. Defender tries to tackle attacker to prevent him reaching end of funnel. Attacker tries to score try at the end and must not run outside funnel sidelines. Second attacker starts when defender has recovered.

(b) Circle Tackle

Groups of 8 to 10. Players numbered and form circle as shown. Two numbers called, 1 sec time-lag between. First number player picks up ball and tries to return to his place. Second player tries to prevent him with a tackle.

(c) Pick-Tack

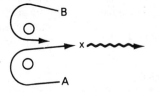

On signal A runs around obstacle (track-suit, post, brick) picks up ball and attempts to score a try. B runs round obstacle and tries to tackle A before a score is made.

3.4 THE SCRUM AND THE BACKS

Skill 1   Scrummaging Progressions

Activities

1   Pairs • 1 v 1 basic scrumming position. Holding opponent's shirt, then without holding each other. On signal push hard against opponent.

2   Fours • 2 v 2 scrum formation, emphasis upon binding and positioning of body.

3   Fives • 2 v 2 scrum with scrum half putting ball in, change positions frequently.

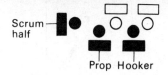

Key points

Shoulder to shoulder, head under opponent's chest, feet wide apart, weight on insides of feet. Drive strongly from legs, keeping low position.

Bind under arm-pits not around neck, grip opponent's shirt with free arm, try to get a flat back.

'Snap' shove when ball is put in (not before), hooker tries to heel ball back with right foot.

Note: Although the R.F.U. recommend the eight man scrum it is acknowledged that many coaches prefer only six. For further information on this point see publications in 6.2.

Skill 2   The Eight Man Scrum

1   Eights • Practise forming the scrumming position. Name the positions.

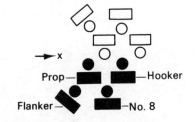

Front row needs to be big and strong, preferably of similar size, flanker and No. 8 bind on.

2   Eights • Pushing competitions. On signal push back over opponents' line.

Turn the feet out and push with inner edges, bend legs well to get low position, all players bind tightly.

3   Nines • Eight man scrum and
scrum half practise 'snap' shove
and heeling ball back.

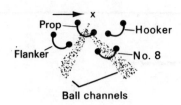

Ball channels

Prop whose side puts the ball in has
his head on the outside of the
scrum, push hard when ball is put
in, look for ball.

Skill 3   The Ruck and Maul

Note: A 'ruck' or 'maul' develops when a player with the ball is caught by the opposition.

Maul — Ball held in hands.
Ruck — Ball on the ground

Activities

Key points

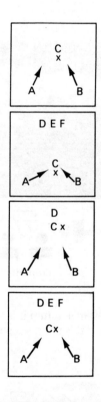

Ruck

1   Fours • C lies beside ball, A and
B drive beyond C and ball. C
joins in ruck and heels ball back.

Drive over player and ball, keep on
your feet, make sure you bind on
and look for the ball.

2   Sixes • As above but D, E, F,
provide opposition, fairly
passive at first trying to gain ball
later.

Try to keep forward momentum
going as opposition is met, bind
tightly together and try to heel
ball back.

Maul

3   Fours • C with ball turns as he
meets opposition D. A and B
drive in hard to form maul.

Bind on and keep pushing, look for
ball and try to hand ball back to
imaginary scrum-half.

4   Sixes • As in 3 but D, E, F,
provide stronger opposition,
trying smother tackles to spoil
maul.

Keep on your feet, try not to let
ball drop to ground, keep forward
momentum, rip the ball clear if
smothered.

Skill 4   Half Back Play

1   Pairs • 5m apart, practise straight
pass where ball is played from the
ground. Pass in turns.

Ball on ground at feet, back foot
close to ball, step towards receiver
with other foot, sweep ball off
ground and swing arms to pass.

2   Pairs • Same as 1 but pass on
signal.

Take up wide stance, sweep up and
pass in one movement as quickly as
possible.

3   Pairs • Dive pass to each other.

Both feet close to ball, drive hard
with legs to gain height and swing
arms.

Skill 5   The Backs: Attack and Defence

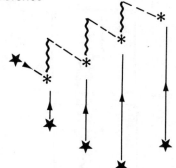

1 Fives • Alignment practice for attack. Passing with deep line from improvised start line to goal line. (30-40m).

Run straight, keep just behind player with the ball, run a few metres with the ball and pass just in front of receiver.

2 Fives • Same as 1 but players practise some simple loops to back up other players.

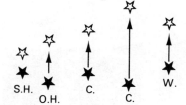

After passing ball move round back of next player or back of whole team and be ready to receive ball again. Change positions frequently.

3 Tens • Alignment practice for defence. Defending backs try to prevent attacking backs breaking through.

S.H. O.H. C. C. W.

Move up in line, tackle opposite number, cover across if opposite number passes. Attack and defence can change often.

Examples of Competitive Challenges

(a) Pushing Competitions

Two, four or eight man scrums. Try to push opponents over their back line. Change opponents often.

(b) Competitive Rucks and Mauls

Two teams of four players in specified area. Place ball on ground equidistant between teams. On signal players run for possession of the ball and try to score from the ensuing ruck or maul.

(c) 5 v 5 Rugby

1 Use 4 grid squares, i.e. 20m x 20m area.
2 Tries scored over opponents' end line.
3 2 forwards, 3 backs. 2 v 2 scrums for infringements.
4 No kicking.
5 Play for 10 min. and change opponents.
6 Otherwise normal rugby rules.

3.5 RUNNING, KICKING AND CATCHING

Skill 1   Beating an Opponent

Activities

Key points

1 Pairs • Use grid square. Beat passive tackler coming from front by a feint and 'swerving' to the opposite side.

Try area

Run fast, make as if to move to left and drive off hard with left leg to the right of defender.

2 Pairs • Same as 1 but tackler now tries to touch attacker with two hands below waist. Change frequently.

Hold ball with two hands, let arms move across body when running, feint to pass before swerving.

3   Pairs • Beat passive tackler
    approaching on an angle by
    feinting as though to run outside,
    and sidestep inside.

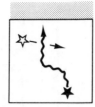

Appear to make a determined
effort to run around tackler, thrust
vigorously with right leg to sidestep left.

4   Fours • Same as 3 but A gives
    ball to D after sidestep is made.
    D returns to sidestep C. D then
    gives ball to B and so on.

Once sidestep is successful try to
straighten up to original direction,
sidestep to the left and right.

5   Fours • Four players in grid
    square, one with ball sidesteps
    and swerves to avoid being
    touched by others with two
    hands below waist.

Encourage player with ball to
feint, swerve, etc. as much as
possible. Player catching the ball
carrier takes over possession.

Skill 2   Catching

1   Pairs • 10m apart, lob the ball to
    partner with a two handed throw.
    Gradually throw higher.

Run to place yourself directly
under dropping ball, reach out with
both hands, as ball arrives bring
arms in close to body, elbows
touching bottom of rib cage.

2   Fours • Players stand just outside
    grid square, one player lobs ball
    high into middle and calls name,
    named player runs in to middle to
    catch.

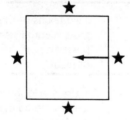

Be alert it could be your catch next,
anticipate dropping ball and bring
arms in quickly to prevent ball
bouncing out of hands.

Skill 3   Kicking and Catching (Kick with both left and right legs)

1   Pairs • 10m apart, 'punt' ball
    accurately to partner, both stand
    on a line and kick along line.

Point ball at partner holding it with
two hands. Drop ball on to kicking
foot stretched out with toe pointed.

2   Pairs • Move back to 20m apart,
    'punt' ball accurately to partner,
    progress to much higher kicks.

Kick with the instep not the toe,
let the leg follow-through high in
air, remember catching technique.

3   Pairs • 'Punt' kick, then chase to
    get to catcher at same time as
    ball.

No throwing ball upwards but let it
drop straight on to kicking foot.

4   Pairs • 10m apart, 'drop kick'
    ball accurately to partner, kick
    along a line.

Hold ball tilted slightly backwards,
let it drop at this angle, kick
immediately it touches ground.

5 Fours • Two players face two others 20m apart, 'drop kick' ball and nominate catcher as ball is in the air.

Keep the head down watching ball, start kicking action as ball is released from the hands.

6 Pairs • 20m apart, 'place kick' accurately to partner.

Tee up ball in upright position, short run-up, place non-kicking foot just beside and behind ball, kick through ball with other foot.

7 Pairs • 'Place kicks' with one player either side of a set of goal posts.

Short approach run, take a long last stride, try both the toe and instep.

Examples of Competitive Challenges

(a) 1 v 1 Kicking

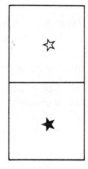

1 Each player stands in a grid square.
2 Try to make ball land in opponent's square or force him to drop a catch, point scored each time this occurs.
3 Ball landing outside square gives point to receiver.
4 Specify type of kick or allow free choice. Kick must go over head height.
5 Play for 5 min and change opponents.
(This can be played with up to 5-a-side on larger playing areas).

(b) Touch Kicking

1 Two players stand on a line, punting distance apart.
2 Each tries to push the other back down the line, kicking position being where ball crosses line.
3 Players may widen the angle before kicking.
4 Practise with both feet.

(c) Howitzer

1 Two teams of two or more players on full mini rugby pitch.
2 Both teams start midway in their own halves.
3 The object is to gain as much ground as possible with kicks, if ball is caught before bouncing, player may take 5 strides before kicking. If ball bounces, kick from where it is stopped.
4 When in kicking distance of opponent's goal-line, attackers may try punt, drop-kick or place kick over posts.

(punt = 1 point, place/drop = 2 points).

5 If score made, resume as at start of play.

4. PROFICIENCY AWARDS

No official award scheme as yet. The following tests are suggested by R. Williams. The R.F.U. have an award scheme in preparation. For details apply to the Technical Administrator.

Test 1:

Equipment: Three lines 10m apart; 1 ball (size 3), 1 stop-watch.

Test: Stand on starting line; ball on the centre line. Run, pick up ball — score a try on the far line. Still carrying ball, turn around, run back to centre line, place ball, run back to touch ground beyond starting line and repeat. Record the total time taken.

Test 2:

Equipment: A 10 metre square marked out on ground, in the centre is a 5 gallon oil drum (weighted so that it cannot be knocked over) standing on a box 60cm high. Four balls (size 3), each one placed 60 cm outside the corner of the square, 1 stop-watch.

Test: Player stands at one corner outside the square and when given the word picks up the ball and does a standing pass aiming to hit the oil drum. One foot only allowed to be in the square. As soon as he has passed he runs to the next corner and so on until he finishes on the original starting point. Count the number of hits and record the total time.

Test 3:

Equipment: A 10 metre square marked out on ground. Four touch flags — one in each corner. In the centre is a 5 gallon oil drum (weighted so that it cannot be knocked over) standing on a box 60cm high. Four balls (size 3) one in each corner, 1 stop-watch.

Test: Starting from one corner pick up the ball and run to another corner: while running pass the ball to hit oil drum. Forward passes do not count and player must not run into the square. Run around the square until original starting point is reached. Repeat, running in the opposite direction. Record hits and total time taken.

Test 4:

Equipment: Four chairs placed at 5, 10, 15 and 20m. One ball (size 3); 1 stop-watch; starting line.

Test: From the starting line run forward dodging in between the chairs, run around the end chair and return dodging between the chairs, score a try over the starting line. Ball must always be carried in two hands except in the actual movement of scoring the try when grounding with one hand is permissible. Record the time taken.

Test 5:

Equipment: Restraining line (goal-line), touch-line, 20m line and 5m line (as on pitch). One ball (size 3).

Test: Stand behind restraining line at least 15m from touch line. Kick ball to touch. Three attempts with right foot to left-hand touch and three to right-hand touch with left foot. Score as follows:

(a)   Ball *direct* to touch nearside of 20m line, 1 point.
(b)   Ball *direct* to touch far-side of 20m line, 3 points.
(c)   Ball pitches far-side of 20m line and then goes into touch, 4 points.

Test 6:

Equipment: Target 60cm square (either nailed on post or painted on wall); bottom of target 6 feet from ground. Three lines marked 5m, 7m and 9m from the target. One ball (size 3).

Test: Throw the ball over-arm (right or left) to hit target. Two attempts from each line. Score 1 point for a hit.

Test 7:

Equipment: A line drawn on a hard surface, e.g. playground or wooden floor.

Test: Standing broad jump. Stand with both feet behind line and with a two-footed take-off jump as far as possible to land on two feet. Measure and record the best of three attempts.

Test 8:

Equipment: 1 set regulation goal-posts. One ball (size 3).

Test: From 20m in front of the posts, using either
foot — 2 place kicks, 2 drop kicks, 2 punts to kick
ball over crossbar between uprights.
Three points for a goal.
Two points for a hit on crossbar or uprights above bar.
One point for a hit on upright below bar.
Record total points.

Teachers and coaches will need to formulate their own
standards as none are available at the moment.

5. TEACHING/COACHING QUALIFICATIONS

5.1 R.F.U. PRELIMINARY AWARD

1 Organising Body   Rugby Football Union

2 Aim   To improve teaching and coaching standards:

    (a) Introducing rugby football to young people;
    (b) Using constructive methods of teaching and coaching;
    (c) Instilling positive attitudes in the true spirit of the game.

3 Syllabus

    (a) *Individual Skills:*
        Handling: Running: Contact: Kicking.

    (b) *Unit Skills:*
        Scrummaging: Line Out: Ruck and Maul: Back Division.

    (c) *Team Skills:*
        Attack: Defence.

4 Duration of Course   Minimum 15 hours plus two practical coaching sessions.

5 Assessment

    (a) *Practical* (30 min.)
        20 min. coaching individual skills and/or in a game of rugby teach/coach/
        referee aspects of play.
        10 min. viva.

    (b) *Theory* (1 hour)
        Simple written paper to assess a candidate's knowledge of rugby football.

6 Applications   Write to Hon. Sec. of Coaching of your Constituent Body,

        or

The R.F.U. Technical Administrator, Rugby Football Union, Twickenham, Middlesex.

6. REFERENCE INFORMATION

6.1 USEFUL ADDRESSES

Rugby Football Union
Secretary: Air Commodore R.H.G. Weighill
        Rugby Road
        Twickenham
        Middlesex TW2 7RQ

Technical Administrator:

        D Rutherford
        Rugby Road
        Twickenham
        Middlesex TW2 7RQ

Rugby Football Schools' Union
Secretary: R R Tennick
        Rugby Road
        Twickenham
        Middlesex TW2 7RQ

Town and Country Productions Ltd.
(for hire of Mini Rugby Films).
        21 Cheyne Row
        Chelsea
        London SW3 5HP

Welsh Rugby Union
(for hire of Mini-Rugby film).
        28/31 St Mary Street
        Cardiff CF1 2PP

6.2 RUGBY REFERENCES

Publication			Description of Mini Game	Skill Descriptions	Teaching Practices	Tactics	Senior Rules
Banks G. 1976	Teaching Rugby to Boys	Bell, Book		*	*		selection
KTG	Rugby Union Football	E.P. Pub. Ltd. Booklet					*
Robinson D. 1975	Rugger: How to Play the Game	R.F.U. Booklet					interpretation
R.F.U. 1975	Better Rugby	R.F.U. Book	small-sided games	*	*	*	
R.F.U.	Coaching Scheme	R.F.U. Booklet	*				
R.F.U.	Laws of the Game	R.F.U. Booklet					*
R.F.U.	Mini Rugby	R.F.U. Booklet	*				
R.F.U.	Mini-Rugby Barbarians Style	Town & Country Productions Ltd. Film	*	*			
R.F.U.	Mini-Rugby — It's the Real Thing	Town & Country Productions Ltd. Film	*	*	*		
R.F.U.	Rugby Post	R.F.U. Newsletter	*	*	*	*	
R.F.U.	The Art of Refereeing	R.F.U. Booklet					interpretation
Scottish R.U.	Mini-Rugby: A Teaching Guide	S.R.U. Booklet	*	*	*		
Welsh R.U.	This is Mini-Rugby	W.R.U. Film	*	*			
Williams G. 1975	Tackle Rugger	Stanley Paul Book			*	*	
Williams R. 1973	Rugby for Beginners	Souvenir Press Book	*	*			simplified
Williams R. 1976	Skilful Rugby	Souvenir Press Book		unit skills		*	

CONTENTS

1. PLAYING AREA

1.1 THE PITCH

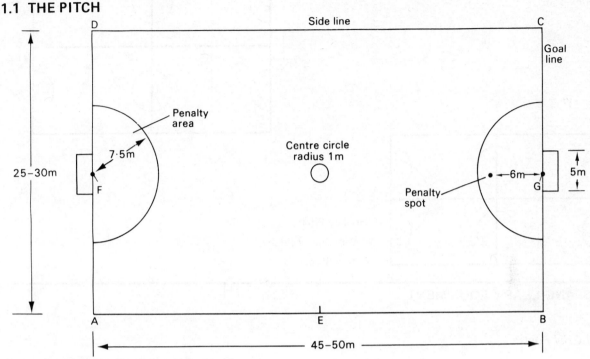

Marking Instructions (For 50m x 25m Pitch)

1 Use two lengths of string:

   (a) 50m with a knot tied at its mid-point.
   (b) 35m with a knot tied at 7.5m.

2 Fix one end of 50m string at A, hold string taut and mark B. Also mark mid-point E.

3 Keep 50m string fixed at A. Fix one end of 35m string at E. Holding the knot of the 50m string and the free end of the 35m string walk away from E. When both strings are taut point D may be marked.

4 Using B as the fixed point for the 50m string do the same to mark C.

5 Mark exterior lines joining ABCD. Mark the mid-points of side-lines AD and BC. Fix 35m string at F. Holding the knot at 7.5m walk around the semi-circle marking the goal area. Do the same at G.

Note: For the English Schools Football Association 6-a-Side Championship senior rules are used and therefore full pitch markings are desirable, e.g. half-way line and rectangular penalty area.

1.2 ADAPTATIONS OF OTHER PLAYING AREAS

———————— original lines to be 'disregarded' in mini soccer

———————• original lines to be 'utilised' in mini soccer

– – – – – – – additional temporary lines required

Soccer Pitch
4 Mini Soccer Pitches
50m x 35m

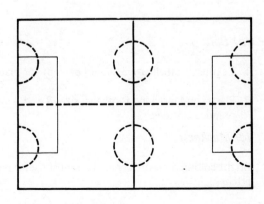

Rugby Pitch
4 Mini Soccer Pitches
50m x 35m

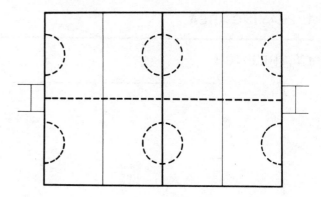

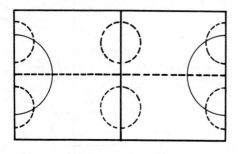

Hockey Pitch
4 Mini Soccer Pitches
45m x 30m

1.3 ANCILLARY EQUIPMENT

(a) Goal Posts:

1 Posts may be constructed fairly easily using the dimensions shown in
   diagram. These may be either: 'permanent' where the uprights are sunk
   into sockets in the ground or 'portable' where supporting lengths of
   timber are attached to the uprights.

2 Portable posts of light tubular metal are also very effective and durable.

3 Brush handles, canes and 1" diameter lengths of wood can be utilised as
   goal posts although slightly more dangerous than 1 and 2.

Note: for the E.S.F.A. 6-a-Side Championship goal posts need to be
6½ m wide and 2 m high.

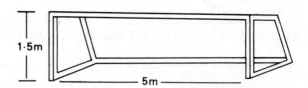

(b) Ball:

1 Leather football size 3 should be kept for matches.

2 Plastic and moulded footballs, sizes 3 and 4 can be used effectively in
   practice sessions.

(c) Markers:

Bright coloured plastic cones are a most useful method of marking out mini
pitches.

2. RULES

The following rules are suggested for Mini Soccer. Note that senior rules are used in the E.S.F.A. 6-A-Side Championship. The complete rules of soccer can be found in the *Referees' Chart and Laws of Association Football* (see 6.2).

2.1 INTERPRETATION OF RULES

Rules

Notes

Object

(1) The main object of the game is to play the ball into the goal of the opposing team.

(1) Goals may be scored from *anywhere* on the pitch.

The Teams

(2) A team has 6 *players*, five on the field and one goal-keeper.

(2) A team may change its goalkeeper during the match provided the referee is informed before the change is made.

(3) During the game *two substitutions* may be made in the case of injury.

(3) Teams should therefore always endeavour to nominate eight players.

Time in Play

(4) Playing time depends upon circumstances. *15 minutes each way* is suggested.

(4) Class time may well dictate the duration of a match but 15-20 mins each way is suggested for 9-11 years, 20-25 mins for 11-13 years.

(5) If a result is required and the scores are equal at full-time, the match shall be decided by penalty kicks.

(5) The 5 players on the outfield at full-time take the penalty kicks. If the scores are still level after 5 penalties the process is repeated until a result is achieved.

Ball in Play

(6) The game shall be started at the commencement of play in each half and after each goal by a *pass from the centre spot* in the centre circle.

(7) Players are free to move *anywhere* on the pitch.

(6) No member of the opposing team may enter the centre circle until the kick has been taken. The pass may be either forward or back.

(7) This avoids the complications of whether or not players have entered or left prohibited areas and the resulting penalties.

(8) There is *no off-side*.

(9) Normal rules for *throw-ins* from touch, *corners* and goal kicks.

(10) All fouls and misconduct shall be penalised by the award of a *direct free kick* taken from where the breach occurred (except for penalty kicks).

(8) This should lead to more open play.

(9) Goal kicks taken from anywhere inside penalty area.

(10) In order to simplify matters there are no indirect free kicks. Players from the offending team should stand not less than *5m* from the ball until it is played.

(11) Any fouls committed inside the penalty area shall be penalised by the award of a *penalty kick* taken from the *penalty spot*.

(12) The goalkeeper may handle the ball only in the *penalty area*.

(11) All the usual rules for a penalty kick apply, e.g. all players apart from the goalkeeper and player taking the kick should stay outside penalty area until kick is taken.

(12) He may leave the penalty area however and play the ball with his feet, head etc.

Referee

(13) The game will be controlled by *one referee*. His decisions are final.

(13) With no off-side the need for linesmen is reduced but may still be utilised.

2.2 REFEREEING MINI SOCCER

1   In addition to learning the rules obtain a copy of
The F.A. Guide to the Laws of the Game which
answers questions on the application of the laws to
situations arising in the course of play.

2   Be positive and cooperative, helping the players
observe the rules rather than seeming to treat them
as criminals.

3   Ensure that the players are clear as to why the
whistle has gone.

4   Maintain the continuity and rhythm of the game
by sensible usage of the advantage law.

5   Operate mainly from the centre of the field to avoid
impeding play in congested areas (e.g. goal area).

6   Two substitutes are allowed in Mini Soccer if injured players have to leave the pitch. No player may
join the game without the referee's permission.

7   Players committing intentional fouls should be
severely reprimanded. For this age group the referee
(along with teachers, coaches and parents) has the
responsibility of instilling desirable attitudes in the
true spirit of the game.

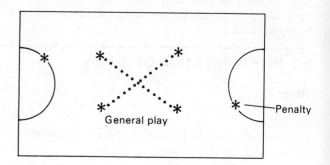

General play

Penalty

3. PRACTICES

3.1 BALL FAMILIARISATION (INCLUDING DRIBBLING)

Skill 1   Close Control

Activities

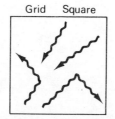

Grid   Square

1 Dribble ball within playing area keeping it less than 1m from body.

2 Dribble amongst other players in specified area. Use both inside and outside of foot.

3 Dribble amongst others in specified area but now emphasise control while changing speed and direction.

4 Any of above but now try to look up as much as possible.

5 Half group stand with legs apart, remainder dribble through and around their legs without touching them.

6 Use any objects to act as obstacles which have to be successfully negotiated (e.g. shoes, satchels, skittles, bricks).

7 Try keeping the ball in the air. First with one bounce allowed and then keep it off ground altogether.

Skill 2   Screening

1 Pairs • Player with ball continually tries to keep his body between ball and opponent.

2 Pairs • As above but play is kept within small restricted area.

Key points

Start moving slowly and build up speed, touch the ball lightly to keep it close.

Keep ball very close, do not lose control, weave in and out of others but do not touch them.

Whistle command could be used to change pace or direction, use inside or outside of foot to change direction.

Keep foot in contact with ball when looking up thus increasing awareness of ball position.

Ball should only be tapped lightly so as not to interfere with others.

Make sure knees are bent when changing direction, use all parts of the feet. Watch for other players.

Play the ball close to the body using the top of the foot, knee or head.

Opponent fairly passive at first, then tries to gain possession, player with ball must angle the body back to give balance and retain close possession of the ball.

Try to prevent opponent from seeing or getting a foot to the ball.

3 Threes ● A passes to B who must
   hold possession for 5 seconds
   before passing back to A. C moves
   around trying to dispossess B.

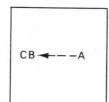

CB ◄── ─A

Make sure of control first, screen
the ball while watching opponent's
position and the movements of A.
Only pass when safe, 5 sec is a
minimum.

4 Threes ● As above but increase
   possession time.

Try feinting in one direction (i.e.
stepping over ball) to send opponent one way while passing in
other direction.

Examples of Competitive Challenges

(a) Beat Your Own Record	How many times can you touch the ball before it falls to the ground?
(b) Put More Players than Balls in Grid Square	Players must maintain or gain possession of ball. Score point if in possession when whistle blown.
(c) Ball Control Relays	Simple 'there and back' type at first. Introduce obstacle relays later. Use small teams.
(d) Who Can Find Most Ways?	Dribbling, changing direction, keeping ball in air.
(e) Possession Ball	In pairs players try to maintain possession in restricted area.

3.2 SHORT PASSING

Skill 1   Short Passing with the inside of the foot

Activities

1 Pairs ● 5m apart. Pass continuously to each other with inside of foot, use both right and
   left feet.

2 Pairs ● 5m apart. Vary the pace
   and make partner move slightly
   to one side to stop.

Key points

Side of foot contacts centre of ball,
non-kicking foot level with ball at
point of contact, arms aid balance.

Head well over ball, try not to lean
back when kicking, ensure follow-
through is in direction of pass.

3 Pairs ● 5m apart. Players pass to each other whilst moving across playing area.

Pass slightly ahead of partner, control ball before passing back, again get non-kicking foot close to ball.

4 Pairs ● 5m apart. As 3 but never stay level with each other, (e.g. A sprints forward, receives pass from B).

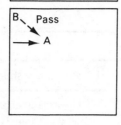

Keep moving but try to pass either forward or back, look to see where partner has moved.

5 Pairs ● Try all activities above with increased distances.

Accuracy even more important, longer last stride before striking ball.

6 Pairs ● Pass with inside of foot at or through target, gradually increase distance and reduce target size.

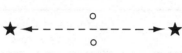

Ensure foot is at right angles to target, try with non-dominant foot, try a first-time pass if successful.

7 Fours ● All move about grid square, pass when appropriate.

Be alert for pass at any time, run into a space and call for the pass.

8 Fours ● 3 v 1, opposition player passive at first to ensure success. Pass from one side of grid to the other.

Pass accurately to player then move behind opponent into a space. Opponent moves around but does not tackle.

Skill 2   *Short Passing with the outside of the foot*

1 Pairs ● 5m apart. Pass continuously to each other with outside of foot, use both feet.

Outside of foot contacts centre of ball, bend at the knee and flick the ball towards partner.

2 Pairs ● 5m apart. As above but pass alternately with left and right feet.

Make sure ball is quite still at first, place non-kicking foot firmly for balance.

3 Pairs ● Pass with outside of foot and move to new position.

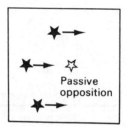

Use arms to aid balance, look up quickly and pass to partner in new position.

4 Pairs ● Pass to each other whilst moving around grid square.

Stay close together, pass just in front of partner, change positions.

5 Threes ● Passing to each other with outside of foot along very narrow corridor.

Imaginary boundary

Use short, flick pass in this tight situation, constantly move in and out of one another passing often.

6 Threes • Use wall pass to beat opponent, use both inside and outside of foot.

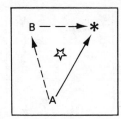

A passes to B and immediately moves behind opponent to receive return pass from B.

Examples of Competitive Challenges

(a) Time Challenges — How many short passes can you make in 30 sec?

(b) Beat Your Own Record — How many consecutive passes can you play through the target? (Skill 1, no. 6).

(c) Races — Cross the grid square 4 times making at least 3 short passes each time you cross.

(d) Competitive 3 v 1, 4 v 1

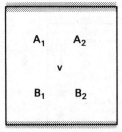

When short pass has developed sufficiently let opponent defend properly. Attackers attempt to stop ball on end grid line.

(e) Possession Ball — 3 players in grid square, two trying to keep possession while third attempts to win ball. Player losing possession (i.e. making the poor pass) goes into middle (3 v 1 or 4 v 1 may be necessary if skill level is low).

(f) 2 v 2 Soccer

1 Use a grid square approx. 10m x 10m.
2 Goal scored by *stopping* ball on opponents' end line.
3 Short side-foot pass only. (Conditions may be imposed to improve movement off the ball e.g. 3 touches or 3 paces only before pass must be made.)
4 If ball crosses side-line, non-offending team simply takes possession at point where ball crossed line.
5 If ball crosses end-line, defending team takes possession at point where ball crossed line.
6 Play for 5 min and change opponents.

3.3 CONTROLLING THE BALL

Skill 1   Foot Control

Activities

1 Pairs • 5m apart. Pass along ground to each other stopping and controlling ball with the inside of the foot.

2 Pairs • 5m apart. As above but partner alternately aims for right and left side of partner.

3 Pairs • 5m apart. As above but vary speed of pass.

4 Pairs • Above activities over greater distances.

5 Pairs • Players move around grid square, pass to partner who controls and passes on again.

6 Fours • Players as in diagram, pass and follow ball, receiver controls and passes on while under pressure from approaching player. Always return to own corner and wait for next pass.

Control and
pass on

7 Pairs • 5m apart. Partner lobs ball into the air for player to receive and control on the instep and pass back to feeder.

8 Pairs • Activities 2, 3 and 4 above but receiving ball in the air.

Skill 2   Thigh Control

1 Pairs • 5m apart. Partner lobs ball for player to control on thigh and pass back.

Key points

Leg placed forward to meet ball, try to 'absorb' impact by relaxing and withdrawing leg quickly.

Achieve balance by spreading arms and getting weight well over stationary leg. Turn foot out to meet ball.

Withdraw foot quicker to take pace off fast ball, stop ball in front of body.

Watch pathway of approaching ball, try to control on both sides.

Decide quickly which foot is to be used for control, do not attempt pass until ball fully under control.

Emphasise following ball and putting pressure on receiver (not too much at first) watch ball and not approaching player.

Simple underarm lob, watch flight of ball, leg put forward to meet ball, 'absorb' impact on the instep by withdrawing foot quickly.

Balance (using arms) very important, practise with both feet.

Watch the flight of the ball, move quickly to get in line, thigh approx. at right angles to this line.

2　Pairs • Partner lobs ball for partner to run to and control with thigh.

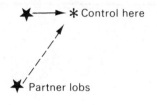

* Control here

Partner lobs

Try to get balanced when controlling by holding arms wide, withdraw leg quickly on impact.

3　Threes • A lobs ball to B who controls with foot or thigh while being closely guarded by C.

C　B ◄ ─ ─ ─ ─ ─ ─ A

B must hold his ground and make an effort to ignore distractions caused by C. Pass back to A.

4　Threes • A lobs to B who controls with foot or thigh, turns with ball and passes to C.

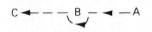

C ◄ ─ ─ B ─ ◄ ─ A

Quick decision whether to use foot or thigh. Keep ball as close as possible when turning and passing.

5　Fours • Players as in diagram, ball is thrown wildly at any player who attempts to control and pass to another player.

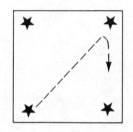

Try to take pace off ball by withdrawing part of body, control as quickly as possible, make an accurate pass to another player.

Skill 3　Chest Control

1　Pairs • 5m apart. Partner lobs ball in the air for player to control on chest and pass. Sometimes high, sometimes bouncing.

2　Pairs • Increase distance and feed more difficult balls to test partner.

If ball is very high, lean back, bend knees and 'absorb' ball on chest. If ball is lower, arch upper body forward so ball drops to ground.

Get in line with approaching ball, hold arms wide, angle chest well forward or well back.

3　Threes • A lobs to B who controls with his chest and passes back to A. C pressurises from different positions.

A mixes up the feeds so that B must control on chest, or, chest down. C fairly passive at first challenging for ball later.

4　Threes • A feeds B with varying types of ball. B controls and passes to C who approaches from behind on either side.

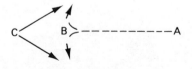

A mixes up the feeds so that B must vary his methods of control. B must look up quickly to find C's position and make accurate pass.

Examples of Competitive Challenges

(a)	Speed Challenges	Which pair is quickest to pass and control ten times?
(b)	Beat Your Own Record	How many consecutive times can you successfully control the ball?

(c) Shuttle Relays

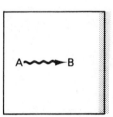

Ball passed by A across specified distance to D who controls, passes back and runs to back of opposite line. All team members do the same. First team back in starting position wins. Condition type of control.

(d)	Ball Juggling	Individual, pair or small groups. How long can you keep the ball off the ground using feet, thighs, chest and head only or combinations thereof?
(e)	Circle Control	As above except ball must be passed around circle.

3.4 CHALLENGING, INTERCEPTING AND TACKLING

Skill 1   Challenging and Intercepting

Activities	Key points
1 Pairs • Player A must dribble ball across grid square. B tries to prevent by challenging. He may *not* tackle but places himself between ball and end line.	Challenger on toes leaning slightly forward, arms angled down to balance. With quick, agile movements he stays between ball and target line.
2 Threes • A and B pass to each other within grid square. C tries to intercept.	Challenger places himself between A and B closing in on player with ball to narrow the angle.
3 Threes • A and B try to stop ball on target line. C tries to prevent them by challenging and inter-cepting.	No tackling allowed at this stage. Try to anticipate dribble or pass by studying movements of opponent.
4 Threes • As above except A and B must pass within 5 sec.	Make use of feint challenges to force player into mistake.
5 Sixes • Players as in diagram, player in middle tries to intercept passes across and around circle.	Try to force player to pass in certain direction and then attempt to intercept that pass.

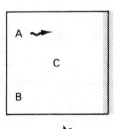

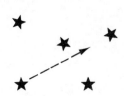

Skill 2   Tackling from the front

1   Pairs ● One player dribbles slowly, other player attempts tackle from front. Try with right foot and then left.

Approach carefully in challenging stance, make a sudden thrust forward when sure of winning ball.

2   Pairs ● As above but player with ball approaches faster and varies direction of the dribble.

Non-tackling foot used as firm base, body leans slightly back, side of foot aims for middle of ball.

3   Pairs ● Players stand either side of ball one pace away. On signal both players thrust their leg forward to gain possession.

Tackling foot must be turned sideways and held firm on contact, weight is brought forward all the time to pressurise opponent.

4   Threes ● 2 v 1 situation. A and B interpass, C tries to gain possession with tackle from front.

Timing of tackle vital to prevent pass or being beaten by dribble, try a feint thrust forward also.

Skill 3   Tackling from the side

1   Pairs ● One player dribbles slowly, other player attempts tackle from side. Try on both sides.

Approach carefully in challenging stance, stretch tackling foot forward to contact ball with side of foot.

2   Pairs ● As above but tackler starts behind player with the ball.

When contact is made try to drag ball away from opponent.

3   Pairs ● Player with ball dribbles along line towards target, defender attempts side tackle before target reached.

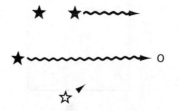

Non-tackling foot very important as pivot to maintain balance, recover quickly if tackle missed.

4   Pairs ● As above but defender attempts slide tackle from the side. Tackle on both left and right sides.

Thrust leg forward into tackle only when contact is certain as recovery is impossible if tackle missed.

5   Pairs ● As above but player with ball now at full speed changing direction if necessary.

Body lands on side, weight being taken on hand and knee, watch ball all the time to ensure contact.

Examples of Competitive Challenges

(a) Funnel Tackling

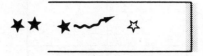

Groups of 4 or 5. Funnel 5m wide and 10m in length. Defender tries to tackle the attacker to prevent him reaching end of funnel. Attacker must not run outside funnel sidelines. Second attacker starts when defender has recovered.

(b) 2 v 1 Funnel Ball

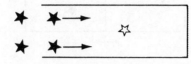

Same as above except two players attempt to take ball through funnel. Defender must tackle or intercept pass. Change defender often.

(c) Individual Retrieve Ball

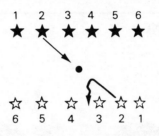

Two equal teams 20m apart, ball equidistant from each team, each team member numbered diagonally. When a number is called the two players assigned that number compete to dribble ball to stop it on their home line. Later two or three numbers may be called at one time.

(d) Circle Pass Out

Children pair off, form circle with one partner standing in front of the other. Player in middle with ball belongs to outside team and tries to pass to a player on the outer ring. Inner ring defenders try to intercept. Each team has 3-5 min, change player in middle often.

(e) 3 v 3 or 4 v 4 Soccer

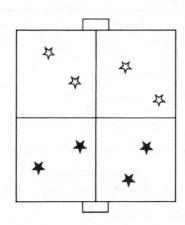

1 Use 4 grid squares approx. 10m x 10m. Total 20m x 20m.
2 Narrow goals (1-2m) may now be used.
3 When a ball passes over side-line throw-ins taken in normal way.
4 When a ball passes over goal-line, non-offending team simply takes possession at point where ball crossed line.
5 No off-side.
6 Conditions may be imposed, e.g. 3 touches and pass.
7 Play for 5 min and change opponents.

3.5 SHOOTING AND LONG PASSING

Skill 1   Driving

Activities

Key points

1 **Pairs** • 15m apart. Drive to each other concentrating on accuracy. Use both legs.

2 **Pairs** • As above but this time try to drive a moving ball.

Use instep to strike ball, toe points towards ground on impact. Swing kicking foot well back for power.

Ensure non-kicking foot is beside ball on impact, body leans forward, arms wide to balance.

3 **Pairs** • Drive through 'gate' target placed equidistant between players. (Use shoes, poles, etc.)

Quickly line up with target, long last step before driving, consistency first greater power later.

4 **Fours** • Players as in diagram. Each may shoot for any of other three goals.

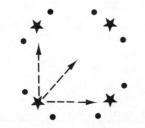

Use both legs, more power when aiming for goal opposite, more accuracy to goals on the angle.

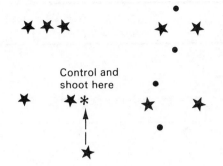

5 Small groups • Players as in diagram. Shoot for goal with drive, retriever feeds ball back.

Short approach run, aim for specific area of goal, change action if inaccurate, change to different angles.

6 Small groups • As above but one of group passes to attacker who shoots. Pass from behind square and in front.

Control and shoot here

Pass must be timed well and paced accurately (no 60 m.p.h. centres). Attacker should control ball but then shoot quickly. Change to different angles.

Skill 2   Chipping

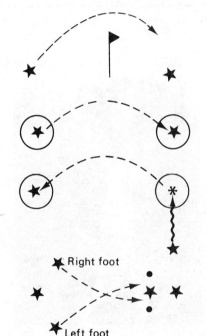

1 Pairs • 15m apart. Chip to land ball on bootlaces of partner. Use both legs.

Ensure the toe strikes the ball underneath and swings through in an upward direction.

2 Pairs • 20-30m apart. Chip over high object (e.g. goals, posts, players) to partner.

Short approach, long last stride, arms wide to balance, swing leg through on slightly curved pathway.

3 Pairs • 20-30m apart. Both players stand in circles. Chip for partner to catch on the full without leaving the circle.

Allow for swerve due to spin put on ball i.e. if right footed aim to right of partner. Aim for as many consecutive catches as possible.

4 Pairs • As above but ball must be dribbled into circle and chipped whilst moving.

Keep close control when dribbling, ensure head is well over ball at impact. Practise with both feet.

Right foot

Left foot

5 Small groups • Players as in diagram. Shoot for goal with chip, retriever feeds back.

Practise with stationary and moving ball, use right foot on left of goal and vice versa. Change positions often.

Examples of Competitive Challenges

(a)	Beat Your Own Record	How many consecutive catches can you make in chipping activity?
(b)	Make Activities Competitive	e.g. Who can score most goals with a drive in Skill 1, no. 4?
(c)	Competitive 3 v 1, 4 v 1 (plus goalkeeper)	Attackers may only shoot from outside goal area. They try to get in a clear drive by passing around to avoid pressure from defender. (Goalkeeper can be used.)

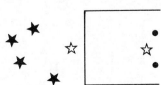

(d) Competitive 3 v 1, 4 v 1	As above except ball must be chipped in from wing and chip shot used.

(e) Shoot

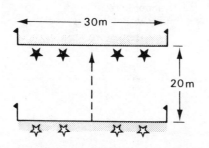

Shooting game for 2-5 a-side. Shot taken from *behind* goal line. All team act as goalkeepers guarding all goal line. Goal scored if ball crosses goal line between posts and below head height.

3.6 HEADING

Skill 1   Basic Heading

Activities

1 Pairs • 5m apart. Partner feeds with underarm throw for player to head back towards body part (e.g. hand, knee).

2 Pairs • 5m apart. As above except feeding is varied so that player must jump to head.

3 Pairs • 5m apart. Continuous heading between the players, stationary and moving.

4 Pairs • 20m apart. Partner chips ball for player to head power-fully back.

5 Fours • Players as in diagram, A and B feed alternately for C to head sideways to goal.

6 Fours • As above but ball must now be headed down, or level or high.

7 Fours • Players as in diagram. A feeds, B heads towards goal, C defends.

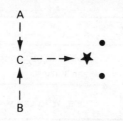

Key points

Lean back, bring head and shoulders forward meeting ball firmly with forehead.

Watch flight of ball, timing of jump important, take arms wide for balance, bring head through crisply.

Get under ball quickly, turn to face partner, head high in the air at first.

Chipping must be very accurate. Watch flight of ball, always meet ball with forehead.

Hand feed unless very accurate with feet. Use side of forehead to strike ball, rotate head and shoulders smartly.

Condition activity to emphasise particular skill. Feed from different angles and distances.

Make C fairly passive at first, B must get to ball before C, watch ball and not opponent.

Examples of Competitive Challenges

(a)	Time Challenges	In pairs, how many headers in 30 sec?
(b)	Beat Your Own Record	How long can you keep the ball in the air when heading?
(c)	Heading Tennis	Teams 2-5 a-side. Playing area divided by net at head height. Heading only, force opponents into making a mistake or so that they are unable to return ball. One bounce allowed.
(d)	Scoring by Heading	Condition small-sided games where goals can only be scored by heading.

3.7 GOALKEEPING

Skill 1   General Handling

Activities

1 Pairs • 10m apart. Partner kicks ball along ground for player to collect with his hands.

2 Pairs • 15m apart. Each player guards 3m goal and receives a shot from partner.

3 Pairs • 15m apart. Goal widened considerably. Players aim to force partner to dive to save.

4 Pairs • 15m apart. Each player guards a goal and receives a lofted shot from partner.

5 Fours • Players as in diagram, A centres high ball for goalkeeper B to catch or punch away.

6 Fours • Players take turns to dribble ball up to the goal. Keeper saves in best way possible.

All these activities can be made competitive.

Key points

Get body in line with approaching ball, legs form second barrier behind hands.

Elbows held in to body, ball is hugged to chest, go down on to one knee if necessary.

Always try to get body behind line of approaching ball, try to hold on to ball rather than merely parrying it.

Ensure body is in line with approaching ball, fingers point upwards when ball is high, thumbs kept close.

Always go wholeheartedly if attempting a catch, use two hands, timing of jump important, bring ball down to chest quickly.

Keeper must come out to meet attacker to narrow the angle, timing all important to seize possession.

4. PROFICIENCY AWARDS

1 Award Scheme Title   Super Skills Awards

2 Organising Body   The Football Association

3 Aim   To guide the practice efforts of all young players who want to develop their skills to the very highest levels.

4 Award Details   There are different awards for different levels of attainment:

1   Blue Award   4   Silver Award
2   Red Award   5   Gold Award
3   Black Award

(Only the *Blue Award* is described here)

Blue Award Each test must be passed

1 Touch Test (Juggling)

Standing and remaining inside a 10 metre square throw the ball into the air. Allow it to bounce on the ground and use any part of your body to start a bouncing sequence going.

Pass = 6 bounces in succession.

2 Heading (In Pairs)

Standing and remaining inside a 10 metre square player A pulls the ball onto his head so that it rebounds to B, standing 3 or 4 metres away, who fields or catches the ball.

Pass = 7 successful out of 10.

3 Passing (Wall and Ground Marks)

Mark a line along a wall 60 cm above the ground. Mark a line along the ground 3 metres from the wall and parallel with it. From behind the 3 metre line pass the ball against the wall so that it always strikes the wall below the 60cm wall line.
Each pass must be made using only three touches of the ball, or fewer if you wish.

Pass = 5 passes in succession.

(Alternative if no wall available)

In threes, players A and B stand together facing player C who stands behind a line 3 metres from A and B.
A and B pass the ball to C who, using no more than three touches, passes the ball back to A or B who stops the ball.
C's pass must arrive at A or B below knee height.

Pass = 5 passes in succession.

4 Controlling and Trapping

Facing the wall and remaining behind the 3 metre line, throw the ball against the wall. Without using any part of your hands or arms stop the ball from bouncing past you.

Pass = 5 successful attempts out of 10 tries.

(Alternative if no wall available)

In pairs and standing no less than 3 metres apart. Using a two handed underhand throw, player A throws the ball gently towards B who must stop the ball from passing him by using any part of the body except hands or arms.

Pass = 5 successful attempts out of 10 tries.

5 Dribbling

Dribble the ball down a 'channel' which is four grid squares long and one square wide (40m x 10m). Turn round a post at the end of the channel and return to the starting point. Up to the turn and after it, the ball must remain within the two side lines of the channel.

Pass = 3 successful runs.

6 Kicking

In pairs, A and B each stand in a grid square (10m x 10m) with one empty square (10m x 10m) between them. Kick the ball to your partner so that it doesn't touch the ground in the empty square.
Your partner must not leave his square to collect the kicked pass.

Pass = 5 successful kicks out of 10 tries.

7 Shooting

Working over four grid squares in line (40m x 10m), player A tries to shoot through a goal 8 metres wide and 1½ metres high (use corner flag posts for uprights) placed on the middle line of the four squares. The ball should be stationary and can be kicked from any position in the end square.
B repeats the test from the opposite end.

Pass = 5 successful shots out of 10 tries.

5 Applications

The F.A. Super Skills Award Scheme,
22-24A The Broadway,
Darkes Lane,
Potters Bar,
Herts.

6 General Details

(a) All children over the age of 7 are eligible to gain an award.
(b) Successful candidates receive cloth badges and/or lapel badges and certificates.
(c) A small fee is charged to cover costs.
(d) Schools, clubs, recognised bodies (e.g. Youth Clubs) and individuals may organise the Super Skills Awards.
(e) The Super Skills manual gives details of all the Awards and may be obtained from the address given above.

5. TEACHING/COACHING QUALIFICATIONS

5.1 TEACHING CERTIFICATE

1 Organising Body   Football Association

2 Aim   To assist a teacher to cope more effectively with a school games lesson.

3 Course Content
(a) The coaching grid, class organisation and control.
(b) Principles of play, conduct on the field and the Laws of the Game.
(c) Coaching in the game.
(d) Dribbling and tackling, marking and dodging.
(e) Passing and kicking.
(f) Bringing the ball under control, organisation of small group practices.
(g) Goalkeeping, 'conditioning' a game.
(h) Lesson planning and organisation.

4 Duration of Course   Minimum of eight 2 hour sessions.

5 Assessment   The Teaching Certificate is not examinable.

6 Applications   Apply to Local County Area Football Associations
or
The Secretary, The Football Association,
16 Lancaster Gate, London W2 3LW

6. REFERENCE INFORMATION

6.1 USEFUL ADDRESSES

English Schools' Football Association
Secretary: A Rice
        4A Eastgate Street
        Stafford ST16 2NQ

Football Association
General
Secretary: E.A. Croker
        16 Lancaster Gate
        London W2 3LW

National Association of Youth Clubs
        30 Devonshire Street
        London W1

Women's Football Association
Secretary: Linda Whitehead
        11 Portsea Mews
        Portsea Place
        Marble Arch
        London W2

6.2 SOCCER REFERENCES

Publication					Description of Mini Game	Skill Descriptions	Practices	Tactics	Senior Rules
Batty E.	1980	Coaching Modern Soccer – Attack	Faber & Faber	Book			*	*	
Brown B.	1981	Successful Soccer	Letts & Co	Book		*	*	*	
Docherty T.	1972	Better Soccer for Boys	Kaye & Ward	Book		*		*	selection
Elliot R.W.	1973	Five-A-Side Football	Midas Books	Booklet					5-a-side
F.A.	1975	Referees' Chart & Players' Guide to the Laws	Pan	Booklet					*
F.A.	1972	The F.A. Guide to the Laws of the Game	Heinemann	Book					*
Gibbon A. Cartwright J.	1981	Teaching Soccer	Bell	Book		*	*	*	
Jago G.	1974	Football Coaching	Stanley Paul	Book				*	
Jarman J.	1976	Junior Soccer	Faber & Faber	Book	*	*	*	*	
Jones K.	1978	How to Play Soccer	Hamlyn	Book		*	*	*	
Keegan K.	1981	Book of Soccer Skills	World Int.	Book		*	*	*	
Vogelsinger H.	1973	The Challenge of Soccer	Allyn & Bacon	Book		*	*	*	
Wade A.	1972	Coach Yourself Association Football	E.P. Publishing	Book		*	*		
Wade A.	1976	The F.A. Guide to Training and Coaching	Heinemann	Book				*	
Wade A.	1978	The F.A. Guide to Teaching Football	Heinemann	Book		*	*	*	
Worthington E.	1980	Teaching Soccer Skills	Lepus	Book		*	*	*	

MINI TENNIS

CONTENTS

1. PLAYING AREA

1.1 The Court

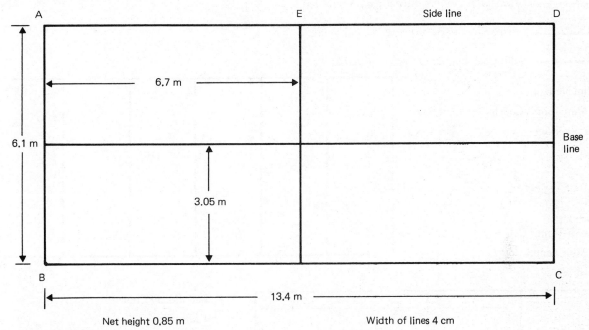

Net height 0.85 m   Width of lines 4 cm

Marking Instructions

1 Use two lengths of string:

   (a) 13.4m long with a knot tied at 6.1m.
   (b) 9m.

2 Lay down the 13.4m string and mark line AD with mid-point E.

3 Fix one end of 13.4m string at A. Fix one end of 9m string at E. Hold 13.4m string at 6.1m knot and free end of 9m string. B is marked where both strings meet when taut.

4 Using D as the fixed point for the 13.4m string instead of A, mark C.

5 Mark lines AB, BC and CD.

6 The remaining lines can now be marked in easily.

1.2 ADAPTATIONS OF OTHER PLAYING AREAS

—————— original lines to be 'disregarded' in mini tennis

—————— original lines to be 'utilised' in mini tennis

— — — — — . additional temporary lines required

Mini Netball Court
6 Mini Tennis Courts
12m x 4.5m

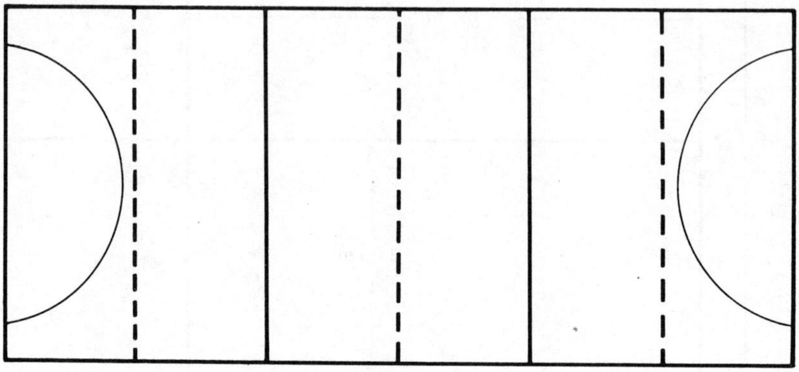

Lawn Tennis Court
4 Mini Tennis Courts
11m x 6m

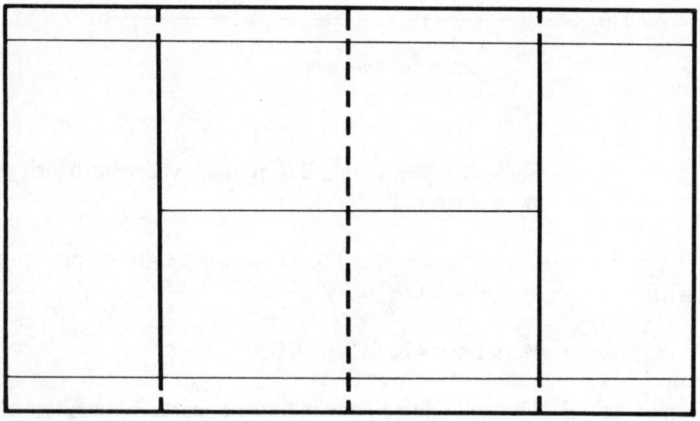

Badminton Court
1 Mini Tennis Court
12m x 5m

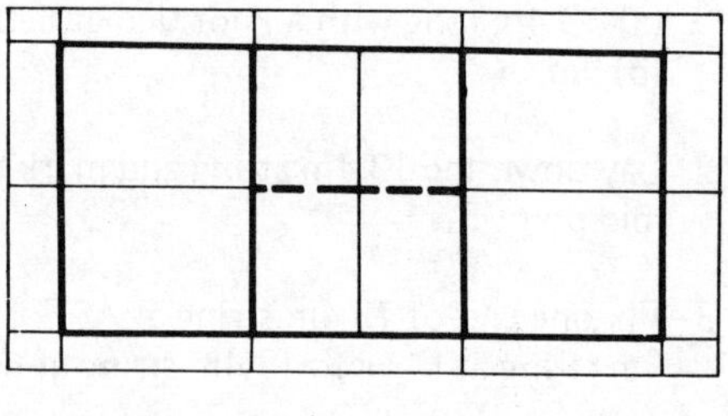

Basketball Court
4 Mini Tennis Courts
14m x 6.5m

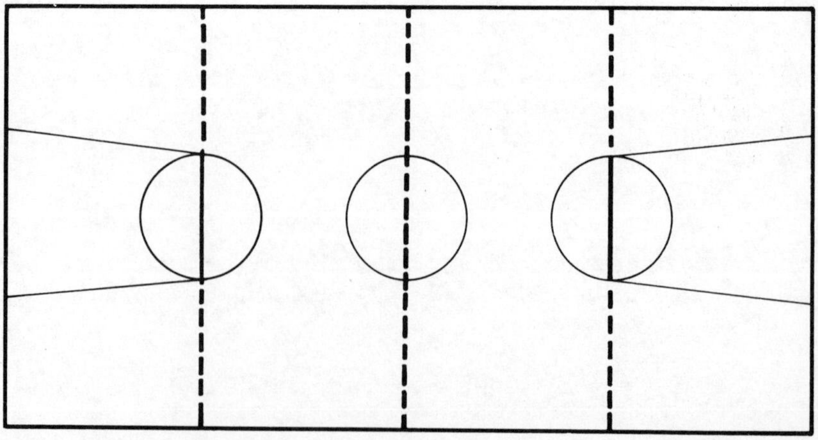

1.3 ANCILLARY EQUIPMENT

(a) Bat:

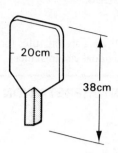

Note that a simple bat shape can be used in mini tennis eliminating the need for an expensive strung racket. This can be cheaply constructed in woodwork department. Short moulded plastic rackets are also available now.

1 Plastic frame with cork facing.
2 ½" marine plywood.

A light, junior tennis racket (12oz) could be introduced around the age of 9 or 10 years.

(b) Ball:

Foam balls used initially with progression on to tennis balls later.

1 Cheap new tennis balls can be bought at local suppliers.

2 Used balls can sometimes be obtained from local tennis clubs.

3 Used balls can also be bought fairly cheaply at tennis tournaments.

4 Light rubber balls and airflow balls (as used for golf practice) make an adequate substitute if tennis balls unavailable.

(c) Posts and Bases:

1 Padder tennis sets can be obtained at local suppliers.

2 90cm x 5cm diameter post of wood or metal. Attach sturdy hook to hold net, encase in large paint tin filled with sand.

3 Longer posts of 110cm. Drill holes in playing area surface. Insert posts in sockets during play. Cover holes with lids when not in use.

4 Utilise existing badminton or volleyball posts. Attach hooks at 85cm.

(d) Net.

1 Padder tennis nets can be obtained at local suppliers.

2 Use benches from gymnasium, two benches give adequate height.

3 Strong cord or tension wire enclosed in 2" webbing or tape, brightly coloured. Provides effective and cheap net height.

4 Tennis/Badminton club throwouts. Handicraft department may be able to repair holes and cut to correct size. Even if nets are in a poor condition the tape part may still be usable.

5 Tie a rope between posts. Least effective but adequate. Attach a fringe if possible (i.e. thin strips of coloured material).

2. RULES

The following are the rules for the game of mini-tennis — known as Short Tennis. Modifications could be made to suit individual circumstances.

2.1 INTERPRETATION OF RULES

Rules

Notes

Object
(1) To play the ball into the opponents' area so that it is out of reach or such that it forces them to play the ball into the net or out of court.

(1) This principle needs little explanation and is usually grasped quickly.

The Teams
(2) Mini Tennis can either be played as singles (1 v 1) or doubles (2 v 2).

(2) 2 v 2 probably most suitable in school.

Service
(3) The player stands behind the baseline. The first service in every game is taken from the *right-*hand side and the ball must land in the half of the court *diagonally opposite.*

(4) Serves then taken from *alternate* sides every point until the game is completed.
(5) *Two* attempts allowed at serving.
(6) The service may be delivered over or under-arm but the ball may not bounce before being struck.
(7) The receiver must allow the ball to bounce.

(8) Service alternates between players every 2 points.

(9) If the serve touches the top of the net and falls 'in' it should be re-taken.
(10) Order of service: *Doubles*

In the event of doubles being played, all rules are the same except the four players serve two points in rotation.

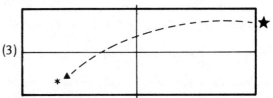

(3)

(4) Emphasise this until rhythm of changing established.

(5) Thus some risks can be taken with the first serve.
(6) Encourage under-arm serves initially. Over-arm serves will be erratic and hinder development of the game.
(7) If the receiver strikes the ball before it bounces he loses the point.
(8) Except when the score reaches 10—10 (see *scoring*) when service would alternate between the players every point.
(9) It is called a 'let' and applies to both 1st and 2nd serves.
(10) Example service sequence

Pair A	Pair B
A[1] serves points 1 & 2	B[1] serves points 3 & 4
A[2] serves points 5 & 6	B[2] serves points 7 & 8

The sequence is then repeated.

Ball in Play

(11) Once service has been correctly returned it can be taken *on the volley* or after *one bounce*.

(12) As soon as the service has been delivered players may move to any position on the court.

(13) In the event of the ball striking the ceiling, walls, or other obstructions, the striker loses the point.

(14) If the ball lands on any part of the line it is counted as *in*.

(11) In the early stages volleying may need to be restricted as it often leads to a premature breakdown in rallies.

(12) Partners do not have to play the ball alternately in doubles but it may be a useful condition to improve footwork.

(13) It is not a fault if, during normal play, the ball touches the top of the net and falls 'in'. Play should continue if possible.

(14)

Scoring

(15) Games are played on a *first to 11 points* basis.

(16) While 11 points are suggested, this figure can be amended (e.g. 9 or 15) to suit individual circumstances.

(17) In the event of the score reaching 10–10, the game should continue until one player has a lead of 2 points (e.g. 13–11).

(18) Players change ends every *8* points.

(15) This simple system is easily grasped by young children.

(16) For example, younger children may benefit from playing to 9 points whilst older children might play up to 15 points.

(17) Service alternates between the players (pairs in doubles) every point.

(18) A rule which need only apply where there is a significant advantage to be gained at one end.

2.2 UMPIRING MINI TENNIS

Normally an umpire is not necessary. Children should be encouraged to arbitrate between themselves. Principles of fairness and trust in an opponent's decision should be constantly commended.

Occasions when umpires are desirable might be:

1 If a child is unfit to play
2 If there is not enough equipment for all to play.

Suggestions

1 Get as much height as possible (e.g. stand on a chair or bench).

2 State the score clearly after each rally.

3 Always give the server's score first.

4 Ensure that players serve from the correct side and in the correct order.

5 Replay any doubtful points.

3. PRACTICES (ALL KEY POINTS REFER TO RIGHT HANDED PLAYERS)

3.1 BALL FAMILIARISATION

Skill 1   Bouncing Ball on the Ground

Activities	*Key points*
1 Hit the ball to make it bounce continually at waist height.	Shake hands with bat to get correct grip.
2 Bounce the ball low (knee height), very low, high, very high (so high you have to jump to hit it).	Hit the ball just after the top of the bounce, hit at arm's length, watch ball very closely, bend knees to get low.
3 Alternate high and low bounces.	Keep the bat face as flat as possible.
4 Bounce ball on a target (e.g. a line, mark on the ground).	Flex the wrist when striking the ball, use non-striking arm for balance.
5 Bounce ball slowly then quickly, very slowly and very quickly.	Find two ways of changing the speed of the bounce.
6 Hit ball at the top of the bounce, before and after the top of the bounce.	Try to find which is more difficult, which is easier.
7 All the above activities performed whilst moving around the playing area.	Start slowly and gradually increase speed, watch out for other players.

Skill 2   Hitting in the air with one bounce

1 Hit ball high into the air letting it bounce once on the ground before hitting. Gradually hit lower and lower.	Watch ball carefully, hit at arm's length with palm upwards, arm bends at elbow with slight flexing of wrist.
2 Hit into the air while walking in and out of other players.	Watch ball but look out for others out of the corner of eye. Only allow one bounce between hits.
3 On the spot, hit high and turn full circle between each hit.	Turn quickly, try to turn in both directions.
4 Hit ball high and let it bounce but keep swopping with partner.	Stay close to partner, hit fairly high to give each other plenty of time.
5 Partner stretches arm out, hit back and forth over partner's arm.	Try to hit with both sides of bat face, move quickly to get bat directly under ball when striking.

Skill 3   Keeping the ball in the air

1 Hit continuously into the air approximately a metre high.

Stand with one foot slightly forward, keep the bat face level.

2 Hit very high at first, then bounce the ball on the bat as low as possible.

Move quickly to get directly under high ball, flex wrist for low bounces.

3 Hit into the air with the back of the bat (i.e. palm facing ground).

Keep well balanced, hit with a smooth action trying not to jerk bat.

4 Alternate bat face for every hit.

Turn wrist over quickly, gradually increase speed.

5 Move in and out of others while hitting into the air. Start slowly, gradually increase speed.

Keep the ball at an even height, use the non-striking hand for balance, watch out for others.

6 On the spot, hit high into the air turning full circle between each hit.

Turn quickly, try to turn in both directions, keep bat level to be ready for dropping ball.

Examples of Competitive Challenges

(a) Beat Your Own Record	How many consecutive hits can you make before ball falls to the ground?
(b) How Many Ways?	How many different ways can you hit the ball into the air?
(c) Time Challenges	Who can make the most hits in 20 sec. when alternating the bat face?
(d) Races, Relay Races	Keeping the ball in the air, walking over set distance.

3.2 BASIC HITTING WITH A PARTNER (INCLUDING SERVICE)

Skill 1   Hitting with hand feed from partner

Activities

Key points

1 5m apart, underarm throw to bounce just in front of and to the left of striker. *Forehand* stroke played back for feeder to catch.

Emphasise accurate feeding, striker stands sideways, left shoulder forwards; move to the flight of the ball, only one bounce then hit.

2 Feeder throws ball slightly further away, making striker move and hit.

Swing bat through to hit ball, stepping on to left leg as shot is hit at arm's length.

3 Underarm throw to bounce just in front of and to right of striker. *Backhand* stroke played back for feeder to catch.

Similar principles as forehand but striker now steps on to right leg as shot is played. Hit just after the top of the bounce.

4 As 2 but feeder throws slightly further away, making striker move to play backhand.

Face the feeder and turn sideways to hit, keep the wrist fairly firm on impact.

5 Feeder mixes throws to forehand and backhand.

Be ready to turn in either direction, emphasise swinging action.

6 Feeds now made more difficult; harder, higher, further away.

Look out for strokes played on the wrong leg. Try to play every ball back to feeder.

Skill 2   Hitting in Pairs (Without Net)

1 5m apart, random hitting to each other emphasising one bounce only.

Stress co-operation, hit carefully and accurately to each other. Turn sideways and swing bat.

2 Play forehands only.

Good backswing and follow through essential, hit across body, aim to forehand side of partner.

3 Play backhands only. (Important to emphasise this activity since backhands often ignored in practice.)

Backswing even more important, swing bat through in horizontal plane, aim to partner's backhand side.

4 Make partner move to play a stroke.

Keep alert on the toes, prepare backswing whilst moving to ball.

Skill 3   Hitting in Pairs (Playing over Net)

1   Activities 1 to 4 of Skill 2

2   Vary the height of the ball over the net. Hit high for a while then as close to net as possible.

3   Play a rally of 'good length' strokes.

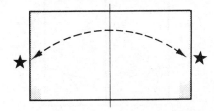

When hitting high over the net start backswing low and follow through higher, when hitting low over net swing more in a horizontal plane.

Try to make the ball bounce deep in your partner's court, stand behind baseline whilst waiting for ball.

4   Alternate long and short length strokes.

Be alert, on your toes, always let the ball bounce but only once, try to hit just after top of bounce.

5   Try to hit the ball at different speeds, e.g. fast, medium, slow.

Use much quicker swing to hit ball harder, but avoid hitting wildly. Stand further back to receive harder hit balls.

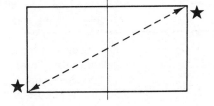

6   Play a rally of cross court strokes on the forehand side.

Turn sideways and hit across body more, always come back to central position behind baseline.

7   Play a rally of cross court strokes on the backhand side.

A more difficult activity, co-operate and play slow high balls until more competent and confident.

8   Now vary the direction, pace and length of shots played.

Try to move your partner about as much as possible, return to a central position after every stroke.

Skill 4   Service

1   Shadow/copy stroke as demonstrated by teacher.

Stand sideways, feet short distance apart, left foot forward, hold bat down just behind right hip.

2   Practise serving into service court diagonally opposite.

Let ball bounce, as it reaches top of bounce swing bat forward smoothly. Keep wrist firm, natural follow through.

3   Practise serving to land ball on target (e.g. box, shoe, stone).

Drop ball to side and just in front of forward foot, weight shifts forward as serve is made.

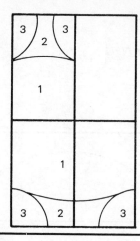

4 Practise serving with opponent receiving. Both server and receiver aim for optimum placements as shown in diagram. Continue rally after service.

Try to vary the serve, placing it on forehand and backhand sides of opponent. Play a strong 1st and safe 2nd serve.

Examples of Competitive Challenges

(a) Beat Your Own Record

Count number of consecutive strokes before rally breaks down.

(b) Time Challenges

Which pair can play most strokes in 30 sec?

(c) Serving Competition

Using chart in Skill 4 no. 4. Each player has set number of serves. Who can achieve the highest total?

(d) Passing While Moving

Which pair can keep rally going whilst walking/jogging up and down playing area?

(e) Simple Conditioned Games

1 Playing only in front section of court. Any player puts ball into play. Point scored for every rally won. Play to 11 and change opponents.
2 Same as 1 but use full court.

(f) Keep the Kettle Boiling

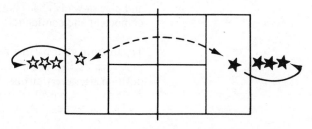

Small team at both ends of court, first child plays and moves to back of team, next player steps forward and does the same, keep going until rally breaks down.

Variation 1 After hitting ball player moves to back of team at 'other' end of court.
Variation 2 Either of above but child loses 'life' when causing breakdown of rally.

3.3 WALL ACTIVITIES

Activities

1 Continuous hitting against a wall with forehand stroke.

Key points

Be alert because ball will come back fast, lob ball high at first, only one bounce allowed.

2 Continuous hitting against a wall with backhand stroke.

All previous points of technique but take bat back earlier in preparation for stroke.

3 Mix up forehand and backhand strokes.

Good footwork of prime importance, turning to step on correct leg.

4 Aim on an angle so that the player must move to the ball.

Move quickly to the ball, try to get balanced when playing stroke.

5 Stand further away from wall and play long drives, stand closer and play shortened strokes.

Same stroke pattern followed but either lengthened or abbreviated according to needs.

6 Aim at targets above net height (e.g. chalked, painted, coloured bricks).

Side of body points roughly at target, aim carefully and take a smooth swing.

7 Any of activities 1 to 6 but alternating hitting with a partner.

Co-operate with partner to keep rally going, move out of the way to give partner plenty of room.

Examples of Competitive Challenges

(a)	Beat Your Own Record	How many consecutive backhands can you play?
(b)	Time Challenges	Who can play most long drives in 30 sec?
(c)	Target Competitions	Who can hit the target most times with a set number of attempts?
(d)	Keep the Kettle Boiling	Continuous hitting against the wall with two or more players alternating.

(e) Adapted Paddleball

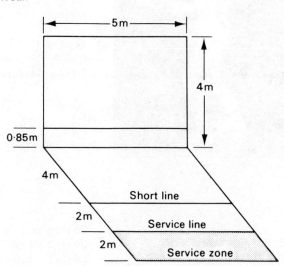

1 May be played by 2 or 4 players on court as shown.
2 Service: player stands in service zone, bounces ball on floor and hits it on to the front wall so that it rebounds to bounce behind the short line. Two serves allowed.
3 In play: ball may only bounce once, players hit the ball alternately, after being struck the ball must not touch the floor before reaching front wall, ball must hit front wall above net height.
4 Player winning rally wins point: first to 11 points wins game.

3.4 VOLLEYING

Activities

1 Partner feeds underhand, play forehand volley for partner to catch.

2 Partner feeds underhand, play backhand volley for partner to catch.

3 Partner feeds underhand, play volley to bounce ball in front of partner, both forehands and backhands.

4 Keep a volleying rally going with partner.

Key points

Bat held up in front of chest, use a short thrusting/punching action keeping wrist very firm.

Bring right shoulder forward, very short backswing, bat held in horizontal position.

Watch ball carefully, transfer weight forward as volley is made, thrust bat downwards slightly across body, short follow through.

Keep the ball off the ground, adjust your wrist quickly as ball approaches at different angles.

5 Keep volleying rally going. Volley high in the air, then low and fast.

6 Volley forehand to forehand with partner.

7 Volley backhand to backhand with partner.

Try to hit at chest height when volleying high. Start slowly and gradually get faster when volleying low.

Play volley with bent arm, hit across body to forehand side of partner.

A difficult activity; start with slow, high volleys, point of impact in front of the body.

8 Player feeds with forehand stroke from baseline, partner plays forehand and backhand volleys down into court.

Be alert with bat up in ready position, watch the flight of the ball carefully, thrust bat downwards.

Examples of Competitive Challenges

(a)	Beat Your Own Record	How many consecutive volleys can you play before rally breaks down?
(b)	Time Challenges	Which pair can play most backhand volleys in 20 sec?
(c)	Make Activity 8 Competitive	Who can win the rally — the player on the baseline or the volleyer?
(d)	Keep the Kettle Boiling	Small team on both sides of the court, players volley and move to back of team, continue until rally breaks down. Note: a difficult activity, restrict to older and more able pupils.
(e)	Volleying Game	Use the front part of the court only, players try to volley all the time. If the ball bounces in the front part of the court player loses point. First to 11 points wins game.

3.5 DOUBLES (2 v 2)

Activities

1 Random hitting to any player.

2 Rallying — each player in the pair hitting alternately.

3 Drive and volley. One pair at the baseline playing drives while the other pair volley at net.

4 Play a game to learn sequence of serving and receiving and basic positioning and scoring.

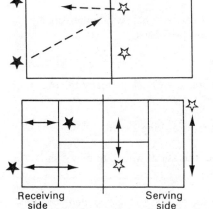

Receiving side   Serving side

Key points

Each player guards one side of the court, call clearly if you decide to play a ball coming down the middle.

Make sure you move out of the way once you have hit the ball.

Co-operate to see how long the drive/volley rally can be continued. Hit to any player.

Serving pair change sides every point, receiving pair move up and back on the same side. Players should aim to position themselves as in diagram but if weak on volleys then both should stay at the baseline until more skilful.

3.6 TACTICAL PLAY

General Points

1 Always try to keep the ball in play: consistency is more effective than erratic play.

2 Play the 'safe' shot rather than the 'big winner'. Statistical research shows that more points are won from opponents' errors than from winning strokes. Accurate placement of the ball is often more successful than sheer speed.

3 Manoeuvre your opponents around by playing the ball away from them.

4 Play to the weakness of your opponents and try to make them play to your strength.

5 Use a variety of strokes (e.g. short, long, straight, angled) to stretch your opponent and force an error.

6 Stand deep in the court and move forward to play a ball; it is more difficult to play a stroke whilst retreating.

7 Never stand admiring your stroke, always be moving and preparing for the next one.

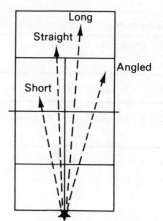

Singles

1 Try to serve deep or on a wide angle to put your opponent on the defensive right from the start.

2 Footwork is all important in singles; always be on your toes with knees bent so that you can move quickly in any direction.

3 Always return to the central base after playing a stroke. This position allows the player to cover all parts of the court.

4 If you play a strong, deep stroke move up to the net and kill (smash or volley) any weak return from your opponent.

5 If you play the ball short move slightly closer to the net: your opponent is ideally placed to play a very short drop shot.

6 Try not to get caught in 'No-Man's Land' (i.e. half way up the court). Either move right up to the net or stay well back.

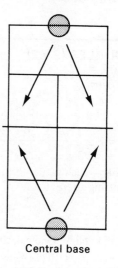

Central base

Doubles

1 Each player guards one side of the court but must be ready to cover if his partner is caught out of position.

2 Keep on your toes when your partner is playing a stroke.

3 Give a clear, early call if there is a doubt about who is to play a shot (e.g. a ball down the middle).

4 On the other hand an attack down the middle of the opponents' court is often a successful strategy as it may lead to confusion on their part.

5 Play doubles as a team, i.e. co-operate, encourage, advise.

4. PROFICIENCY AWARDS

1 *Award Scheme Title*   Lawn Tennis Performance Award Scheme

2 *Organising Body*   Professional Tennis Coaches' Association

3. *Aim*   To further interest in Lawn Tennis amongst the younger generation.

4. *Award Details*   The examination is divided into four sections, each of which must be passed to gain either (a) *yellow elementary award* (b) *white advanced award*

SECTION 1:

Forehand Drives:
5 fed from service line — to be returned into singles court
5 fed from base line — to be returned into singles court

Backhand Drives:
5 fed from service line — to be returned into singles court
5 fed from base line — to be returned into singles court

Service:
5 pairs served from right court — first or second serve to count
5 pairs served from left court — first or second serve to count

Forehand Volleys:
3 balls fed from base line — to be returned into singles court

Backhand Volleys:
3 balls fed from base line — to be returned into singles court

Alternate Volleys:
6 alternate forehand and backhand volleys of greater difficulty fed to simulate a
6 stroke rally — to be returned into singles court

Scoring
1 point for each successful stroke.
Total marks possible = 42
Elementary pass mark = 28
Advanced pass mark = 35

SECTION 2:

Rallies:
Player rallies with examiner.
Elementary Award pass for a rally of 10 strokes of which 3 must be backhand
drives.
Advanced Award pass for a rally of 20 strokes of which 5 must be backhand
drives.
4 attempts allowed; examiner starts each rally; examiner's strokes counted.

SECTION 3:

Scoring:
Examiner plays 2 games with player. Each serves one game and the player
calls the score. Ability to score gives pass.
For Advanced Award the player should also show a reasonable understanding
of the correct approach to the smash and volley.

SECTION 4:

Ability in the Game:
Based on the games played in section 3.
Examiner assesses ability as POOR/FAIR/GOOD.
Elementary Award pass if assessment is FAIR or GOOD.
Advanced Award pass if assessment is GOOD.
(Player should also show some appreciation of spin).

5. *Applications*

Should be made to a qualified Examiner.
Details from:
Mrs P. M. Bocquet
21 Glencairn Court, Lansdown Road,
Cheltenham GL50 2NB

6. *General Details*

1 Elementary Award should be within reach of most youngsters within their first year of playing tennis.
   Advanced Award should be for players of reasonable school team standard.
2 A small fee is charged for the examination.
3 Successful candidates will receive a certificate and badge.

5. TEACHING/COACHING QUALIFICATIONS

5.1 L.T.A. ELEMENTARY TEACHERS' TRAINING CERTIFICATE

1 Organising Body

Lawn Tennis Association

2 Aim

To improve the standard of teaching and coaching in lawn tennis.

3 Duration of Course

Minimum of 18 hours instruction followed by an examination.

4 Applications

To attend national residential courses apply to the L.T.A., Barons Court, West Kensington, London W14 9EG

To attend regional courses apply to the appropriate Regional Office of the Sport Council.

6. REFERENCE INFORMATION

6.1 USEFUL ADDRESSES

The British Schools Lawn Tennis Association
Secretary: Miss Nicolette Leslie
            'Monksilver'
            Boxgrove Road
            Guildford
            Surrey

Lawn Tennis Association
Secretary: J.C.U. James
            Barons Court
            West Kensington
            London W14 9EG

Lawn Tennis Foundation
Manager: J Coates
            The Queen's Club
            West Kensington
            London W14

Professional Tennis Coaches' Association
Secretary: Mrs P Bocquet
            21 Glencairn Court
            Lansdown Road
            Cheltenham
            Gloucestershire
            GL51 2NB

6.2 TENNIS REFERENCES

Publication					Description of Mini Game	Skill Descriptions	Practices	Tactics	Senior Rules
Cox M.	1975	Lawn Tennis	William Luscombe	Book		*		*	
Dewhurst E.	1972	Common Sense Lawn Tennis	Dewpool School of Tennis	Book		*			
Ellwanger	1973	Tennis up to Tournament Standard	E.P. Pub. Co.	Book		*		*	
Fraser N.	1975	Successful Tennis	Pelham	Book		*		*	*
Georgeson D.		A Tennis Professional's Notebook	Georgeson	Booklet		*			
Georgeson D.		Tactics for Tennis	Georgeson	Booklet				*	
Georgeson D.		Tennis Practices & Exercises	Georgeson	Booklet			*		
Jones C.M.	1973	Improving Your Tennis	Faber & Faber	Book		*			
Jones C.M. Buxton A.	1975	Starting Tennis	Ward Lock	Book		*		*	
Know the Game		Lawn Tennis	E.P. Pub. Ltd	Booklet					*
Kramer J.	1977	How to Play your best Tennis	Deutsch	Book		*		*	
Metzler P.	1972	Getting Started in Tennis	Sterling	Book		*		*	
Mottram T.	1971	Play Better Tennis	Stanley Paul	Book		*			
Murphy C. Murphy B.	1975	Tennis for the Player, Teacher & Coach	Saunders	Book	variations	*	*	*	*
Roy H.	1974	Tennis for Schools	Pelham	Book		*	*		*
Tilmanis G.	1975	Advanced Tennis	Lea Febiger	Book			*	*	

MINI VOLLEYBALL

CONTENTS

1. PLAYING AREA

1.1 THE COURT

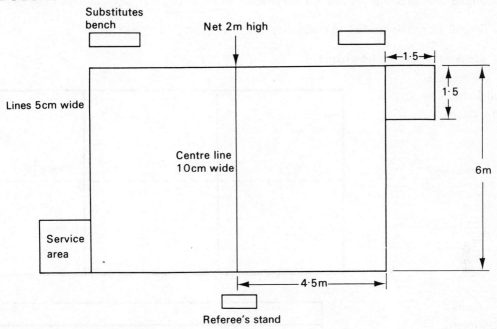

Net height 2m for both boys and girls.

With a playing area of length 9m and width 6m three mini volleyball courts will fit across a senior volleyball court. Other measurements can be used provided they are in the same proportion to one another.

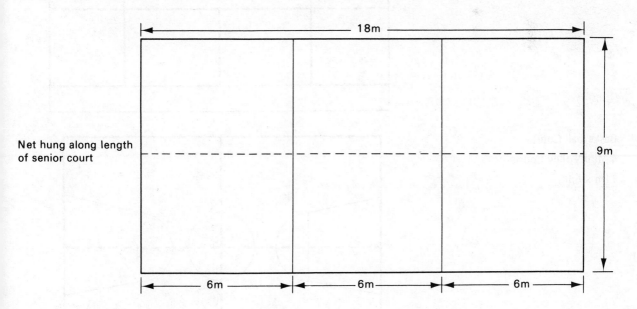

1.2 ADAPTATIONS OF OTHER PLAYING AREAS

——————— original lines to be 'disregarded' in mini volley

————— original lines to be 'utilised' in mini volley

- - - - - additional temporary lines required

Mini Netball Court
6 Mini Volley Courts
10m x 6m

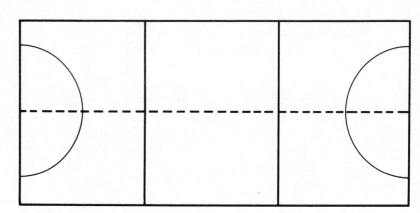

Lawn Tennis Court
4 Mini Volley Courts
10m x 6m

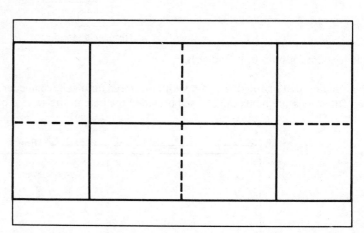

Basketball Court
4 Mini Volley Courts
11m x 6m

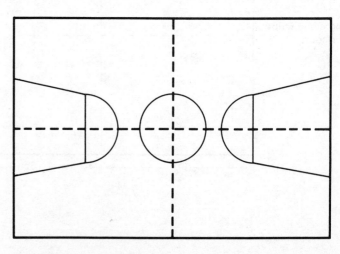

1.3 ANCILLARY EQUIPMENT

(a) Ball:

1 PVC and cloth covered foam balls are suitable for introducing young children to volleyball.

2 Cheap, light plastic balls adequate for practice.

(b) Posts and Bases:

1 Utilise existing senior volleyball posts. Attach hooks at 2m (or slightly higher if net cannot be brought completely taut).

2 Utilise existing netball or basketball posts. Attach hooks at 2m (or slightly higher if net cannot be brought completely taut).

3 2.20m x 5cm diameter post of wood or metal. Attach sturdy hook to hold net. Use wide base supported by weights or rocks for stability.

4 Tie net to permanent attachments (e.g. wall bar, wall fittings, window fittings).

5 Fit brackets or hooks to walls at appropriate height.

(c) Net:

1 Strong cord or tension wire enclosed in 2" webbing or tape, brightly coloured. Provides effective and cheap net height.

2 Tennis/Badminton Club throwouts. Handicraft department should be able to repair holes and cut to correct size. Even if nets are in a very bad condition the tape part is normally still usable as guideline.

3 Tie a rope between posts. Least effective but adequate. Attach a fringe if possible (i.e. thin strips of coloured material).

2. RULES

The rules of Mini Volleyball are very similar to senior volleyball but slightly less complicated. Match rules will be given with notes added for interpretation or less formal play. The full rules of Senior Volleyball can be found in the *Official Rules Book of the E.V.A.* (see 6.2).

2.1 INTERPRETATION OF RULES

Rules

Notes

Object

(1) To play the ball into the opponents' area so that it is out of reach or such that it forces them to play the ball into the net or out of court.

(1) This principle needs little explanation and is usually grasped quickly.

The Teams

(2) Each side has *3 players*. (For matches a team consists of 6 players. 3 players play in the first set, and the other 3 players play in the second set. Any 3 may play in the 3rd set.)

(2) 3 players are suggested although different set ups would be needed at times (e.g. with large class groups).

Service

(3) Each rally is started by the server of one team putting the ball into play. The player stands in the service area, and, with one hand, hits the ball over the net into the opponents' court.

(3) Service is lost if the ball touches:

1 the net
2 one of the server's team
3 any object above or to the side of the playing area
4 the ground outside the court.

It is a fault to step into the court *before* hitting the ball, or to hit the ball *off* the hand.
(Encourage underarm serving — overarm is too difficult for this age group.)

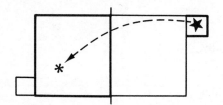

Ball in Play

(4) After the service the ball may be played with both hands, one hand, one arm or with any part of the body *above* the waist. Only *simultaneous* and *instantaneous* contact is allowed. The ball may *not* be caught, pushed, carried, held, lifted or scooped.

(4) In the early stages very strict application of the simultaneous contact rule may stifle the game. Nevertheless players should be continually encouraged to strike the ball cleanly.

(5) The ball may be returned over the net after either *one, two or three touches*. Only after a block (defensive action at the net) may the ball be touched twice in succession by the same player.

(5) Always encourage the use of 3 touches to develop teamwork and build up attacks. Even allow 4 touches in the early stages as this can extend rallies and give more enjoyable games. After blocking the ball a team is still allowed 3 touches.

Play at the Net

(6) Except on service, the ball remains in play when it touches the net. A player may *not touch* the net, but may play the ball after it has bounced off the net, provided that he did not play into the net, and provided that his team has at least one more touch left.

(6) Keep players alert to the possibility of playing the ball on the rebound from the net.

(7) Players may only touch their opponents' court with their foot/feet provided the foot/feet remain *in contact* with centre line. Players may only reach over the net when attempting to block a ball.

(8) If two opponents touch the ball at the same time above the net, the team on whose side the ball lands has the right to *3 more hits*.

Interruptions to Play

(9) Each team is allowed *2 time-outs* of 30 seconds each per set.

In the first 2 sets substitution may only be used in case of injury. 3 substitutions may be made in the third set.

Scoring

(10) A team scores a point if it is *serving* and *wins the rally*. This team continues to serve and scores points until it makes a fault. When this happens a change of service *(side out)* takes place and no point is scored.

(11) On change of service the team to serve will *rotate one position clockwise* before serving.

(12) A team wins the set by scoring at least *15 points* and gaining a two point advantage over the opponents (15/13, 16/14). A team wins the match when it has won 2 sets (2/0, 2/1).

(7) In other words the player's foot may not land completely *over* the centre line but can land on it.

No reaching over the net on the overarm smash.
(8) It is sometimes thought that there are only 2 hits allowed after a simultaneous confrontation at the net — as can be seen from the rule this is not so.

(9) Time outs should only be used for positive coaching points.

(10) This scoring method should be encouraged from the beginning and can be easily maintained once the rhythm is established.

(11)

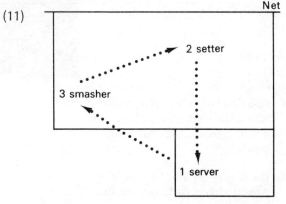

(12) 7 or 11 points may be more appropriate during lessons so that teams may change round to play different opponents.

2.2 REFEREEING MINI VOLLEYBALL

1 Get as much height as possible (e.g. stand on a chair or a desk if no referee's stand is available).

2 Players may not question the referee's decisions.

3 The referee blows his whistle to commence play. (The server must wait for the whistle before serving).

4 The referee also blows his whistle to indicate that the ball is dead (i.e. ball out of play or fault committed).

5 If conversant with the hand signals the referee should

then immediately indicate the nature of the fault. (See *E.V.A. Rules Book*.)

6 State the score clearly and frequently.

7 Always give the server's score first.

8 Balls landing on the line are counted as 'in'.

9 The referee should watch carefully for players touching the net or crossing the centre line with their feet.

10 Replay any doubtful points.

3. PRACTICES

3.1 BALL FAMILIARISATION

Activities

Key points

1 Throw up and catch (one metre, a few metres, very high).

Two handed underarm lob, try to catch just above forehead.

2 Throw up and catch while moving (forwards, sideways, backwards).

Move quickly to position yourself under dropping ball. Move lightly on toes without crossing legs.

3 Throw up and catch after one bounce.

Get down low to catch above forehead. Use the fingers only, not the palms.

4 Throw up and catch after two bounces.

Get down low to catch above forehead. Point the fingers upwards.

5 Basketball dribbling, using both hands. (On spot, forwards, backwards, sideways, high, low, fast, slow).

Flex fingers as much as possible. No slapping. Develop nimble footwork to maintain your balance all the time.

6 Use fingers to push ball around on ground (player stationary and then moving).

Emphasise the use of the fingers to develop and maintain control.

7 Pass ball around body and through legs on ground, in the air.

Try not to lose control, start slowly and gradually increase speed.

8 Keep the ball off the ground using any part of the body above the waist.

Ball must be hit cleanly, no catching, carrying or holding.

Examples of Competitive Challenges

(a)	Beat Your Own Record	How many consecutive catches can you make before ball falls to the ground?
(b)	How Many Ways?	How many parts of the body (above the waist) can you use to keep the ball in the air?
(c)	Races, Relay Races	Basketball dribbling with two hands over set distances.

3.2 VOLLEYING (INCLUDING 1 v 1 AND 2 v 2)

Skill 1   Individual Volleying

Activities	Key points

1 Throw up from above forehead and catch above forehead.	Fingers point upward, hands cup-shaped and close together.
2 Volley above head as many times as possible.	Diagram shows positioning of fingers and amount of contact made with ball.
3 Volley above head varying the height.	Sight the ball through the hands; legs, trunk and arms extend in one continuous action, wrists and fingers relaxed.
4 Volley high, let ball bounce, volley again.	Bend legs, get right below ball, straighten arms and legs as ball is thrust upwards.
5 Volley above head whilst walking (forward, sideways, backwards).	Always try to volley ball above forehead, hands follow ball, wrists rotating on final contact.
6 On the spot, volley high, turning full circle between each volley.	Turn quickly, try to turn in both directions.
7 Keep volleying, kneel and stand up.	Watch ball closely, kneel slowly and carefully, good balance essential.
8 Keep a volley rally going against a wall.	A difficult skill: encouragement and practice needed, volley must go very high.

Skill 2   Volley Pass with a Partner

1 Hold ball in front of forehead, throw to partner aiming for forehead, partner catches and passes back. (2m apart).	Emphasise catching ball with cupped hands in front of forehead. Throw from forehead position, wrists rotating and little arm movement.

2 Same but over high rope (hung between basketball rings, window ladders).

3 1 v 1 pass and catch activity in small court (4m x 2m). Ball must be caught in front of forehead. First to 5, then change opponents.

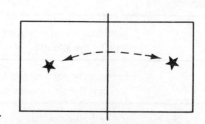

4 Throw ball short distance into the air and volley, partner catches above forehead and does the same.

5 1 v 1 two touch game, when ball received volley to self and then volley back to opponent.

6 Co-operative rally using volley pass only. (2m apart)

7 1 v 1 volley competition, small court, first to 5. Start rally with volley.

Move quickly to get under dropping ball, same catching position and throwing action as 1.

Quick movement essential. Development of basic tactics i.e. playing ball into spaces away from opponent.

Throw straight up in the air, volley high by flexing fingers and straightening arms and legs.

Try to extend legs and arms, keep fingers relaxed and flexible, take pace off ball with 1st touch, then volley back over net.

Still aim to take ball in front of forehead, volley high to give partner time to get in position.

Do not allow underhand lifts, sideways volleys or one handed play.

Skill 3   Variations of the Volley Pass

1 Pairs • Volley to each other increasing the distance apart (e.g. ½m, 1m, 3m from net).

2 Pairs • Volley to partner whilst moving sideways.

3 Pairs • Volley alternately against wall, one bounce allowed before next volley played. Later no bounce allowed.

4 Threes • Form triangle as in diagram, players volley around triangle (both directions).

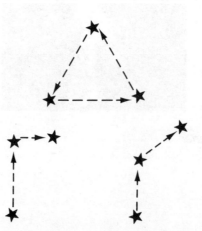

5 Threes • Form right angled and obtuse angled triangles to practise turning 90° and more. Change positions regularly.

Try not to slap the ball, use extra extension of the legs, arms and fingers.

Start slowly and gradually build up speed, try not to cross legs.

Get down low to ensure ball is played above forehead, move out of the way quickly when volley has been played.

Emphasis upon turning to face the way the ball is to be passed, ball should not be played sideways.

Turn quickly to face direction of pass, position yourself directly under dropping ball, otherwise technique similar to straightforward volley.

Skill 4   More Advanced Volleying

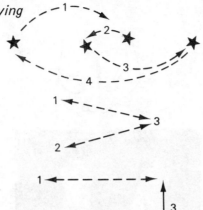

1 Fours ● 4 players in line, volleying over different distances.

Throw and catch initially to learn
sequence. Height in passes really
needed to allow for mistakes.

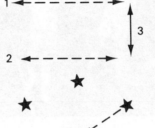

2 Threes ● Pressure on one player
   to volley in different directions.
   Players 1 and 2 feed 3 rapidly.

Feed with accurate volleys. Player
3 must turn quickly to face direction of pass.

3 Threes ● Pressure on one player
   to move quickly to new volleying
   position and players 1 and 2
   feed straight. 3 must move in line
   with them and play straight back.

Feed accurately but not too fast.
Player 3 must move quickly, stop,
turn and face direction of intended
volley.

4 Circle of players, one in middle.
   Player in middle must volley out
   to different person from one who
   volleys in.

Be thinking ahead about the next
pass. Keep the ball off the ground
for as long as possible.

Examples of Competitive Challenges

(a) Beat Your Own Record | Number of consecutive volleys played around triangle.

(b) Time Challenges | Who can volley most balls in 30 sec?

(c) 2 v 2 Volleyball

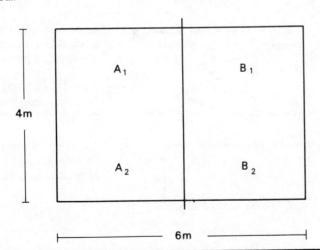

1 Court size approximately
   6m x 4m.
2 Volleying only.
3 On serve one handed overarm
   push (simply push ball over
   with fingers) may be used (or
   continue two handed volley
   serve).
4 Minimum of two touches to
   encourage passing.
5 Proper scoring system (Points
   only scored when team is serving
   and opposing team makes a
   fault.) Play to 5 points and
   change opponents.

3.3 DIGGING

(Because the ball may sting the arms in the early stages of this skill it is recommended that only short periods of
digging practice be included at first).

Skill 1   Basic Digging Technique

Activities

Key points

1 Pairs • Ball lobbed to player who digs back to area of partner's forehead.

Hands clasped, fingers of one hand placed on fingers of other, thumbs down and together.

2 Pairs • Ball lobbed slightly to side of player who digs back to partner.

Ball played on arms *between* wrists and forearms. Be alert on balls of feet, knees bent, one leg forward. Play ball back high.

3 Pairs • Ball lobbed slightly in front of player who moves in and digs back.

Arms always *straight* and together. Elbows locked to prevent arms bending.

4 Pairs • Change pace of feed e.g. a lob, straight and firm, much faster.

Be alert to the type of feed, always be ready to move forward if necessary. Keep arms straight.

5 Pairs • Each player of pair volleys and digs alternately, keeping rally going.

Try not to swing arms at ball, power provided by extending legs and lifting platform formed by arms.

6 Pairs • Give more difficult feeds (deep, short, to side).

Move quickly into position, player should be stationary when dig is made.

7 Pairs • Sit down on bench — rise to dig lobbed ball.

Develop extension of legs rather than swinging of arms.

Skill 2   More Advanced Digging

1 Pairs • Player runs in to specified position, digs and returns to original position.

Emphasise height on dig pass, gradually increase pace to put player under pressure.

2 Threes • Two players put pressure on one, feeding quickly.

Turn to face feeder, try to extend legs rather than swinging arms through.

3 Threes • Pressure on one player to move quickly to new digging position. Players 1 and 2 feed straight. 3 moves in line with them and plays straight back.

Try to get outside leg forward as position is reached and dig is made. Feed accurately but not too fast.

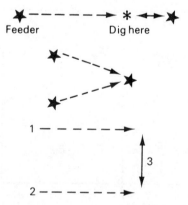

4 Threes • Feed, dig and catch above forehead.

Dig must now be played away from direction of feeder, still concentrate on height and accuracy.

5 Threes ● Feed, dig and volley
   back to feeder who catches.
   Repeat five times and then
   change positions.

6 One player throws rapidly to
   semi-circle of players who must
   dig back to area of forehead.
   (3 to 6 players).

7 Same as 6 but feeder strikes ball
   with overarm hit using heel of
   hand.

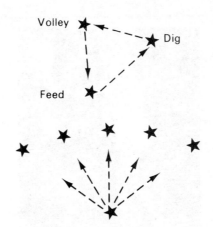

An introduction to the passing
sequence of the game. Gradually
make the dig more difficult.

Feeding must be rapid and lively.
Encourage calling, throw between
players and gradually make feeds
more difficult.

Feeder needs to turn wrist over
quickly, not so much arm movement needed now with dig as
ball will rebound off quicker.

Examples of Competitive Challenges

(a)	Beat Your Own Record	How many consecutive, accurate digs can you play?
(b)	Keep It Up	Which group can keep the ball off the ground the longest using digs only.
(c)	Time Challenges	e.g. How many successful digs in 30 sec. for Skill 2 no. 3?
(d)	Ring Volleyball	Up to 5 players try to volley or dig ball through basketball ring. Each score gives 3 points; if ball touches floor penalty point deducted from group's score
(e)	3 v 3 Volleyball	1 Mini-volley court 9m x 6m or similar.

2 Volleying, digging and push serve (or simple underarm
   throw).
3 Proper scoring, play up to 8 or 11 points in class to enable
   change of opponents.
4 Minimum 2 touches may still be desirable if ball is being
   played straight back over too often: maximum 3 touches.
5 Introduction of court positions and rotation.

*Serving
positions*

Attacking
volleyer

Ⓥ Setter

①
Server

*Initial
receiving
positions*

Ⓝ Setter

③ ①

On change of service (when team serving loses the rally)
the team to serve will rotate one position clockwise before
serving.

*After
service
change*

③

①

②

3.4 SERVING

Activities

Key points

1 Pairs • 5m apart, serve to each other with underarm pendulum action. Stand along line to ensure accuracy.

Ball held in left hand and flipped up into path of hitting hand. Ball may be struck with any part of hand, clenched or open. Ensure that hitting hand follows through in same line that ball is travelling.

2 Pairs • Move further apart and work over net.

Body-weight should move forward as ball is struck.

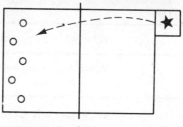

3 Pairs • Move to baseline of mini volley court, place targets on opponent's court.

Try to hit through centre of ball so that ball floats and does not rotate. Keep the head down looking at ball.

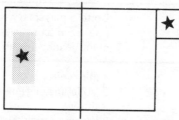

4 Pairs • Practise serving to partner who attempts dig. Server aims for optimum placements as shown in diagram.

Swing arm through in line with partner, try to strike the ball with the heel of the hand, try to be consistent rather than spectacular.

Overarm service may be taught with better players — care needs to be taken if this causes a breakdown in the game.

3.5 SMASHING AND BLOCKING

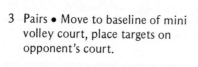

Skill 1   The Smash

Activities

Key points

1 Pairs • Player holds ball high with left hand, overarm hit with heel of hand to partner's feet.

Overarm action as if throwing a ball, elbow starting high, cupped hand whipping through quickly.

2 Pairs • Players stand 3m from wall, partner holds ball high, lets go just before player smashes.

Hit at full height, wrist kept very flexible, hand follows through downwards.

3 Pairs • As 2 but player now takes one step before double foot jump to smash ball.

Jump as high as possible by bending legs and thrusting up hard, good timing important.

4 Pairs ● As 2 but extend to two steps before double foot jump to smash.

Sequence for right-handed player is right foot, left, then both together. Both arms swing vigorously upwards.

5 Pairs ● As 2 but start moving before partner releases ball. Aim for target (e.g. shoe, chalk mark).

Ball struck with open hand directing ball downward, elbow of striking arm held high at start of action.

6 Threes ● Players as in diagram. 1 feeds with high underarm throw, 2 smashes and 3 retrieves.

Underarm feed must be high and accurate, hitting arm on follow through is pulled back clear of net.

7 Threes ● As 6 but target placed on court (e.g. box, shoe, track suit).

Ball hit at height of player's reach, try to maintain correct footwork, wrist guides ball in required direction.

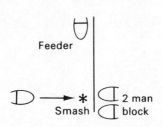

8 Class ● Full court smashing practice. Feeders now 'set' with high volley, smasher retrieves own ball.

Pick best volleyers for setting, smashers aim straight to avoid other players, smashers collect ball and move to back of opposite line.

Skill 2   The Block

1 Pairs ● Two players stand facing each other across net, jump up and clap hands.

Two footed jump, no arm swing (to avoid hitting net), hands starting at net height.

2 Pairs ● As 1 but players pass ball over net as they meet at the top of their jump.

Arms are angled over net (without touching it), the ball being pushed down into opponent's hands.

3 Pairs ● One player stands 2m from net, lobs ball underarm to skim top of net, partner blocks.

Try to attain correct timing, push ball down into court, immediately pull hands back to avoid touching net.

4 Threes ● As 3 but two players form the block.

Both players must jump together, timing therefore important.

5 Fours ● One player feeds for 2nd player to smash, other two players block smash.

Jump for block must be slightly after smasher's take-off, keep eyes open.

6 Blocking can be done with all smashing practices.

Most effective for both skills as this situation will occur in game.

Examples of Competitive Challenges

(a)	Target Hitting	Count number of targets hit in smashing/serving practices.
(b)	Smash v Block Practice	Who is best at this?
(c)	Volley-Squash	1 v 1 playing against wall: volleys, digs or smashes (pick one only or combine) with or without one bounce, failing to hit wall gives fault and point to opponent, play for 8 or 11 and change opponents.
(d)	Combination Rallies	Combinations nominated by class members — groups keep ball off ground as long as possible, e.g. volley, dig, dig, smash: volley, smash, volley, dig.
(e)	Skittle-Volley	Line skittles up 1m from base-line, groups have specified time to knock over as many skittles as possible with smashes.

3.6 TACTICAL PLAY

With teams of three in Mini Volleyball children can learn the basic tactics of the adult game. Children should be taught to play as members of a team and not as individuals. It is vital that they realise the importance of building up an attack through the three touch sequence of dig, volley and smash. The teacher's job is difficult because efforts to achieve this will, in the early stages, lead to the breakdown of rallies and possible losses to 'one touch' teams of inferior skill. It is essential to persevere however as three touch tactics have been undoubtedly proven as superior in the long run.

Basic positions for service and service reception already given in 3 v 3 introduction.

Team Tactics for Building Attack:

(a)

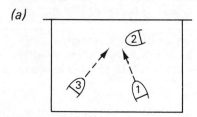

Service receivers 1 and 3 try to dig ball to Setter 2

(b)

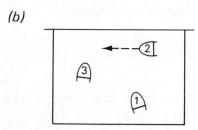

Setter 2 tries to set ball parallel to net for player 3 to smash.

(c)

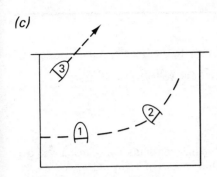

As player 3 smashes players 1 and 2 move across to cover. If smash is not completely successful and opposing team start to build an attack players will need to take up defensive positions.

Team Tactics for Defence:

(a)

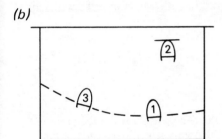

Positions when defenders have no block and there is a soft smash or no smash.

(b)

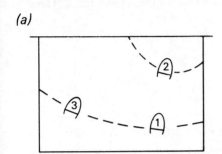

Positions when defenders apply a block (No. 2) and there is a hard smash.

(c)

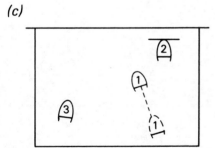

Positions when defenders apply a block (No. 2) and there is a soft smash or tip.

4. PROFICIENCY AWARDS

The English Volleyball Association is preparing an award scheme. For details apply to the General Administrator.

The following is a suggestion for teachers and coaches wishing to run their own basic volleyball skills test.

The scheme consists of five sections:

Section 1:

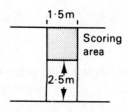

Volley Pass

For 1 minute attempt to volley the ball continuously against a wall over a line 2.5m high and keeping within an area of 1.5m width.

The test is begun by throwing the ball above the 2.5m line. If an error occurs the player must first throw the ball against the wall and then continue volleying.

Over 40 = Excellent
31-40   = Good
20-30   = Fair

Section 2:

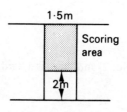

Dig Pass

For 1 minute attempt to dig the ball continuously against a wall over a line 2m high and keeping within an area of 1.5m width.

The test is begun by throwing the ball above the 2m line. If an error occurs the player must first throw the ball against the wall and then continue digging.

Over 40 = Excellent
31-40   = Good
20-30   = Fair

Section 3:

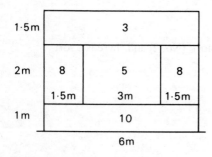

Service

Perform ten serves. The court is divided up as shown in the diagram. Total score obtained by adding the points scored from each of the ten serves.

Over 70 = Excellent
51-70   = Good
40-50   = Fair

Section 4:

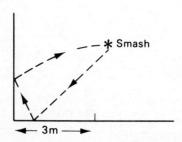

Smash

For 1 minute, jump in the air, hit the ball downward hard enough for it to rebound from the floor to a wall and back behind a 3m restraining line. This may be continuous if the player is skilful enough. The player must be in the air when striking the ball which must also be above chest height.

Over 20 = Excellent
15-20   = Good
10-14   = Fair

Section 5:

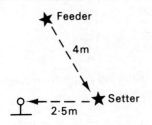

Setting

Attempt to set volleyball into mini basketball basket 2.60m high. The set should be taken from the side so the backboard cannot be used and from a distance of 2.5m. A feeder should provide an easy underhand throw for the setter from approximately 4m. Set five from the right side and five from the left. Score 3 points for a basket, 1 point if ball hits rim.

Over 20 = Excellent
15-20   = Good
10-14   = Fair

5. TEACHING/COACHING QUALIFICATIONS

5.1 TEACHERS' AWARD

1 Organising Body   English Volleyball Association

2 Aim   To improve the standard of teaching in volleyball especially through the use of small sided games in the class situation.

3 Syllabus

(a) Six part scheme for the introduction of volleyball to complete beginners.
(b) Basic technique of the volley pass, dig pass, smash, block and serve.
(c) The tactical principles of setting the ball up for the smash, executing a smash, covering behind the smasher, covering behind the block, serving — receiving service.
(d) Class organisation for volleyball.
(e) Competition organisation.

4 Duration of Course   18 hours instruction.

5 Assessment   Theory examination.

6 Applications

(a) Regional Coaching Administrator
(b) Local Sports Council Volleyball Liaison Officer
(c) English Volleyball Association,
   128 Melton Road
   West Bridgford
   Nottingham

6. REFERENCE INFORMATION

6.1 USEFUL ADDRESSES

English Schools' Volleyball Association
Secretary: Zbig Pagacz
    4 High Trees House
    Nightingale Lane
    London SW12

English Volleyball Association
General Administrator:
    128 Melton Road
    West Bridgford
    Nottingham NG2 6EP

E.S.V.A. Minivolley Development Officer
    Dave Joy
    62 Meadow Lane
    Trentham
    Stoke

E.V.A. Chairman of Technical Commission
    Rob Youngs
    2 Odell Road
    Sharnbrook
    Bedford

6.2 VOLLEYBALL REFERENCES

Publication					Description of Mini Game	Skill Descriptions	Practices	Tactics	Senior Rules
Anthony D.	1973	Success in Volleyball	John Murray	Book	short summary	*	*	*	
E.S.V.A.		The Rules of Mini-Volleyball	E.S.V.A.	Booklet	*				
E.V.A.		Official Rules Book	E.V.A.	Booklet					*
E.V.A.		Volleyball — Notes for Teachers	E.V.A.	Booklet	small sided games	*	*	*	
Hartman P.E.	1968	Volleyball Fundamentals	Merrill	Book		*	*	*	
Keller V.	1972	Point, Game and Match	Creative Sports Books	Book		*		*	
K.T.G.		Volleyball	E.P. Pub. Ltd.	Booklet		*			*
Nicholls K.	1973	Modern Volleyball	Henry Kimpton	Book		*	*	*	*
Odeneal W.T. Wilson H.E. Kellam M.F.	1969	Beginning Volleyball	Wadsworth	Book		*		*	*
Sandefur R.	1970	Volleyball	Goodyear	Book		*		*	*
Shondell D. McManama J.	1971	Volleyball	Prentice-Hall	Book		*		*	Summary
Slaymaker T. Brown V.H.	1970	Power Volleyball	Saunders	Book		*		*	*
Sotir N.	1973	Winning Volleyball	Stanley Paul	Book		*	*	*	

ORGANISATION OF TOURNAMENTS

The following different types of tournaments can add an extra incentive to practical sessions:

1 *Handicap:* Each player/pair/team is given a handicap for the session/tournament. Especially suitable for groups of uneven ability. No need to worry if handicaps are slightly incorrect, children will try to prove them wrong anyway.

Example: Player/Team A = +7   A starts 4-0
B = +3   in game.

Different forms of handicap necessary for cricket and tennis.

2 *Round Robin:* Players/teams play all other players/teams. Most victories give overall winner(s). Sample fixture list shown in table below.

Key:
(a) Read down vertical columns for fixtures in each round.
(b) AB indicates team A versus team B.
(c) Bye A indicates that team A does not play in that particular round.

Total Games

3 Teams

AB	CA	BC		Each team	
bye C	bye B	bye A		plays 2 games	3

4 Teams

AB	CA	AD		Each team	
CD	DB	BC		plays 3 games	6

5 Teams

BA	AC	DA	AE	CB	Each team	
CD	BE	EC	BD	ED	plays 4 games	
bye E	bye D	bye B	bye C	bye A		10

6 Teams

BA	AC	DA	AE	CB	Each team	
CD	BE	EC	BD	ED	plays 5 games	
EF	DF	FB	CF	AF		15

7 Teams

AB	CA	AD	EA	AF	GA	BG	Each team	
CD	DB	BC	FB	BE	EC	CF	plays 6 games	
EF	GF	EG	GC	DG	FD	DE		21
bye G	bye E	bye F	bye D	bye C	bye B	bye A		

8 Teams

AB	CA	AD	EA	AF	GA	AH		
CD	DB	BC	FB	BE	EC	BG	Each team	
EF	GF	EG	GC	DG	FD	CF	plays 7 games	
GH	HE	FH	HD	CH	HB	DE		28

3 Knockout: Pairings arranged by using a draw.
Make sure losers are occupied e.g. plate competition for 1st round losers.

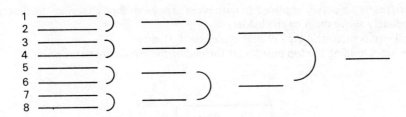

4 American   Can be played in many ways: two examples given.
Tournament: Aim is to move players/teams around, winners combining with losers to give success to as many
players as possible.

Individual Sports

1   Split players into two sections (not teams) e.g. boys
and girls.

2   One player from each section play together on any
court for one round.

3   After each round:

(a) Winning boy moves clockwise to next court.

(b) Winning girl moves anti-clockwise to next court.

(c) Losing boy and girl stay on the same court but
oppose each other in the next round.

(d) When winning players have moved to new court
winning boy partners losing girl and winning girl
partners losing boy.

Team sports (6 players in team)

Split players into two sections (not teams) e.g.
blue and red. Form these into groups of three
players.

One group of three from each section play
together on any pitch for one round (i.e. 3 red
and 3 blue form a team).

After each round:

(a) Winning blue group of 3 moves clockwise to
next pitch.

(b) Winning red group of 3 moves anti-clockwise
to next pitch.

(c) Losing red and blue groups stay on the same
pitch but *oppose* each other in the next round.

(d) When winning players have moved to new pitch —
winning blue group of 3 joins up with losing
group of red.
Winning red group of 3 joins up with losing
group of blue.

4   Play another round and repeat this process in the time available.
Each round might consist of 10 min. playing time.
Total games/matches won at the end provide the winners.

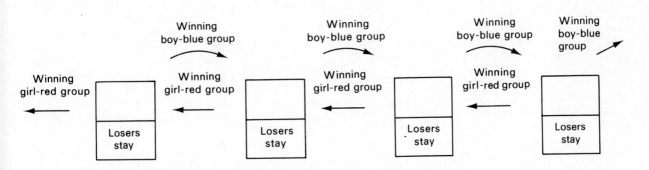

5 Leagues   Players/teams placed in small groups (perhaps six players/teams).
                   Draw up a fixture list as in the Round Robin where each player/team plays every other
                   player/team. Play one round each day/week/fortnight. Group winners play off in finals.

6 Ladder: Players/teams are drawn or placed in rank order. They can then challenge the player/team
                   immediately above them on the ladder.
                   If challenge is successful they change places on the ladder.
                   Player/team holding the top position at the end of the season are the winners.

1	—	Blue
2	—	Green
3	—	Black
4	—	Yellow
5	—	Red
6	—	Purple
7	—	White
8	—	Orange

GENERAL REFERENCES

1 Anderson, M.E.,   *Games Skills*, Chambers, Edinburgh, 1971.
2 Edmundson, J.,   *Games and Activities*, Pitman, London, 1974.
3 Frith, J.R. and Lobley, R.,   *Playground Games and Skills*, Black, London, 1971.
4 Johnson, F.J.M. and Trevor, M.D., *A Suggested Games Scheme for Juniors*, Blackwell, Oxford, 1972.
5 Latchaw, M.,   *Movement Activities for the Elementary School*, Prentice-Hall, Englewood Cliffs, 1970.
6 Lenel, R.M.,   *Games in the Primary School*, University of London Press, London, 1969.
7 Mauldon, E. and Redfern, H.B.,   *Games Teaching*, Macdonald & Evans, London, 1969.
8 Sykes, R.,   *Minor Games and Relay Activities*, E.P. Publishing, Wakefield, 1976.
9 Wise, W.M.,   *Games and Sports*, Heinemann, London, 1972.